TEXT EDITING, PRINT AND THE DIGITAL WORLD

Digital Research in the Arts and Humanities

Series Editors
Marilyn Deegan, Lorna Hughes and Harold Short

Digital technologies are becoming increasingly important to arts and humanities research, expanding the horizons of research methods in all aspects of data capture, investigation, analysis, modelling, presentation and dissemination. This important series will cover a wide range of disciplines with each volume focusing on a particular area, identifying the ways in which technology impacts on specific subjects. The aim is to provide an authoritative reflection of the 'state of the art' in the application of computing and technology. The series will be critical reading for experts in digital humanities and technology issues, and it will also be of wide interest to all scholars working in humanities and arts research.

Forthcoming titles in the series

The Virtual Representation of the Past
Edited by Mark Greengrass and Lorna Hughes
ISBN 978 0 7546 7288 3

Modern Methods for Musicology
Prospects, Proposals and Realities
Edited by Tim Crawford and Lorna Gibson
ISBN 978 0 7546 7302 6

Text Editing,
Print and the Digital World

Edited by

MARILYN DEEGAN
King's College London, UK

KATHRYN SUTHERLAND
University of Oxford, UK

ASHGATE

Published by
Ashgate Publishing Limited
Wey Court East
Union Road
Farnham
Surrey, GU9 7PT
England

Ashgate Publishing Company
Suite 420
101 Cherry Street
Burlington
VT 05401-4405
USA

www.ashgate.com

British Library Cataloguing in Publication Data
Text editing, print and the digital world. - (Digital
   research in the arts and humanities)
   1. Criticism, Textual 2. Electronic books
   I. Deegan, Marilyn II. Sutherland, Kathryn
   801.9'59

Library of Congress Cataloging-in-Publication Data
Text editing, print, and the digital world / [edited] by Marilyn Deegan and Kathryn Sutherland.
      p. cm. -- (Digital research in the arts and humanities)
   Includes bibliographical references and index.
   ISBN 978-0-7546-7307-1
   1. Editing. 2. Criticism, Textual. 3. Transmission of texts. 4. Electronic publishing. I. Deegan, Marilyn. II. Sutherland, Kathryn.

   PN162.T434 2008
   808'.027--dc22

                                                                      2008024692

Transfered to Digital Printing in 2010

ISBN 978-0-7546-7307-1

Printed and bound in Great Britain by
MPG Books Group, UK

Contents

List of Figures and Table

Figures

Table

Notes on Contributors

Gabriel Bodard (PhD, Classics, University of Reading) is trained in Classical literature and history. His research interests include Greek religion, magic, epigraphy and papyrology, with a focus on the early Greek world; XML design and analysis, electronic publication, and language and text encoding. He is founder and editor of the Digital Classicist community, an active participant in the EpiDoc Collaborative, guidelines for the encoding of ancient epigraphic documents in XML, and on the Technical Council of the TEI. He works at the Centre for Computing in the Humanities and in Classics, King's College London.

Linda Bree is the Literature Publisher at Cambridge University Press. She is the author of *Sarah Fielding* (1996) and editor of Sarah Fielding's *The Adventures of David Simple* (2002) and (with Claude Rawson) of Henry Fielding's *Jonathan Wild* (2004), as well as of Jane Austen's *Persuasion* (2000).

Dino Buzzetti teaches medieval philosophy at the University of Bologna. He has published essays on medieval logic and metaphysics and the history of logic in general. He has also taught document representation and processing in the Faculty of Preservation of the Cultural Heritage in Ravenna and gives humanities computing courses to philosophy students. He has published articles on digital editions of manuscript texts and digital text representation. He is a member of the Executive Committee of the Association for Literary and Linguistic Computing.

Mats Dahlström is associate professor at the Swedish School of Library and Information Science, UC Borås/Göteborg University. His research concerns digitization, bibliography, text encoding, knowledge organization and new media studies. His 2006 PhD thesis investigates how scholarly editors define and reproduce source material, the reasons for conflicts between editors' varying expectations of media types, and the connections and demarcations between scholarly editions and reference works such as bibliographies. He is consultant for, teaches and supervises cultural heritage digitization projects within the framework of libraries and archives and has published studies on e-books, textual theory, media theory, open access and document architecture. He is the editor-in-chief of the open access peer review journal *Human IT* (<http://www.hb.se/bhs/ith/humanit.htm>).

Marilyn Deegan has a PhD in medieval studies where her specialism is Anglo-Saxon medical texts and herbals. She has published and lectured widely in medieval studies, digital library research and humanities computing. She is currently Professor of Humanities Computing and Director of Research Development at the Centre for Computing in the Humanities at King's College London and was formerly Digital Resources Director of the Refugee Studies Centre at Oxford University. She is Editor-in-Chief of *LLC: The Journal of Digital Scholarship in the Humanities* and Director of Publications for the Office for Humanities Communication based at King's College London.

Paul Eggert FAHA is Professor of English at the University of New South Wales, Canberra. He is general editor of the Academy Editions of Australian Literature and chair of the AustLit database Advisory Board. He has edited critical editions in the Cambridge Works of D.H. Lawrence and the Academy Editions series. He is the author of *Securing the Past: Conservation in Art, Architecture and Literature* (Cambridge: CUP, 2009).

Juan Garcés is Curator at the Department of Western Manuscripts of the British Library, London, where he is currently coordinating the *Codex Sinaiticus* Project. In 2003, he received a doctorate in Biblical Studies from the University of Stellenbosch, South Africa. He has since gathered experience in the field of Digital Humanities as analyst, consultant, and adviser in relation to digitally based research projects, particularly in the field of Greek texts.

James McLaverty is Professor of Textual Criticism at Keele University. He is the author of *Pope, Print, and Meaning* (2001) and a general editor of the Cambridge Edition of the Works of Jonathan Swift.

James Mussell is lecturer in English at the University of Birmingham. He was postdoctoral researcher on the Nineteenth-Century Serials Edition. He is the author of *Science, Time and Space in the Late Nineteenth-Century Periodical Press* (Ashgate 2007) and has taught at King's College London, Birkbeck College and Middlesex University.

Espen S. Ore has a degree in Humanities from the University of Oslo and has worked in Humanities Computing since 1981, mainly with multimedia/ hypermedia and text encoding and electronic editions. He was *pro tem* director of the Bergen electronic edition of Wittgenstein's *Nachlass* in 1995 and a member of the editorial board of the new edition of Henrik Ibsen's Writings until he started full-time work at the National Library of Norway in Oslo in 2001. At the Library he has been responsible for electronic publications from the special collections and for parts of current work to digitize extensive collections at the Library.

Suzanne Paylor has a PhD in epistemology and authority of 'common knowledge', especially scientific knowledge, in nineteenth-century popular culture. Suzanne is a postdoctoral researcher on the Nineteenth-Century Serials Edition. She has worked on several large academic digital projects and for the Leeds Electronic Text Centre and teaches postgraduate level digital humanities. Her current specialisms include nineteenth-century print culture and digital scholarship and editing. She is also involved in the development of the user interface of the British Library/JISC Archival Newspapers Project, sits on several digital project advisory boards and is the Communications Secretary to the British Society for the History of Science.

Elena Pierazzo has a PhD in Italian Philology: her specialism is Italian Renaissance texts and text encoding, and she has published and presented papers at international conferences in Renaissance literature, digital critical editions, text encoding theory and Italian linguistics. She is currently Associate Researcher in the Centre for Computing in the Humanities at King's College London and lead analyst of a dozen research projects; she is also teacher of XML related technologies both at undergraduate and master level. Formerly she was Researcher at the University of Pisa, engaged in both teaching and research. She is involved in the TEI user-community, with a special interest in the transcription of manuscripts.

Charlotte Roueché is Professor of Classical and Byzantine Greek at King's College London. She works on a range of Greek texts, with a special interest in those inscribed on stone. Since the early 1970s she has been involved in recording and publishing the inscriptions from Aphrodisias, a Graeco-Roman city in south west Turkey. The exceptional richness of the material from this site led her to explore the possibilities of online publication, working with Tom Elliott (University of North Carolina, Chapel Hill) and Gabriel Bodard (King's College London). The full corpus of inscriptions was published in summer 2007: <http://insaph.kcl.ac.uk/iaph2007>.

Kathryn Sutherland is Professor of Textual Criticism at the University of Oxford and a Professorial Fellow in English at St Anne's College, Oxford. Her research interests include the fictional and non-fictional writings of the Scottish Enlightenment and Romantic periods; textual criticism and theories of text; and aspects of digital culture. She is the director of the AHRC-funded Jane Austen Digital Fiction Manuscripts Project. Her most recent book is *Jane Austen's Textual Lives: From Aeschylus to Bollywood* (Oxford: Oxford University Press, 2005; paperback edition 2007). Her edited work includes the essay collection *Electronic Text: Investigations in Method and Theory* (Oxford: Clarendon Press, 1997). She is currently collaborating with Marilyn Deegan on a book for Ashgate, *Transferred Illusions: Digital Technology and the Forms of Print*, due out in 2009.

Edward Vanhoutte studied Dutch and English language and literature and medieval history. His main research interests include the history, nature, and theory of humanities computing and electronic textual editing, the encoding of modern manuscripts, letter editing and genetic criticism. He has lectured and published widely on these subjects. He is currently Director of Research in the Royal Academy of Dutch Language and Literature (Belgium) where he heads the

Centre for Scholarly Editing and Document Studies. He lectures in humanities computing at the University of Antwerp. He is Associate Editor of *LLC: The Journal of Digital Scholarship in the Humanities.*

Series Preface

Text Editing, Print and the Digital World is volume 13 of *Digital Research in the Arts and Humanities*. Each of the titles in this series comprises a critical examination of the application of advanced ICT methods in the arts and humanities. That is, the application of formal computationally-based methods, in discrete but often interlinked areas of arts and humanities research. Usually developed from Expert Seminars, one of the key activities supported by the Methods Network, these volumes focus on the impact of new technologies in academic research and address issues of fundamental importance to researchers employing advanced methods.

Although generally concerned with particular discipline areas, tools or methods, each title in the series is intended to be broadly accessible to the arts and humanities community as a whole. Individual volumes not only stand alone as guides but collectively form a suite of textbooks reflecting the 'state of the art' in the application of advanced ICT methods within and across arts and humanities disciplines. Each is an important statement of current research at the time of publication, an authoritative voice in the field of digital arts and humanities scholarship.

These publications are the legacy of the AHRC ICT Methods Network and will serve to promote and support the ongoing and increasing recognition of the impact on and vital significance to research of advanced arts and humanities computing methods. The volumes will provide clear evidence of the value of such methods, illustrate methodologies of use and highlight current communities of practice.

Marilyn Deegan, Lorna Hughes, Harold Short
Series Editors
AHRC ICT Methods Network
Centre for Computing in the Humanities
King's College London
February/March 2008

About the AHRC ICT Methods Network

The aims of the AHRC ICT Methods Network were to promote, support and develop the use of advanced ICT methods in arts and humanities research and to support the cross-disciplinary network of practitioners from institutions around the UK. It was a multi-disciplinary partnership providing a national forum for the exchange and dissemination of expertise in the use of ICT for arts and humanities research. The Methods Network was funded under the AHRC ICT Programme from 2005 to 2008.

The Methods Network Administrative Centre was based at the Centre for Computing in the Humanities (CCH), King's College London. It coordinated and supported all Methods Network activities and publications, as well as developing outreach to, and collaboration with, other centres of excellence in the UK. The Methods Network was co-directed by Harold Short, Director of CCH, and Marilyn Deegan, Director of Research Development, at CCH, in partnership with Associate Directors: Mark Greengrass, University of Sheffield; Sandra Kemp, Royal College of Art; Andrew Wathey, Royal Holloway, University of London; Sheila Anderson, Arts and Humanities Data Service (AHDS) (2006–2008); and Tony McEnery, University of Lancaster (2005–2006).

The project website (<http://www.methodsnetwork.ac.uk>) provides access to all Methods Network materials and outputs. In the final year of the project a community site, 'Digital Arts and Humanities' (<http://www.arts-humanities. net>) was initiated as a means to sustain community building and outreach in the field of digital arts and humanities scholarship beyond the Methods Network's funding period.

List of Abbreviations

AHDS	Arts and Humanities Data Service
AHRC	Arts and Humanities Research Council
ASCII	American Standard Code for Information Interchange
BEE	Bergen Electronic Edition (of Wittgenstein's *Nachlass*)
CCH	Centre for Computing in the Humanities
CEAA	Center for Editions of American Authors
CIL	Corpus Inscriptionum Latinarum
DTD	Document Type Definition
EEBO	Early English Books Online
EPAPP	EPidoc APhrodisias Project
ERA	Entities, Relations and Attributes
GPL	General Public Licence
HIW	Henrik Ibsen's Writings
HTML	HyperText Markup Language
HTTP	HyperText Transfer Protocol
IFLA	International Federation of Library Associations
IP	Intellectual Property
IT	Information Technology
JITAM	Just-In-Time Authentication Mechanism
JITM	Just-In-Time Markup
JPEG	Joint Photographic Experts Group
KWIC	Key Word in Context
NARA	National Archives and Records Administration
NCCH	Norwegian Computing Centre for the Humanities
NL	National Library (of Norway)
OCR	Optical Character Recognition
ODNB	Oxford Dictionary of National Biography
OED	Oxford English Dictionary
OHCO	Ordered Hierarchies of Content Objects
OSCE	Open Source Critical Editions
PDF	Portable Document Format
RDF	Resource Description Framework
SDSC	San Diego Supercomputer Center
SE	Scholarly Edition
SGML	Standard Generalized Markup Language
TEI	Text Encoding Initiative
TIFF	Tagged Image File Format
TLG	Thesaurus Linguae Graecae

UML   Unified Modelling Language
XHTML   eXtensible HyperText Markup Language
XML   eXtensible Markup Language
XSL   eXtensibe Stylesheet Language
XSLFO   XSL Formatting Objects
XSLT   XSL Transformations

In memory of Julia Briggs (1943–2007),
Professor of Literature and Women's Studies at De Montfort University,
who was part of this conversation.

Introduction

Marilyn Deegan and Kathryn Sutherland

This collection of essays is intended as an appraisal of the current state of digital editing, considering from a number of perspectives its benefits and drawbacks in the development of complex editions. It draws upon presentations given at several seminars on textual editing and the new possibilities offered by digital technologies held by the ICT Methods Network at King's College during 2006. Contributors to the seminars, leading practitioners in the fields of text management, textual studies and editing, discussed a range of issues from diverse, and not always concordant, perspectives. This diversity and range of opinion marks the essays presented here.

There has been much debate in recent years about the use and value of the computer in the preparation and presentation of scholarly editions of literary works. Traditional critical editing, defined by the paper and print limitations of the codex format, is now considered by many to be inadequate for the expression and interpretation of complex, multi-layered or multi-text works of the human imagination. So much so, that many exponents of the benefits of new information technologies suggest that in future all editions should be produced in digital and/or online form: that digital tools give scholars, critics, teachers and non-professional readers better representations of and access to the literary works which inform our cultures. Others point to the sophistication of print, after more than five hundred years of development, not only in storing and presenting knowledge and information in complex and accessible ways, but also in setting the agenda for how we continue to think about text, even in its non-print forms.

Several of the contributors to this volume consider whether and how existing paradigms for developing and using critical editions, many of them resting on theories and practices shaped under the shadow of the codex and of print, are changing to reflect the increasing commitment to and assumed significance of digital tools and methodologies. Our ideas of what constitutes a literary work are under revision: what factors determine its boundaries and shape, what we mean by 'text' and what features define it. Conversely, and in the face of the new technological hype, it is also timely to reconsider with renewed critical discrimination the older technologies: the status of the book or codex as a valuable and durable witness to our textual traditions and its relationship to the more fluid but impermanent digital record; and the book's witness to expertly selected or digested argument over the quantification and machine-analysis of data.

If digital scholarship in the literary field is significantly challenging the way in which theories of text editing are formulated and editions are researched, compiled and disseminated, the scholarly support models within the academy have yet to be modified to reflect the shift in approach and working practices this enjoins. Text editors have more experience than most of the invisibility and collaborative nature of their work. The prior, factual nature of texts was for a long time a confident assumption of a scholarly and a reading community, with the intervenient and critical work of the editor largely disregarded. Only in the last few decades have we submitted the practicalities of editorial procedure to more vigorous reassessment and recovered, for the wider community, a better understanding of the subjective and interpretative functions of editing. This has had the ambivalent effect of raising the status of editing as critical activity at the same time as it has called the authoritative status of editions into question. Again, digital scholarship seems to open up timely avenues for development: the storage or facilitation of multiple critical perspectives on text or even of 'raw' text, and the promotion of new models for collaboration.

The essays in this collection address these issues from a range of disciplinary perspectives and commitments to old and new media. These are some of the questions we set ourselves in our conversations during the seminars:

- How seriously in the current mixed environment do we envisage the falling away of print in respect of the electronic edition?
- What do we envisage the cultural status of the electronic edition to be? Do we see it serving the needs of general readers as well as expert users?
- What new kinds of edition are made possible through the electronic medium?
- What constitutes an edition in the electronic medium? How is this related to the notion of an electronic archive?
- Is the role of the editor changing in the electronic environment?
- What new kinds of editing partnerships are emerging?

Part I: In Theory

In her opening chapter, 'Being Critical: Paper-based Editing and the Digital Environment', Kathryn Sutherland calls for a historically grounded scepticism and points to a long-standing paradox in literary studies. She stresses the basic fact of the centrality of the critical edition to literary criticism and the contradictory truth that although literary judgements are inevitably based on texts, the assumptions underpinning those texts remain remarkably invisible to or unexplored by users and readers. Even editors themselves fail to engage with theoretical issues, or with the textual criticism that underpins literary criticism. Moreover, the fluidity or evanescence that characterizes literary criticism contrasts sharply with the expectation that editions will endure. Sutherland cites the example of R.W. Chapman's 1923 edition of the novels of Jane Austen, which continues to serve as the textual ground for literary judgements without any accompanying interrogation of the editorial principles and assumptions underlying it – as if Chapman's text were somehow neutral, a benign or pure representation of the author's intentions. She gives a summary of the development of 'New Bibliography' which attempted to stabilize a text against the adventitious processes of its transmission through time, producing an ideal or 'clean' text purged of corruption and made up of various textual states according to the editor's judgement about the intentions of the author. Subsequently, she notes, an increasing interest in cultural studies led to an acceptance of the equal validity of different textual versions according to their production at a particular moment in time. Simultaneously, technological developments made it possible to archive such states electronically, with no single version being hierarchically privileged over another. However, such developments were not accompanied by adequate attention to the question of how texts exist, how they mean and the modes of engagement they produce or facilitate. Sutherland suggests that electronic materiality may actually hinder the kinds of engagement prompted by print versions, and that we have not yet thought hard enough about the purposes electronic editions might serve, nor what assumptions about texts underlie their production. We urgently need an electronic equivalent of textual theory that will take into account the essential difference between print texts and digital texts. Some texts lose an essential aspect – their 'bookishness' – by translation into an electronic variant; in some cases the reading experience seems inseparably related to the physicality of the book as an object; and assumptions about the advantages of electronic editions have left such issues unexamined.

The nature of a scholarly edition, as of any bibliographical tool, is determined by the historical, technical, social and rhetorical dimensions of the genre. This situatedness puts constraints on the validity of scholarly editions: what they can and what they cannot do. Claims have been made for the potent reproductive force of scholarly editions, as well as for the making of massive digital facsimile and transcription archives that can be used as platforms for producing new critical editions. Mats Dahlström in his chapter, 'The Compleat Edition', questions the legitimacy of such assumptions when combined with idealist notions of documents, texts and editions. That the nature of editions is rhetorical rather than neutral, social rather than individualistic, and one of complex translation rather than simple transmission, for instance, suggests that the versatility and reproductivity of the edited material itself will be limited by significant factors. Recognizing this makes us better equipped at subjecting digital editions, libraries and archives, along with the claims some of their surrounding discourses make, to critical inquiry.

While one of Sutherland's underlying arguments is that users have more resistance to electronic editions than their producers care to believe, it is precisely this resistance and an attempt to find a solution that forms the topic of Dino Buzzetti's contribution. Buzzetti begins 'Digital Editions and Text Processing' by stating that his goal is to develop a semiotics of digital text rather than a sociology of text. He argues that it is necessary to transfer to the machine part of the reader's 'competence', and that attempts to do this using, for example, XML semantics have not been entirely successful because the role of markup itself has been understood in only limited and fairly mechanical ways. Current practices tend to be conventional, with the assumption that markup is no more than a limitedly iterative technical tool. On the contrary, the relationship between markup and a string of characters can more profitably be understood as dynamic rather than passive. Assumptions need to change; humanities' scholars specifically need to engage with the challenge of developing tools that allow for the multi-dimensionality of markup to be exploited to its fullest scope. Thus Buzzetti, like Sutherland but from a quite different perspective, argues that users (in this context, humanities' scholars) must imaginatively engage with the question of the purposes served by electronic editions in order to ensure that they do serve their real needs and, therefore, gain wider acceptance.

Paul Eggert opens his chapter, 'The Book, the E-text and the "Work Site"', with a timely reminder of the scholarly satisfaction that derives from completeness in the production of a paper-based edition. In the 'finished' print edition, 'every part of the volume [is] enlightened by every other part, all of it seamlessly interdependent and unobjectionably cross-referenced, nothing said twice, all of it as near perfectly balanced as you could ever make it'. By comparison, there is no deadline for an electronic edition, and further editorial intrusions can be made at any time. Does this mean, he questions, that the scholarly rigour brought to bear in the print world will be relaxed? And what of the interactive and multi-author possibilities engendered by electronic editions? Can we engage in these new ways of doing things *without* compromising traditional standards of accuracy and rigorous reasoning?

Eggert argues that there must be some clear way of authenticating electronic editions and preserving their integrity, just as in the print world the fixed and stable nature of the book preserves the integrity of the work. He proposes the use of what has come to be known as 'just-in-time-markup' (JITM) to ensure the accuracy and authenticity of the electronic text. This system runs counter to common practice in markup, where tagsets are inserted into the text and travel along with it when it is transmitted or transformed. JITM keeps markup and texts separate, and any corruptions or changes in the text are detected instantly using algorithmic methods (checksums) to keep track of even the slightest difference. JITM also has the advantage that various interpretative 'perspectives' in the text can be generated at will, leaving the underlying text unchanged.

In 2006 a group of scholars within the Digital Classicist community began to meet, first electronically and then physically, to discuss a range of issues and strategies that they dubbed 'Open Source Critical Editions'. Gabriel Bodard and Juan Garcés, in 'Open Source Critical Editions: A Rationale', consider the interests of this active community and focus on three core matters: (1) the sense and implications of the Open Source model; (2) the connotations of 'critical' in this context; (3) the question of what kinds of edition should be included in such a project – defined by them as literary, eclectic or individual manuscript editions – and what this means for the technologies and protocols adopted.

The use of the term 'Open Source' in their discussion is deliberately provocative: the authors argue that the principles of the Open Source movement are basically those of scholarly publication, which conventionally requires full documentation of sources, references and arguments, and allows – nay requires – the reuse of these sources from and reference to previous editions in any future publications on the same topic. If a project were to publish digital critical editions without making its source data available, therefore, it would arguably be in conflict with those principles of scholarly editing and publication upon which the academy is based. Open Source is not innovative, it is traditional. Presenting the rationale of the Open Source Critical Editions by way of unpacking these three key issues suggests important implications for standards of data sharing and transfer and policies for collaboration in the electronic environment, and it brings the arguments to a wider public, in order to lay the foundation for future projects and discussions.

In the final chapter of Part I, 'Every Reader his own Bibliographer: An Absurdity?', Edward Vanhoutte asks the question 'who buys editions, and why?' He supports Sutherland's point that most users or readers are not interested in textual bibliography, and posits that the reasons for consulting a scholarly edition are first for access to a reliable text, and second for the annotations and commentary. For most readers, the more arcane issues of variants and genesis of a text rarely factor in the choice of edition. On the contrary, Vanhoutte argues, scholarly editing as a discipline is in disharmony with the importance of the scholarly edition as a cultural product. He further claims that there is a notable scholarly resistance to the production of what he calls a 'minimal edition': academic focus is on the 'maximal' edition, and although the two types serve different and equally valid purposes, they are viewed hierarchically. Electronic editions could follow a different model, but so far they have notably failed to do so. They have not freed themselves from the layout economies invented for the printed page nor from the kinds of documentation and presentation of data agreed upon for the print format. Like printed scholarly editions, they are of value academically but not culturally: that is, they do not provide reading editions but, rather, large archives that include multiple documentary witnesses and images. In fact these archives are even less likely than scholarly editions to be used as reading texts because they simultaneously present multiple texts or different states of a given text, which are better suited to computational interrogation than to straightforward reading.

Vanhoutte suggests it is time to propose the use of electronic scholarly editing as a mode for reintegrating (or integrating) the scholarly edition with the reading edition without any compromise of academic value. The example he uses is the electronic edition of the Flemish novella *De Trein der Traagheid* by Johan Daisne. In this edition, the collaborative product of three scholars, Ron Van den Branden, Xavier Roelens and Vanhoutte, the user is able to manipulate multiple variables in order to produce exactly the reading edition she requires; the site maintains a record of the user's interventions so that precisely the same edition can be reproduced (thus circumventing the problem of there being no agreed text on which to base interpretation or discussion among multiple users); and, for stability and durability of reference, an edited reading text is provided by the editors as an anchor for scholarly debate.

Part II: In Practice

Espen Ore's chapter, '... they hid their books underground', begins with the extreme examples of the management policies of two ancient book deposits, those at Scepsis and Alexandria, adduced in order to address the issue of electronic editing from a library or storage perspective. Ore compares the closed edition book project that ends with the finished product and is typically very costly (for example, the centenary edition of the works of Heinrik Ibsen) with the electronic product that is also intended as a basis for future work – the text archive that can be taken further and modified as new information becomes available. The benefits are not all in one direction, however. Books have the advantage of being (relatively) inert; the electronic edition or archive can be plagued by the problem of the longevity (or lack of it) of proprietary software. Electronic products must be stored in such a way that their future use-value does not diminish and they do not risk obsolescence. Libraries are the ideal resource for preservation; they can maintain and update or provide user support. Ore identifies other storage issues, including the harvesting of web pages which have no physical manifestation but will be lost as cultural products unless some attempt is made at preserving them in usable form, and he discusses a wide range of editing and digitization projects recently completed or currently under way in Norway.

By contrast, Linda Bree and James McLaverty argue a more cautious use of electronic data storage and make the case for the continued importance of the print edition within a hybrid textual environment. The future of the scholarly edition, they maintain, lies in the creation of complementary print and electronic text versions. Basing its discussion on the Cambridge Edition of the Works of Jonathan Swift, which will appear in 15 print volumes, with an electronic archive of variant texts, their chapter argues the desirability of uniting the authority of the traditional print edition with the searchable multiple texts made possible by electronic publication. The scholarly print edition continues to serve the vital role of defining a canon and summarizing the state of scholarship in a form accessible to a wide range of readers. Its design and economies of production (both intellectual and financial) lead to production decisions that engage both publishing and academic expertise, and its production costs are covered by sales on a tried and tested model. While it generates no maintenance costs, the limitation of the print edition is space. This is where the electronic model comes in: an electronic archive giving detailed assistance to its users through an apparatus of introductions and menus can make a diversity of texts available for consultation and collation. Such a hybrid edition (where the elements complement one another but can stand alone) will undoubtedly serve the scholarly community well at a point of transition, before the modes of publication of electronic texts (evaluative, financial and technical) become satisfactorily established. Uniting as it does the resources of academics and publishers, properly funded, the hybrid edition points to a future in which large scholarly projects remain viable, with the capacity to meet both new and continuing needs.

The final three chapters in the collection are each concerned with varieties of text that in some important sense defy printing or reprinting in conventional paper form or whose enhanced functionality, outside the book, is clearly demonstrated. In 'Editions and Archives: Textual Editing and the Nineteenth-Century Serials Edition (ncse)', Jim Mussell and Suzanne Paylor examine some of the particular characteristics of non-book print publications (in their case, historical periodical or journal publications) which make their editing and continued accessibility problematic in non-digital domains. These printed objects ask different questions of editors from those posed by books, and they demand different treatment from other kinds of published print products, which means that new models are needed for republishing periodicals in the digital world. Mussell and Paylor consider whether what should be provided are archives and gateways, rather than actual editions in the more conventional understanding of the concept.

The Nineteenth Century Serials Edition project is producing an edition of around 100,000 printed pages from six periodical titles, impossible to publish on paper for many reasons: the different objects which make up the periodicals have complex relationships with each other, and the content is associated with certain 'moments'. The relationships within the titles are structured around dynamic hierarchical, generic and thematic indices; meaning is also constructed through layout and typography. Further, the authority embodied in the periodical is constituted from highly complex prosopographical relationships between people: printers, publishers, editors, contributors, illustrators, engravers and paper merchants. The challenges of representing this diversity are huge in any format. Some titles, for instance, approach the codex model while others are more like newspapers. Some titles do not have a linear sequence of numbers distributed according to familiar temporal units (daily or weekly issues) and publish up to nine different editions of a single number (nine editions in one day). The creative visual material in these publications – fancy typographies and rich illustrations – also forces new approaches to computational analysis and demands imaginative editorial solutions.

Existing structures for the digitization of historical newspapers and periodicals tend to be on the archive model, with diverse content held in a database and delivered to users in a manner that often masks or suppresses some of the formal and other complexities integrally associated with this genre. In their chapter Mussell and Paylor explain how their experience of the form and genre of the periodical is encouraging them to move beyond the old digital model for mere content preservation, and instead to use the electronic medium to produce editions of serials that respond sensitively to what is distinctive in the old medium of print.

Charlotte Roueché's 'Digitizing Inscribed Texts' is a practical review of her own discovery of the potential of digital presentation to serve as a vital tool for recording, preserving and rendering accessible images and transcriptions of Greek and Latin inscriptions on stone. Roueché contends that it could be argued that epigraphers 'invented' markup and established the conventions by which texts are presented electronically. Epigraphers, she avers, know that everything they do is a compromise because they have to 'squeeze stones onto paper'. As witnesses to objects whose survival is fragile, they necessarily and constantly engage with questions of human decisions about what to record and preserve. In their case, the move to e-publication was made because its flexibility and capaciousness allow for the presentation of *all* material, including images, which is simply impossible in print because of the prohibitive cost. Roueché notes an interesting but unintended result of digitization, which is that while in the past Classical Studies had tended to regard inscribed texts as not literary in the same way as material preserved on paper, electronic publication has worked to change this, with overall benefit for scholarship. She argues that any electronic project must grow out of an identified need and a full assessment of the purposes and audience such a project would serve. She also raises the thorny issue of scholarly acceptance of such projects; for her own site, she has secured an ISBN to facilitate library cataloguing.

Elena Pierazzo brings the volume to a close with a consideration of the encoding of time in authors' working or draft manuscripts. The distinction between manuscripts as text carriers and their printed, book copies is a distinction between the physical singularity that characterizes any holograph manuscript and reproducibility, which is the essence of print. Working manuscripts contain vital clues to how authors worked and writings evolved – clues that the production processes of print regularly erase. In reading manuscripts we get closer to certain aspects or signs of creativity. While such interest in working or genetic processes is not new, it is something that digital surrogacy can promote; and not just by making copies of unique manuscript pages more available to more readers. There is a kind of allegiance, against print, between the digital environment and working manuscripts, both of which favour looser or hybrid expressive forms and resist the stability that print prefers. Representation in print tends to confer a solidity or finality on working materials that is not intrinsic: careful consideration of how to present manuscripts in electronic form should enable the preservation of their dynamic and axiological qualities. Pierazzo turns her attention to one specific and difficult issue: how to represent and encode time, or manuscript layers (of change, revision or development), in electronic manuscript transcription.

Like Mussell and Paylor, and Roueché, Pierazzo begins from an identified need or problem: in this case, the challenge of capturing the discontinuous nature of writers' working documents. Several other chapters in the volume return, either by means of theory or practice, to the connection between the intellectual formulation of knowledge within an edition and the medium that conveys or manifests this, with the suggestion that the two – medium and content – are mutually informing. By this way of thinking, an edition in paper would imply a set of assumptions distinct from those that pertain in the digital environment. Sometimes this is so; but it is worth pointing out that not all electronic editions are either flexible or innovative, and many paper editions, some dating back to the earliest days of print, are hypertextual and remain startlingly fresh. As Mats Dahlström (p. 29) reminds us, when we think about the 'compleat edition', whether we are drawn to think by preference either of print or digital forms, we must be careful not to assume that the medium is always the message:

To even talk about *digital* editions as one particular type of edition is debatable. Current discussions on digital editions tend to talk about the genre as based on media form and publishing technology, whereas traditional discussions in editorial theory rather identify the genre as based on its epistemological foundation and theoretically based strategy. Discussions therefore end up mixing apples and pears: digital editions versus, say, eclectic editions. This presupposes one predefined function and theoretical base for the digital editions to counter the ones identified in printed editions, when in fact many kinds of editorial approaches – both traditional and innovative – are being tried out and simulated in the realm of new media.

PART I
In Theory

Chapter 1

Being Critical: Paper-based Editing and the Digital Environment

Kathryn Sutherland

Textual criticism is that branch of literary studies charged with establishing the status of texts – traditionally of literary works disseminated as written and printed documents, though in the last few decades we have extended 'text', and our critical enquiries, to the complex of cultural practices whose codes are not necessarily written but nevertheless amenable to analysis or close reading, as though they were part of the written record. Obviously, visual, oral and numeric data (film, music, recorded sound, prints, photographs), will be included; but also buildings, clothing, dance, rituals of various kinds, whose codes of influence are inscribed at a farther remove from the world of writing and print.[1] In its older and more limited application, textual criticism's concern is to establish the authority of written or printed verbal texts according to particular sets of principles, and its practical outcome has conventionally been their preparation for consumption – in the form of critical editions. In English studies, with the massive exception of Shakespeare, textual criticism is a discipline reserved almost exclusively for graduate work; even at this level many graduate schools currently prefer its more modish cultural studies formulation, History of the Book, to an engagement with textual theory, analytical bibliography or issues in editing, the various conventional sub-disciplines of textual criticism. Yet decisions drawn from the nature and phenomenology of text and how best to represent texts within scholarly editions underpin and pre-delimit every literary critical judgement we make, whether we know it or not.

The single most important feature of textual criticism is that it is critical: that is, it involves prejudiced speculation, however rigorously controlled its prejudices and pre-judging assumptions or ideologies might be. Like any branch of literary criticism, textual criticism begins from a set of assumptions on which theories and practices are built. In the case of textual criticism, we can say that its assumptions have to do with identifying what text is. In this sense, it is the foundational critical practice: it comes before any other textual engagement we may make, to this

---

1 See, for example, the arguments in D.F. McKenzie, *Bibliography and the Sociology of Texts* (1986; Cambridge: Cambridge University Press, 1999); J. Grigely, *Textualterity: Art, Theory and Textual Criticism* (Ann Arbor: University of Michigan Press, 1995); and D.C. Greetham, *Textual Scholarship: An Introduction* (New York and London: Garland Publishing, 1994), pp. 295–346.

extent always informing our subsequent critical performances, whether we know it or not. In English studies, textual criticism, like the principles and practices of literary criticism, is largely a twentieth-century discipline. As long ago as 1912, Walter Greg, an Elizabethan scholar, addressing the Bibliographical Society in London, described the amalgam of specialisms grouped under bibliography and textual criticism as 'the grammar of literary investigation'.[2] For Greg, working chiefly with the material transmission of texts as printed books, 'Textual Criticism and Critical Bibliography are synonymous';[3] and like grammar, they articulate and give structure to our critical acts. Very soon Greg was successfully arguing the case for bibliography and textual criticism to the postwar British government Committee on the Position of English in the Educational System of England, as that aspect of literary studies which underpins the subject's claims to be 'research'. Grounding its own critical acts in what Greg called its 'self-conscious' reflection into the instability of textual states, textual criticism laid claim to being the stable basis of critical enquiry because it conducted its own enquires at a profounder level. The Committee's report of 1921 distilled and quoted his observations thus:

> 'bibliography may be defined as the systematic study of the transmission of the written word whether through manuscript or print, and it aims at the evolution of a critical organon by which the utmost possible results may be extracted from the available evidence. It forms the greater and most essential part of the duty of the editor, but its value in criticism is by no means confined to the editor. It will be found of service in every field of investigation, and cannot be neglected even by the "aesthetic" critic without loss.'

And the Committee concluded: 'We are convinced that in every University where research work in English is undertaken provision should be made for instruction in bibliography.'[4] A combination of rigorous abstraction and intensive empiricism, drawn from the 'facts' and observation of text and book-making through the ages, bibliography and textual criticism would anchor the lighter-weight, subjective and impressionistic, activities of the literary critic. It might seem at this point that the textual critic had taken the high ground in the emerging new field of English Studies. And yet …

Why have we as literary critics, trained in close reading and the niceties of interpretation, traditionally cared so little about the standing of the documents on which we exercise our judgements? Is there any other interpretative discipline where the status and provenance of the interpreted object is so carelessly disregarded or simply taken on trust? Would historians or Classicists be so cavalier? This disregard remains an enduring feature of literary studies with no obvious detrimental effect

───────────────

2 W.W. Greg, 'What is Bibliography', in J.C. Maxwell (ed.), *Collected Papers* (Oxford: Clarendon Press, 1966), p. 83.

3 Greg, 'Bibliography – an Apologia', in *Collected Papers*, p. 254.

4 Quoted in Greg, 'The Present Position of Bibliography', in *Collected Papers*, p. 211.

on the seriousness with which we, the insiders, assemble, validate and broadcast our readings, and no loss of authority in the general reception accorded those readings. Even where we admit the editorial model into our critical practices, much, if not most, editing is done piecemeal, with little reference to the theoretic dimensions of the task or the wider implications of the various techniques for rigorous textual appraisal. Contextual annotation, often dismissed as a frivolous extra by serious editors, who see their proper concern as the establishment of the text, its variants and transmission history, is at the same time the kind of editing most in favour with student readers, general readers and commercially minded publishers, to all of whom it is perceived as adding value. In textual critical terms, however, it is largely worthless.

Most instructive of all is the persistent occlusion of the critical work performed by the scholarly editor on text by the very demand that such work stand outside our regular critical practices. The crudest demonstration of this is shelf-life: the scholarly edition of a literary work is expected to have a far longer life than any other critical study or opinion. The economics of adoption, as it is called in the trade, demand that an edition serve several markets over several decades: issued first as a massive and expensive multi-volume Clarendon Press hard-cover edition, say, before being stripped of its more arcane textual critical apparatus and condensed into paperback with a newly added literary critical essay under the World's Classics imprint. The intriguing point here is not that editions date or fall out of fashion, but that they do so with glacial slowness. For example, over the last 80 years, a plethora of critical readings, including most recently postcolonial and queer interpretations, have let down anchor in R.W. Chapman's carefully colonized 1923 text of the novels of Jane Austen without any voiced objection by the makers or readers of those readings that his text, based on long outmoded critical assumptions and interventions, will not support them. Chapman undertook the restoration of the texts of Austen's novels as a deliberate exercise in canonization. His syntactic regularization of her prose and quirky, belle-lettristic annotation placed her within a particular élite, male, Augustan and non-novelistic tradition, and effectively cut her off from the work of her female contemporaries. In the immediate aftermath of World War I such narrow attribution made some cultural sense. But Chapman's hyper-corrected texts have also, contradictorily, served her post-1970s' feminist revaluation as an altogether riskier and more experimental writer.[5] Oxford University Press continues to market them, unfashionable though they are, into the twenty-first century. They are readable, that is, against the grain of Chapman's earlier editorial intention. In other words, not only is there no necessary congruence between the work of the textual and the literary critic, but the latter may (and does) regularly labour in cheerful disregard of the critical procedures by which the former shaped and delivered the text. The

---

5 For a fuller account of Chapman's textual work, see K. Sutherland, *Jane Austen's Textual Lives: From Aeschylus to Bollywood* (Oxford: Oxford University Press, 2005).

qualified conclusion must therefore be that the textual critic does and does not predetermine the terms of our engagement as readers.

We might explain this coincident pre-emption of and irrelevance to the text by suggesting that practitioners within the dominant twentieth-century Anglo-American tradition of scholarly editing (New Bibliographers, as they used to be called) were simply victims of the logic of their own theorizing when, in their editorial practice, they attempted to establish a resting place in the relentless change and attendant corruption that represented the historical fate, as they saw it, of text's material transmission. Their faith lay in ideal stasis, achieved by means of the eclectic text, an emended and cleansed composite made up of several witnesses. This they aligned with a previously unrealized or betrayed authorial intention, but which might be seen, from our digital vantage point, as a kind of compressed, synoptic and editorially selected archive of variant textual states functioning as the authorial work. Thus, to take a conservative and unremarkable example, the 1984 Clarendon Press edition of Charlotte Brontë's *Villette*, prepared by Herbert Rosengarten and Margaret Smith, is based upon the text authorized by Brontë in the first printed edition of 1853. The editors emend this text with readings taken from three other states: the holograph manuscript, a further copy of the first edition made up in part of proof sheets, and an advance copy of the first edition into which Brontë at a later date inserted corrections and revisions. In other words, they take as their copy text the first edition and, as they see fit (that is, according to their informed views of her best intentions), they mix into it readings from these earlier and later states, correcting backwards and forwards, with hindsight and foresight, as it were, and confecting a text that at different points represents within it both pre and post-publication forms. Described thus, theirs is a routine eclecticism undertaken in the interests of the author. As is often remarked, this kind of editorial activity, by challenging and reversing the likely mishaps of historical transmission, results in a text that never has been. But highly interventionist though it was, its well-theorized defence effectively neutralized or naturalized the critical basis of its own labour. In claiming to represent or restore authorial intention, editors working from these principles denied their own share in shaping the text; at the same time, their intentionalism denied the eclectic text's status as critical interpretation. Though now generally disfavoured as a method, the long shelf-life of printed scholarly editions ensures that the New Bibliographic model continues to infuse the bulk of the major literary works that constitute the common ground for our critical interpretations. Perhaps this should disconcert us.

Two particular developments have helped to shift the emphasis in textual criticism and, more cautiously, in critical editing in the last three decades from ideal stasis to historical metastasis, and to suggest at the same time a potential synergy or area of cooperation between the textually engaged literary critic and the critically engaged textuist. One is the articulation of a sociological or cultural studies strain of textual criticism, represented by the following statement:

Just as there is no single, correct, or best approach to editing an author's work, there is no universal best text for a critical investigation: the choice of a text, or texts, is necessarily related to the kinds of questions being asked, and these questions themselves frequently change in the course of reading ... Textual criticism and bibliography could therefore be redefined as disciplines that study manifestations of difference in cultural texts, wherein 'difference' does not presuppose a genre or a system of values.[6]

The other development is the rapid expansion of electronic storage and dissemination as a textual device. The interesting thing is how these two – the sociological (with its robust rejection of permanent evaluative criteria) and the electronic – have become mutually implicating in the world of literary texts: that is, how the contingent and material appear to find expression and critical purpose through the digital. The very idea is deeply problematic, that the electronic archive's storage capacity might convert, through the accessing, manipulation and analysis of multiple documentary surrogates, into a strictly materialist approach to the question of how texts of a work exist and differ one from another. It is indeed as problematic as the now discredited New Bibliographic faith in an eclectic text's ability to defy the same historical fate that befell its component parts. It is sometimes hard, when confronted with such claims, to resist the impression that textual critics are oppositional by training: one constant element in their diverse procedures and purposes over the last hundred years appearing to be an adversarial engagement with the materials of their enquiry – texts – and with the real range of activities that most readers wish to perform upon them. Hence the renewed importance of being critical.

This enduring oppositionism leads to some interesting reasoning. For example, where the physical limits of the book as both a technology and a critical tool (for representing texts and for assessing the consequences of their representation through time in other books) supported the development of a theory and practice grounded in textual idealism, now the spatial liberation proposed by computer storage and dissemination persuades at least some of us that it gives access to something that turns the terms of that earlier engagement inside out: in place of synoptic abstractions, the historical versions of texts as real things; and digital facsimiles as faithful or trustworthy equivalents of originals. In the words of Martha Nell Smith, executive editor of the *Dickinson Electronic Archives*, 'the ability to provide artefacts for direct examination (rather than relying on scholarly hearsay)' is a present 'boon' that alters both the general perception of the usefulness of computation to the humanities and our expectations of editions.[7] This verdict is worth pondering on several counts. Firstly, it assumes that, unlike the book, the computer is a totally mimetic space unshaped by the constraints of its own

---

6 Grigely, *Textualterity*, p. 48.

7 M.N. Smith, 'Electronic Scholarly Editing', in S. Schreilbman, R. Siemens and J. Unsworth (eds), *A Companion to Digital Humanities* (Oxford: Blackwell, 2004). Available online at <http://www.digitalhumanities.org/companion/>, accessed 20 July 2007.

medium. Secondly, it redistributes specialist knowledge, reducing the status of the evidence provided by the print editor to 'scholarly hearsay' in favour of 'artefacts for direct examination' available in the electronic archive. Taken together, such arguments amount to a demotion of the expert human processor in favour of an alliance between mechanical means and the unknown user. Greg's 'critical organon by which the utmost possible results may be extracted from the available evidence' supposed a blend of informed system-building and refined critical imagination located in the person of the textually trained scholar; in the electronic world this translates into something more like complex computer functionality at the service of multiple use. The electronic edition's claim to a new kind of definitiveness is marked by a rebased authority, in which the emphasis shifts from intervention and interpretation to full information display. Of course, principles of selection will still apply: no electronic repository, however massive, can hold everything; and in any case, definitions of everything are subjective and perspectival. Nevertheless, many engaged in large electronic text projects celebrate their openness or facility for exhibition as a good in itself. *The Hypermedia Archive of the Complete Writings and Pictures of Dante Gabriel Rossetti*, under development at the University of Virginia, is an elegant example of a lightly edited collection of this kind, described thus on its webpage:

> When completed in 2008, the Archive will provide students and scholars with access to all of DGR's pictorial and textual works and to a large contextual corpus of materials, most drawn from the period when DGR's work first appeared and established its reputation (approximately 1848–1920), but some stretching back to the 14th-century sources of his Italian translations. All documents are encoded for structured search and analysis. The Rossetti Archive aims to include high-quality digital images of every surviving documentary state of DGR's works: all the manuscripts, proofs, and original editions, as well as the drawings, paintings, and designs of various kinds, including his collaborative photographic and craft works. These primary materials are transacted with a substantial body of editorial commentary, notes, and glosses.[8]

Such statements of principle and practice mark a shift in focus from the old book-bound author–editor alliance to an editor–reader/user partnership, brokered by the computer. Yet in our heroic efforts to grapple with the monumental technical obstacles to digitizing our high literary heritage within such archives or editions, we have scarcely begun to consider the compelling arguments that might suggest the limited worth or usefulness of so doing.

We are paying insufficient attention to electronic difference at almost every stage of our engagement with the architecture and functioning of the electronic edition because we are too enamoured of electronic simulation. Electronic materiality, the difference that electronic instantiation makes, is currently far more of a hindrance to textual engagement than any articulated limitation in the robust,

---

8 <http://jefferson.village.virginia.edu/rossetti/>, accessed 20 July 2007.

versatile and sophisticated medium of print. At the same time, we have not yet thought hard enough about who will use electronic editions or how often or for what real purposes. We know they bring delight and funding to those who compile them, but who, beyond the few compilers, are their obvious users? If we have lived through a century of cheerful disregard for or simple trust in our major paper critical editions by most professional readers (and I do not think this is an exaggeration) what makes us believe that a new medium will provoke a new, engaged response? In an important, sceptical study published in 1999, *The Internet: A Philosophical Inquiry*, Gordon Graham drew on well-tried concepts from political and moral philosophy to examine the place of electronic technology in human culture. He argued that among 'the marks of a truly transforming technology' is 'the ability to serve recurrent needs better (qualitatively as well as quantitatively)'; and he further suggested that the principles by which we evaluate the usefulness and worth of change must be objective rather than subjective: that is, not constituted simply by our desires (since people can genuinely desire worthless things) but in the form of real benefits. Real benefits are values 'which will command agreement or consensus after a process of widespread social deliberation and debate'.[9] By this way of thinking, the real world of electronic editing (electronic editions delivered as electronic editions rather than as stages in the preparation of print, that is) is still some way off. Can we really go forward into an age of digital editing with a model that suggests that each user is (or wants to be) her own editor? And if we do not (if, that is, we accept that electronic editions enact further controlling interpretations and theories about what text is), how will we equip the user to understand (and critique) those theories and interpretations? How will we equip the user to work with and against the new kind of materiality that digitization attributes? How will we make electronic editions worth desiring by more than a few developers?

Of course, not all electronic editions imply a break with the organizational structures of print, just as not all print editions impose eclectic principles. In neither case is the connection between medium and editorial approach a rigid one: electronic editions might be eclectic, editor-centred and profoundly directive; print editions are often hypertextual. In fact, one problem as I see it is that at a deep level, our definitions of text, for all their apparent extension to other media, still habitually assume print as 'the baseline'.[10] We hear this regularly in the howls of protest (or misattributed enthusiasm) when a classic novel is transposed onto film. Textual criticism has refined its theories over many centuries under the shadow of the printing press. Print expectations have shaped much of our thinking about alternative graphic forms: manuscripts, epigraphic inscriptions, even illustrations. Yet texts are always and inevitably changed by the material basis of their generation, and there can be no complete equivalence or identity between either the vehicles

---

9 G. Graham, *The Internet: A Philosophical Inquiry* (London: Routledge, 1999), pp. 37, 60.

10 Cf. the criticism offered by N.K. Hayles, *My Mother Was a Computer: Digital Subjects and Literary Texts* (Chicago: University of Chicago Press, 2005), p. 93.

which carry text or the texts themselves as self-identical objects across media. If materiality means different things in different media, then it follows that text does too. It does so more than ever if we give any credence to the assertion, offered recently by Dino Buzzetti and Jerome McGann, that the electronic domain can perform the sociological dimension that print-based critical editing cannot practically implement, but which they, along with many others, currently believe represents text's true state. What is the nature of the correspondence that the computer's simulation properties enact between a text and its non-computational carrier? How might this compute an old sociology of text (the social and documentary aspects of the book) as distinct from performing a new?

As far as I understand it, the only aspect of the book-bound text that the computer appears to simulate with any high degree of success is the visual. This can of course include many of those features we currently call, after McGann, bibliographic codes:[11] page size, fount, the placing of the type block on the page, leading, gutters, etc. However, not only does the navigational functionality of the computer screen make it clear that the way we access these visual properties is completely unlike accessing print, the visual itself is only one dimension of the book. For example, how a book feels, its volume and weight, are crucial elements in a literary work's signifying structures. Those early twentieth-century definitions of text that concentrated exclusively on its linguistic aspects provided a way of legitimating text's portability over its locatability, a means of transcending the stabilizing force of print and its vehicles of transmission – books. Ironically, not only are McGann and others currently using the computer to fetishize the book as object (a bizarre enough notion), it seems they are also currently looking to promote electronic storage and delivery *as* text's locatability, where user logs will function as 'an even more complex simulation of social textualities'.[12] This is to displace onto the e-reader those aspects of production which, in print, situated text within a socialized workforce. No New Bibliographer ever imagined an act of such attentive textual surveillance. But none of this sleight of thinking actually confronts the real issue: how texts as non-self-identical material objects can be replicated satisfactorily across material space.

Of course, if we work with literary texts our expectation is almost always zoned to print; we may need another hundred years of electronic creativity to nurture into existence a really sophisticated textual model zoned to the computer. Against McGann and his followers, I would suggest that the real advantages of electronic editing will only become apparent as we shed ideas of how digitization enhances aspects of the functionality of print culture, or releases aspects of text that print transmission betrays. This current and curiously self-contradictory obsession, by which the computer both

---

11 J.J. McGann, 'What Is Critical Editing?', in *The Textual Condition* (Princeton, NJ: Princeton University Press, 1991), p. 56.

12 D. Buzzetti and J. McGann, 'Electronic Textual Editing: Critical Editing in a Digital Horizon', in L. Burnard, K. O'Brien O'Keefe and J. Unsworth (eds), *Electronic Textual Editing* (New York: Modern Language Association of America, 2006), p. 71.

simulates and releases text from its bookishness is bound up with the seductive powers of the screen delivery of high-quality images. But, as Diana Kichuk remarks, from her careful study of Early English Books Online (EEBO):

> Claims for an identical relationship between a digital facsimile and its original, and the transparency of the user-resource experience, ignore the myriad transformations that occur when producing a facsimile in another medium. The process of remediation lowers a digital veil of varying opacity between the scholar and the original work. The scholar, gazing through that veil, seduced by the transformations wrought by remediation, suspends disbelief in order to advance the study of the text. Successful remediation depends on the witting and unwitting complicity of the viewer.[13]

At the same time, we need to remind ourselves of the restricted usefulness of the thesis posed by McGann in his widely disseminated and much-quoted essay, 'The Rationale of Hypertext'. First published in 1997, and written 'in a consciously revisionary relation to W.W. Greg's great essay "The Rationale of Copy-Text" [1950], which had such a profound influence on twentieth-century textual scholarship',[14] the highly charged rhetoric of McGann's argument relies (*contra* Greg) on our willingness to accept the exception as the rule. Where Greg, whatever we now think of his conclusions, attempted to propose principles and make policy from what he regarded as the *commonly* divided practice in the treatment of textual witnesses, McGann regularly invokes the *rare and exceptional* limitations of book technology in the service of texts. Adherents of his approach seldom note what is at least as obvious and compelling, that for every literary work that frets at its bookishness (the usual examples are Burns, Blake, Dickinson, Rossetti), a thousand others insist upon it, as a vital component of their makeup and meaning. In these everyday cases, and in the words of Geoffrey Nunberg, 'it is precisely because these [electronic] technologies transcend the material limitations of the book that they will have trouble assuming its role ... A book doesn't simply contain the inscription of a text, it *is* the inscription.'[15] For example, bibliographic accommodation, being situated within the confines of a book, is an integral feature of the narratives of most nineteenth-century novels. The feel and weight of the book's volume and its metonymic properties as a stand-in for the individual life are knit into our classic novels: 'my readers', writes Jane Austen, 'will see in the tell-tale compression of the pages before them, that we are all hastening together to perfect felicity'.[16] Print, too, can give a fair simulation of 'this drop

---

13 D. Kichuk, 'Metamorphosis: Remediation in *Early English Books Online (EEBO)*', *Literary and Linguistic Computing* 22/3 (2007): 291–303, pp. 296–7.

14 J.J. McGann, 'The Rationale of Hypertext', in K. Sutherland (ed.) *Electronic Text: Investigations in Method and Theory* (Oxford: Clarendon Press, 1997), p. 46 n. 9.

15 G. Nunberg, 'The Places of Books in the Age of Electronic Reproduction', *Representations*, 42 (1993): 13–37, p.18.

16 J. Austen, *Northanger Abbey*, vol. 2, ch. 16 (ch. 31).

of ink at the end of my pen' with which George Eliot begins to write *Adam Bede*. First-generation digital texts display equivalent poetic allegiances to the formal properties of electronic storage and transmission, as William Gibson's *Agrippa* and Michael Joyce's *afternoon* demonstrate. We need to get beyond our computer-driven simulation of bookishness, in all its forms, and begin to think openly and rigorously in directions that the computer's own materiality, architecture and functioning determine.

This kind of thinking is just beginning. Against what already looks like outmoded postmodernism, I would set Paul Eggert's recent call for an electronic equivalent of a theory of textual criticism as distinct from the electronic modelling of an old textual sociology. Eggert writes:

> Leaving aside the operations on texts performed by computational stylisticians and linguists, it is true to say that, in the main, digital texts are still serving only as surrogates for printed texts and indeed are often delivered, by preference, in that form. Existing methods of research are tacitly assumed. This is partly because the inherited consensus on what texts are and how they function has not changed with the technology.[17]

In a related move, Matthew Kirschenbaum has set out to confront some of the shibboleths current in the critique of electronic textuality. Crucial to his argument is the fundamental materiality of digital writing technologies, and therefore of electronic texts. His contention, that electronic texts are artefacts or mechanisms which, like the older technology of the book, are amenable to material and historical forms of investigation, challenges textual critics to respond to the new medium in terms of its own materiality, architecture and functioning, as distinct from those of print. The implication is that we need an electronic-sensitive theory of textual criticism (something that advances us beyond 'screen essentialism'), and that its contours will only become apparent as we shed assumptions of how digitization enhances or betrays aspects of the functionality of print.[18]

Electronic editions are still in an early stage of design; for that reason their worth is limited. That need not be a problem if, for the present, we see them as restrictedly useful depositories of data and generators of print editions. For most reading and scholarly purposes the stable or stabilized paper text is currently not only sufficient, it is best. For most purposes the fact of textual variance does not lead inevitably to the importance of variance; often it leads to its opposite. Most reading and scholarly purposes require a stable text. It is on notions of stable textual identity, persisting as shared cultural property, that reading communities are built. Contrary to much current thinking, stability is a function of print, and it is a useful one that we should not give up lightly. Ironically, too, stable print

---

17 P. Eggert, 'The Book, the E-Text and the "Work-Site"', Chapter 5 below.

18 See M.G. Kirschenbaum, 'Editing the Interface: Textual Studies and First Generation Electronic Objects', in *TEXT*, 14 (2002): 15–51; and M.G. Kirschenbaum, *Mechanisms: New Media and the Forensic Imagination* (Cambridge, MA: MIT Press, 2008).

texts have always provoked variance in interpretation, while it is even possible that shifting between multiple electronic versions within a complexly linked archive will freeze our selective capacities as readers, redirecting them towards a wilderness of locally variable and meaningfully inert features. At an extreme, each user will choose, expertly or ineptly, her own variant text to prove her own critical point (everyone her own editor),[19] a direct route to silencing critical dialogue and the shared life of our discipline.

In formulating his philosophical inquiry into the benefits of new technology, Graham built on an earlier critique of 'technopoly' by Neil Postman, who suggested that we should always ask of any new technology the following question: what is the problem to which it is a solution? Postman defined technopoly as 'a state of culture'. He continued:

> It is also a state of mind. It consists in the deification of technology, which means that the culture seeks its authorization in technology, finds its satisfactions in technology, and takes its orders from technology. This requires the development of a new kind of social order, and of necessity leads to the rapid dissolution of much that is associated with traditional beliefs. Those who feel most comfortable in Technopoly are those who are convinced that technical progress is humanity's superhuman achievement and the instrument by which our most profound dilemmas may be solved. They also believe that information is an unmixed blessing, which through its continued and uncontrolled production and dissemination offers increased freedom, creativity, and peace of mind. The fact that information does none of these things – but quite the opposite – seems to change few opinions, for unwavering beliefs are an inevitable product of the structure of Technopoly. In particular, Technopoly flourishes when the defenses against information break down.[20]

Refining Postman's and Graham's inquiry to one privileged category of information, the critical edition, we might ask: what use do we have as professional and general readers of literature for powerful electronic scholarly editions or archives? Will our uses of texts as mediated by the new technology serve any pre-existent ends or will they transform the way we think about texts; and if so, is this transformation desirable? Will it make for a better world or, more modestly, will it change our relationship to our textual heritage for the better? If it is the case, as it seems to be, that as literary critics we do not care greatly to quarrel with the status of the texts of the literary works we examine, are we likely to care more when offered a menu of texts to choose from or to collate for ourselves (and possibly even create as new eclectic forms) within an electronic repository? The advantage of the fixed printed scholarly edition was the passive reliance it enjoined. If as critical readers we rarely dip into the apparatus of the print edition to question a textual emendation, will we wish to use the computer tools that urge us to investigate text as complex or at

---

19 Against this line of reasoning, see E. Vanhoutte, 'Every Reader his own Bibliographer – an Absurdity?', Chapter 7 below.

20 N. Postman, *Technopoly: The Surrender of Culture to Technology* (New York: Vintage Books, 1993), pp. 71–2.

least multiple processes of composition, production and dissemination? And if we do, how will the results from this searching of the data be brought into reasonable conversation with anything worth saying or worth sharing? Is large-scale electronic editing as currently conceived anything more than the revenge of the textual critic?

It does not follow that, because the stabilized text of traditional scholarly editing provoked diverse interpretations and engaged debate around its composite form, a decentred or unstable text will lead to anything richer or more persuasive than solipsistic self-communing. On the contrary, procedures that restrain individual impulse in certain areas and insist upon a measure of conformity may be essential; real debate depends on real consensus. Similarly, the editor's exercise of a proper expertise may be more liberating for more readers than seemingly total freedom of choice. To borrow Postman's words, it may be that the editor, someone with skill born of long training and specialized knowledge employed responsibly, is one of our necessary 'defences' against information.

For most critical purposes we want stable reading texts that remain stable over considerable periods of time (decades), because it is this stability that encourages sustained critical reflection. There are important exceptions, of course, and some of these are represented in other essays in this collection: texts that really do defy reprinting in conventional paper forms or never had a bookish dimension and, unlike many literary works, do not depend critically upon that; and texts whose enhanced functionality within the electronic environment is already widely appreciated. In most cases, these will be texts whose main use is non-sequential reading – old runs of newspapers, dictionaries. The inscriptions represented in the Aphrodisias in Late Antiquity Project, while vitally dependent on their stone vehicular forms, cannot be adequately represented in print. The textual dynamic of working manuscripts, too, responds well to electronic storage and display. On the other hand, many literary texts actually lose a valuable critical dimension, their inhering bookishness (though they gain analytic functionality), when they are digitized. Another significant group, though less legitimate in terms of any internal match between the requirements of the text and the technology, are texts that print publishers refuse to commission because they do not expect them to have a shelf-life: electronic repositories can make these available in print-on-demand form. What I see the electronic as best serving (at the moment) is the storage and display of a level of variance which for some of us will remain the detritus of the stable text and for others its supplement or occasional extension, a kind of textual laboratory. I am thinking of projects like the *Cambridge Edition of the Works of Jonathan Swift* (described elsewhere in this volume) and the *Cambridge Edition of the Works of Ben Jonson*, described by David Gants as 'two complementary but materially distinct projects that together attempt to participate in the continuing editorial dialogue: a six-volume traditional edition that will be published in print form, and a networked electronic edition that … will continue to develop dynamically on its own [sic] as scholarship and technology advance'.[21]

One of the overwhelming challenges facing the world in the twenty-first century is storing, recycling or otherwise disposing of the accumulated by-products of our consumerist existences. These might be waste products of various kinds. In our world of textuality, one of the problems will be who will manage and make selections from the huge amount of information that the electronic archive stores and makes available. In the paper edition there is an assumption (widely seen and shared) that an editor will have done some (probably much) of this work; for most purposes even the diligent scholar will not worry about what she does not see. What remains on display in the printed edition is carefully sectioned away, to be examined or ignored by the reader. Hence a print edition, even one that is complexly structured, can be used with relative ease by a range of different level readers, and for different purposes. Currently, most electronic editors have not grappled with this; they assume a sophisticated editor-user. That in itself is ironic given the general drift away from a disciplined knowledge of textual critical principles even among those who assemble such deposits. Because the capacity of the technology allows selection to be postponed, and requires kinds of competence (complex encoding, for example) beyond many editors' range of abilities, even those who assemble the edition may well not know how the parts, under their technical control, interconnect intellectually. This may lead, for the first time, to the real neutrality of the editor. But even the very few informed users may need the assistance of a bank of helpers to sort through the sheer amount of information that any interrogation of the electronic deposit is likely to throw up. So I do not see that the economics (in a wide sense) of the thing really add up as yet. As supplement to or, as it now regularly is, as begetter of the critical paper edition, the electronic depository is currently best seen as a recyclable wastebank, one that can be scavenged by scholars for particular purposes, and, as required, mined for new critical editions. Currently and forseeably these will most usefully (most usefully, that is, for most people and most reading practices) continue to be stabilized, printed, paper critical editions.

---

21 'Drama Case Study: *The Cambridge Edition of the Works of Ben Jonson*', in Burnard, O'Keefe and Unsworth (eds), *Electronic Textual Editing*, p. 123.

Chapter 2
The Compleat Edition[1]

Mats Dahlström

Scholarly editions (SEs) based on textual criticism have historically been developed in intimate relationship with particular script and print-based technologies and distribution logistics. In consequence, editorial theories and strategies are intertwined in their scope, rhetorics and strategies with particular media materialities and epistemologies. This relationship was certainly there in the temporarily stabilized universe of print media, but was rarely discussed. It is now becoming so to an increasing degree. We are currently experiencing not one but several parallel introductions of new media and technologies, exhibiting radically different logistics and parameters for document production and distribution than previous media ecologies do. For instance, new media and web distribution promise vastly to enhance the spatial confines of SEs, or even to annihilate them altogether. What changes are we witnessing in the division of labour between the people involved in scholarly editing and the tools they use, and in the various media outputs from such endeavours?

The making of SEs and archives using new media seems to have opened up new kinds of communication between academic and professional communities that were formerly more or less isolated from each other. Programmers and software designers on the one hand and textual critics and bibliographers on the other have come to work together in several digital editing projects, creating grounds for new kinds of negotiation of competence and power. Editing and editions make use of many different technologies and media. Types of edition also stand in delicate relation to each other due to particular historical ecologies of media. The organization and architecture of SEs as well as the task division between different media change as the ecology changes.

Looking at, for instance, current Scandinavian national editing projects that publish on the web, on discs, as e-books and in print, such as the Ibsen or Almqvist projects, one sees the forming of a new division of labour between various display and distribution solutions, a changed balance between the variants of edition types. The web edition turns into a large resource archive and editorial laboratory, and even more often into a more or less temporary interface to a changing, dynamic digital archive. This affects the scope and function of the editorial material being printed. The printed version does not have to include the laboratory material of the

---

1 An earlier version of this paper entitled 'How Reproductive is a Scholarly Edition' appeared in *Literary and Linguistic Computing*, 19/1 (2004): 17–33.

editors (variants, alternative versions, minor paratexts, illustrations and so forth), but rather confines itself to a single, uniform reader's text with a minimum of editorial tools and paratexts. The digital cumulative archive, on the other hand, assumes the role of the primary, with or without a web interface, from which static spin-offs are secondarily launched in print, on CD, as e-books or on the web. The digital archive is thus able to play with various document forms as outputs.[2] A printed codex edition embodying the principles of one particular editorial theory is therefore no longer the only possible output of the editing endeavour, but rather one potential output from among many that, at least in theory, might satisfy several different and perhaps even rival theoretical ideals.

One of the questions we ask ourselves in the light of this development is whether the SE can and should continue to fulfil the same functions. To what extent, if any, might the logic and capabilities of new media affect the essence of scholarly editing? Do we need editions any longer, or should we rather invest our human, economic and textual resources in massive, long-term digital archives? Any attempt at answering such questions will need to begin by reconsidering the nature of the SE, what forces it has and has not, what limits it has and what kind of factors determine its possibilities and limits. This chapter attempts a tentative discussion of such forces and limits of the SE, and specifically looks at its supposedly representational and reproductive force. The aim is to identify poles of extreme positions in editorial discourse and thereby to map out the fields of tension and perhaps conflict that lie between them. Since I come from the field of bibliography and library and information science, I will also make an argument for the bibliographical dimension of the SE.

The scholarly edition

The SE is, and has been for a long time, a complex and diverse family of document types. Many technologies, professional practices and academic areas converge in it. The result is a spectrum of variant types ranging from facsimile, diplomatic, synoptic, genetic, critical, variorum editions to large-scale digital archives on compact discs or mounted on the web. There is little general agreement as to the classifications. A division of critical versus non-critical, for instance, might render the impression that non-critical editions, whereby diplomatic and transcription types are usually designated, somehow escape implementing the scrutiny of textual criticism or of critical inquiry. More to the point, the labelling of the results of digital editing seems, as has been pointed out,[3] to further blur some of these

---

2 J. Svedjedal, *The Literary Web: Literature and Publishing in the Age of Digital Production. A Study in the Sociology of Literature* (Stockholm: The Royal Library, 2000).

3 P. Robinson, 'What Is a Critical Digital Edition?', *Variants: The Journal of the European Society for Textual Scholarship*, 1 (2002): 43–62, p. 45ff.; E. Vanhoutte, 'Display or Argument: Markup and Visualization for Electronic Scholarly Editions', in T. Burch, J.

classifications. To even talk about *digital* editions as one particular type of edition is debatable. Current discussions on digital editions tend to talk about the genre as based on media form and publishing technology, whereas traditional discussions in editorial theory rather identify the genre as based on its epistemological foundation and theoretically based strategy. Discussions therefore end up mixing apples and pears: digital editions versus, say, eclectic editions. This presupposes one predefined function and theoretical base for the digital editions to counter the ones identified in printed editions, when in fact many kinds of editorial approaches – both traditional and innovative – are being tried out and simulated in the realm of new media.

There is little room or intention in this chapter to elaborate further on the classifications of SEs. Perhaps we can at least agree on their quality as tools and results of scholarly inquiry, enabling us to refer to them as *scholarly* editions (while the term *critical* editions in this chapter refers to the historical-eclectic edition type). I would argue that there is also another common denominator for SEs: their nature as *bibliographical* instruments.

The scholarly edition as bibliographical tool

There is obviously a historical bond between, on the one hand bibliographic activity, and on the other, scholarly editing based on textual criticism, from Alexandria and onwards. Scholarly editing and textual criticism were indeed originally conceived within a bibliographical transmission activity in a library institution context, a historical connection revived with the currently intense digitization activity in libraries. Particular branches of bibliography have collaborated closely with scholarly editing, such as textual and analytical bibliography. But there are also deeper epistemological bonds.

Editing is an attempt to produce a document that bibliographically constitutes other documents. The declared principles and explicit concepts and ideals of editorial theory are, in a sense, statements of bibliographic ideals. Its concept levels and hierarchies overlap considerably with those of bibliography. The way reference bibliography structures works and documents by making bibliographies and catalogues is strikingly analogous to the way scholarly editing structures works, documents, versions and variants by making critical editions. A critical edition is a statement as to the extent and confinements of a particular work. That is why it is central to both bibliography and editing to understand and define the concepts of works, texts and documents. That is also why concept relations and conceptual analyses are crucial ingredients in the emerging theory development within both fields.

Fournier, K. Gärtner and A. Rapp (eds), *Standards und Methoden der Volltextdigitalisierung. Beiträge des Internationalen Kolloquiums an der Universität Trier, 8./9. oktober 2001* (Stuttgart: Franz Steiner, 2003), pp. 71–96.

Several bibliographical and editorial activities and functions correspond, such as the classification of what makes up a particular work, version management and hierarchical ordering of documents. The typology of editions furthermore represents a division of bibliographical labour and interests: the critical, historical-eclectic, operates at the work level, the transcription edition at the text level, and the facsimile edition at the graphical and material document level. The way the SE manages work-version-document relations is analogous to the way a catalogue manages bibliographic relations[4] or the way the International Federation of Library Associations' *Functional Requirements for Bibliographic Records* talk about them.[5] There are, however, also areas where scholarly editing and bibliography differ in this respect. In particular reference bibliography displays much less interest in *texts* than scholarly editing does, and consequently has few or no instruments that equal the variant categories of textual criticism to determine versions and works or to identify and delimit the significant text in a work or a document.

The two fields consequently share a set of problems, such as difficulties in specifying the work level, the battle to define text and ambivalence to the materiality of documents. This ambivalence makes it awkward, for instance, to demarcate text and version, and to explain and manage distortion. The connections between the fields can be further identified in their respective theoretical frameworks, tenets and scientific ideals. In bibliography, however, the idealistic, unbiased and objectifying tradition is even more prominent than in scholarly editing.

The scholarly edition as icon

But editing and bibliography are not only clustering activities. There is a related outcome of the way bibliography, primarily enumerative bibliography, and editing based on textual criticism are similar activities, or in effect two variants of the same activity: *iconicity*. This is one of the chief objectives of both activities, which is to produce surrogates by iconic representation. As the late Ross Atkinson pointed out in his stimulating 1980 article,[6] bibliographic records, catalogue posts and text-critical editions all function as simile representations, ranging from the single catalogue entry, via full-text records in databases, via facsimile editions, transcriptions, critical editions, variorum and synoptic editions, over to full-scale exhaustive databases or digital archives. There is obviously a considerable scale of exhaustiveness and completeness, but nevertheless a commonality in iconicity.

---

4 R.P. Smiraglia, *The Nature of a 'Work": Implications for the Organization of Knowledge* (Lanham, MD: Scarecrow Press, 2001).

5 International Federation of Library Associations (IFLA), *Functional Requirements for Bibliographic Record: Final Report*, UBCIM publications, vol. 19 ns (München: Saur, 1998). Available online at <http://www.ifla.org/VII/s13/frbr/frbr.pdf>, accessed 2 October 2007.

6 R. Atkinson, 'An Application of Semiotics to the Definition of Bibliography', *Studies in Bibliography*, 33 (1980): 54–73.

'An enumerative bibliography,' Atkinson writes, 'reproduces its Object in microcosm; it is a reflection, a picture of its Object. As such, the relationship between sign and referent in enumerative bibliography is one of *similarity* and may consequently be designated iconic.' The same really goes for *descriptive bibliography*, he continues, and interestingly enough also for the way *textual criticism* is a reflection, a picture of the edited work as perceived and constructed by the editor in one or several documents. '[T]he document (in its various conditions),' Atkinson goes on, 'is approached as a set of representable characteristics – a raw material – from which a product, the description, is to be created.' The difference between reference and descriptive bibliography as activities is quantitative. If you take into account the consequences and assume the process is carried out exhaustively to the greatest degree, what you end up with is textual criticism. Again, there is only a theoretical scale of exhaustiveness. From this angle, textual criticism is a natural extension of bibliography, and Atkinson in fact posits a constellation of iconicity as EDT (Enumerative bibliography, Descriptive bibliography and Textual criticism).

Atkinson's is one of the few argumentations I have seen for the epistemological denominator of iconicity between textual criticism and bibliographical activities, and it deserves merit for this quite simple but important observation. Let us grant that the boundary between a critical edition and a reference bibliography is not entirely sharply defined, and that there are many further commonalities between editions and bibliographies, such as multi-sequentiality, referentiality and modularization into fragments that can be separately referenced. I would, however, only follow Atkinson up to a point: scholarly editions and reference works such as bibliographies do position themselves at different places on a scale from reference to referent. The edition simultaneously refers to a work and manifests it, becoming a referent. Bibliographies and reference works cannot reasonably claim this.

The scholarly edition as media translation

The potency of simple iconicity is, however, open to inquiry. Iconic representations are bridges between documents (as interfaces to the works at hand), striving to maximize the degree of similarity when transporting the perceived work contents between them – but how potent are our tools at achieving such similarity? Representation in this case is an instance of the activity of copying, reproduction or what I will refer to as *media translation*. Metaphors convey something of the underlying understanding of the process. The translation metaphor emphasizes the derivative status of the results of the process, whereas metaphors such as transmission or transition suggest that what is being transferred goes through more or less intact (or they are indifferent to whether there is a change or not).

Using documents, we hope to be able to access repeatedly some of the originally intended qualities of a work, and we also intend for these original qualities to be repeated in more or less the same manner every time we access the document. If the process is repeated in the 'same manner', we are satisfied that we have had access to the work. If, however, the manner of the process deviates far enough, we sense that it no longer conveys the same work. But as long as each document manifestation is more or less adequate, a tangible, readable, accessible instance of the work is presented to the world. In other words, with documents we hope to be able to keep the work alive, or rather to keep the memory of the acted work alive.

Needless to say perhaps, documents are also media and matter, and so documents are also subjected to the natural decay true of all matter. They crumble away and die. If the material instantiation of a work dies, the work it contains dies with it *unless* we keep it alive in the internal memories of people or in external memories, i.e. re-instantiating the work in a new document or set of documents.

Media translation goes from a departure document to a target document. It entails many phases: for example, scrutinizing a document, trying to establish what particulars in the document are substantive elements of the work we suppose the document contains, and then using a new document (from the same type of medium as the departure document or from a different type of medium) into which we try to carve text and other signs in order to manufacture a target document that purports to be a remake of the departure document and, to some extent, of the work the latter contained. But it is vital to recognize that the target document is always *derivative* in relation to the departure document. (I am referring here to intentional sequential rather than to mechanical parallel media transition.)

There are many types of media translation at use now and in history: monastic hand-copying, microfilming or digitization such as scanning are all examples of media translations using departure and target documents. Translation brings about transmissional noise. Although rather unproblematic in an abundance of genres, such noise, however, tends to become considerably awkward in cultural heritage works and other material that particularly calls for the critical inquiry of human subjectivity. Textual criticism is a historical solution for coming to terms with such noise. There are vast numbers of potential parameters introducing noise and constraining the target document and its text:

- the socio-cognitive, psychological, linguistic particulars of the *individual(s)* responsible for carrying out the translation;
- socio-cultural and socio-technical particulars of the *situation* in which the translation takes place (e.g. culture and tradition, purpose, specific audience, media environment);
- the material and technological particulars of the departure and target *media* (such as supporting matter, longevity, compatibility, document architecture);
- physical or symbolic *tools* at use in the process (such as practices and techniques, software, platforms, requirements, regulations and rules), and so on.

In particular, this is so if by text is implied not only the linguistic text expressed in linear sequences of alphanumeric characters along with punctuation, but also the accidental textual particulars (expressed by typography and other visual markers) that McGann labels bibliographic codes.[7] If the former aspect is normally subject to authorial intention, the latter is more often the result of collaborative acts, including those of typographers, printers and editors. The bibliographic codes are probably subject to media translational changes to a higher degree than are the linguistic characters we normally define as the pure text.

Each medium as well as each document type produced within and for that medium brings to the text a semiotic system of its own. In the translation process, certain features of the work are preserved that can be carved into the flesh of the new medium and can be expressed by its architecture and the language of its web of signs, while others are treated as noise, obscuring the substantive signals. If translation is successful (in the sense that a human agent accepts the target document as representing the same work as the departure document) we feel the work has been kept alive for yet a little time, namely the time span of the new document instantiation. Then the work is translated again and again, perhaps even across centuries and millennia. At the same time, it is being reinterpreted by new readers and users and thus brought to new life, each new manifestation mirroring particular contemporary medial, social or cognitive settings. But when no more translations take place, no more new documents refresh the work and the old documents finally die, the externally memorized work has ceased to be. And this is how we have lost the vast majority of the works produced in history. Alongside the preservation of the original document, media translation is a crucial instrument for bringing external memories of past works across generations.

The scholarly edition as scientific tool

Scholarly editing is an important instrument in such media translation processes, and the SE is consequently subjected to the constraints discussed above. These are recognized by much editorial theory, but far from always explicitly acknowledged in the SEs themselves. Particularly in idealistic editing discourse, SEs have often been presented as neutral 'scientific' instruments. Scheibe,[8] for example, claimed that scholarly editing must maintain the objective approach to texts that has become impossible within literary studies. He therefore called for the mass production of definitive historical-critical editions that would not need to be renewed to fit every new interpretative act or theoretical position.

---

7 J.J. McGann, *Radiant Textuality* (New York: Palgrave, 2001).

8 S. Scheibe, 'Zu einigen Grundprinzipien einer historisch-kritischen Ausgabe', in G. Martens and H. Zeller (eds), *Texte und Varianten: Probleme ihrer Edition und Interpretation* (München: Beck, 1971), pp. 1–44.

An SE does contain introductory essays, statements of editorial principles and reports of the methods that were implemented in the task of editing; but these do not always address issues of subjectivity in the editorial function, such as how the editor contributes to shaping the edited work through his/her deliberate choices about versions, forms, granularity, media and presentation. Rather, the impression one gets from reading many SEs and their statements is one of presumed inter-subjectivity, reusability and cumulative force. This is realized through the use of the critical apparatus, the stemma and the editor's account of techniques and methods applied, the level of textual granularity chosen and the specific paths taken. All this is to enable the user-as-editor, as it were, to follow the same paths or to tread different paths than those trodden by the editor. With adequately and carefully applied methods and techniques, the scholarly editor supposedly draws the 'correct' text of the edited work from one or several documents, affecting its text only in as much as she/he washes it clean from the dirt of corruption.

One outcome of this is the idea that editorial practice and textual criticism are recreating original material, be it an abstract intentional authorial text or a particular document text such as the reception text or a manuscript text. An extreme but increasingly moot conviction claims it to be both possible and ideal to confine the editorial task to mere discovery and proliferation of the original, to being somewhat of a transparent medium in which the work can safely be transported to its readers. The editor then goes on to report his/her work and reproduce the work in a new document, the edition, which in turn can be used as working material for new scholarly endeavour. But we must keep in mind the simple fact that rather than recreating the departure documents themselves, scholarly editing engages in creating new, target documents, 'similar' but all the same derivative from the departure material.

Arguments as to the degree of representational force of the SE work along an axis. At one pole, editing as textual transmission between documents is a relatively uncomplicated matter. The real challenge is then to generate methods and technologies for the transmission to be performed with little or no noise – that is, transmissional noise can be annihilated. At the other pole, scholarly editing is an undertaking inevitably constrained by many medial factors, making transmissional noise inevitable. From the point of view of the philosophy of science, the axis is related to, on the one hand, *idealism* (where a simplistic Platonist variant regards contents as disembodied, separable from their physical document carriers and hence transportable in their entirety to other carriers) and, on the other, *materialism* (where the extreme position would argue that texts are not only media typical but even exclusive to particular material media).

Given the promises of new media and web distribution vastly to enhance the spatial confines of the editorial material, or even to annihilate them altogether, a subscriber to the idealistic view might be tempted to plead for the making of 'total' digital archives, where every document witness and variant of every work of an author can be accessed in digital form in all manner of display and modes and for all kinds of purpose. This is akin to Kanzog's famous call[9] for the makings of archive editions that would include all versions and variants of a work to such an exhaustive degree that any future editor of the work would settle for the edition as a surrogate for the departure documents themselves. The idea is also to enable a user to generate practically any type of edition she/he desires and thus partly or wholly to fulfil the editorial task him/herself. But in order to provide such a carte blanche to the unknown future user-as-editor, the archive would have to supply the user with access to all the departure documents in their entirety, supporting any kind of analytical aspect. An impossible task: you cannot possibly computerize and encode all possible aspects of a document. Such ideas run the risk of turning into 'mimetic fallacies'.

In an email discussion list thread on digitization and text encoding, Willard-McCarty[10] referred to two recurring fallacies in digitization debates and media theory as the 'complete encoding fallacy' and the 'mimetic fallacy'. I think both make way for simple replacement models. The complete encoding fallacy was defined by McCarty as 'the idea that it is possible completely to encode a verbal artefact', the mimetic fallacy being 'the idea that a digitized version will be able to replace its non-digital original'. The two are closely linked. If it is possible to 'completely' identify, formulate and unambiguously encode every aspect of an artefact, say a document, into another document, then by logic the target document ought to be in every aspect equivalent to the departure document. And if it is indeed equivalent, it follows that to users it is of no importance whether they get their hands on the one or the other. And if that is of no importance, then there is little need for retaining both the departure and the equivalent target document in a collection. The target document can in other words *replace* the departure document because it is a perfect mimic of it, or at least perfect enough to get rid of the old one. Conversely, you cannot make a case for mimetics if you do not believe it is possible to transfer *all* the potentially relevant aspects between media and between documents.

To these fallacies, the idealistic disembodiment viewpoint is of course an intellectual necessity: you cannot legitimize mimetics if you do not subscribe to the possibility of completely separating document from information. In all fairness, these are just ephemeral names and were probably not intended by McCarty to be regarded as definitive models of the state of affairs in current media theory, but rather as mere handles with which to manage the particular discussion thread at hand and to make some rhetorical points in that particular context. Nevertheless, I

---

9 K. Kanzog *Prolegomena zu einer historisch-kritischen Ausgabe der Werke Heinrich von Kleists: Theorie und Praxis einer modernen Klassiker-Edition* (München: Hanser, 1970).

10 W. McCarty, 'Data Modelling for the History of the Book?', *Humanist Discussion Group* 16 (26 February 2003), 509 (London: King's College, Centre for Computing in the Humanities, 2003). Available online at <http://www.kcl.ac.uk/humanities/cch/humanist>, accessed 2 October 2007.

think 'mimetic fallacies' is useful as an explicit label when discussing problematic tendencies so far only hinted at implicitly in many discourses on the various processes involved in the production, digitization, distribution, consumption and indeed translation of works, documents and their texts.

The scholarly edition as rhetorical tool

Particularly in the textbooks and classrooms of bibliography and the adjacent fields of library and information science, textual studies or historiography, there is a tendency to treat bibliographical tools as more or less neutral instruments. They are referred to as being impeccably beyond the limitations of spatial, material, medial, historical, social and ideological constraints, and free from the biases and tastes of any author. Any close reading of the tools as *texts*, however, reveals their situatedness: their dependency on particular historical media settings, their sociocultural roles and functions, or their argumentative, even *rhetorical* dimension.

For instance, the tools have been developed as solutions to problems in specific historical media situations. The parameters of new media technologies and the logistics of distributive networks make us aware of the medial and technical constraints of the tools. Their shape and architecture at a given moment in history are not haphazard but a result of particular media settings. New media contain and distribute the genres and architectures of older media. Perhaps needless to say, they also impose constraints on what is both theoretically and pragmatically achievable with the bibliographic tools. Further, the tools are never genre neutral, but on the contrary steeped in certain genre assumptions and respective social functions.[11]

There are social and historical dimensions in the tools of bibliography as well, as these are instruments performing on various social arenas, mediating between communities. The tools are also always to some extent hermeneutical documents, subjective interpretations, in two senses: they carry with them a history of ideology and a hermeneutical heritage, and they also exert an interpretative influence over the objects they are designed to manage.

This gives us an opportunity to return to Atkinson's article. His, I would say, is an incomplete recognition of the various aims and functions of textual criticism. It is also unfair to infer from Atkinson that scholarly editing and SEs always depend on textual criticism and therefore share its aims and functions. SEs are produced for a number of reasons by and for a number of professions and groups in society, using a variety of media, bibliographical levels in the scope of the edited material selected, granularity, editorial strategies and theoretical programmes. In short, an SE is not only an iconic representational device, but a social and inter-communal instrument as well.

---

11 J. Andersen, 'The Materiality of Works: The Bibliographic Record as Text', *Cataloguing and Classification Quarterly*, 33, 3/4 (2002): 39–65.

Furthermore, if we regard the SE as a genre, there are useful perspectives in genre theory to analyse bibliographical tools such as the SE. Among the many genre perspectives around in literary theory, linguistics, sociology and new rhetorics, Carolyn Miller's much-quoted idea of a genre as 'typified rhetorical actions based in recurrent situations'[12] strikes me as particularly fruitful. It emphasizes both a functional perspective of documents in use and the rhetorical dimensions of genres. Genres are more than the commonality of textual and visual patterns in documents, and Miller points to the socio-rhetorical situations that give rise to the documents. I think we can bring this perspective to analyse bibliographical tools such as the SE.

In a 2000 conference talk, Bethany Nowviskie made an interesting comment on the nature of SEs: '[A] scholarly edition contains an editorial essay, which makes an argument about a text or set of texts, and is then followed by an arranged document that constitutes a frozen version of that argument ... [T]he text of a scholarly edition is an embodied argument being made by the text's editor.'[13] This is as straightforward as it is important as an observation, and it is in line with Miller's observation on the rhetoricity of genres. When the SE is looked upon as an embodied argument made by an authoritative instance of responsibility (a Foucaldian 'editorial function'), one can regard the SE as a *text* of its own, approaching the status of a bibliographical work in its own right. The edited work is, then, incorporated into the edition-as-work, or more precisely: the text of the edited work becomes a sign in the editor's text.

An editor might suppress or acknowledge her presence and influence in the SE, but the subjectivity is still there. The tension between acknowledged presence and presumed absence of the editor has a long history in textual criticism and scholarly editing. To intervene or not to intervene might, in David Greetham's use of words,[14] be described as a choice between an Alexandrian and a Pergamanian editorial ideal. The former accepts and even presupposes intervention and corrections, laying the ground for eclectic editing, while to the latter interventions and corrections are theoretically awkward (and even come close to heresy), making way for the school of facsimile and best-text editing. The more explicit in an SE an editor's presence, the more the genre achieves authorial status. Conversely, the more an editor seemingly withdraws from the scene, the lesser its status as an authorial text. Going back to the idea of total digital archives based on diplomatic and facsimile editions: if in academic discourse scholars appear to want to 'hide' their role as narrative writers, then such an archive promises – or threatens – to enable them to vanish altogether, inviting readers to step in and fill the creative,

---

12 C.R. Miller, 'Genre as Social Action', *Quarterly Journal of Speech*, 70 (1984): 151–67, p. 159.

13 B. Nowviskie 'Interfacing the Edition', available online at <http://jefferson.village. virginia.edu/~bpn2f/1866/interface.html>.

14 D. Greetham, *Theories of the Text* (Oxford: Oxford University Press, 1999), p. 50f.

authoritative editorial function. As noted by Bjelland,[15] there might in such cases be problems when, in an attempt to achieve user-friendliness, the archives seek to hide their markup, scripts and programming details, which actually disarms the user-as-editor.

Atkinson's description of textual criticism and scholarly editing activity has an idealistic flair about it, as if it were the sole objective of textual criticism and scholarly editing to recreate as accurately as possible one or several documents in a new document. As Henrikson reminds us,[16] if the purpose of an SE is little more than to carry the linguistic text of the work between generations of readers and media as accurately and objectively as possible, then there are certainly fast, cheap and reliable methods for accomplishing this by means of automation. But SEs, including the ones based on textual criticism, are more often than not producing new rhetorical documents. The users of the edition are not only perfectly aware that the edition text deviates from the departure document texts. Indeed, this very reconfiguring, repositioning and recontextualizing of the edited work is conceived of as a core value of the editorial work. An SE is rather an attempt at positioning the work in contemporary literary or philological discourse.

So while I agree with Atkinson on the iconical denominator, I would contend that textual criticism and scholarly editing are also hermeneutical and rhetorical activities. The tools and documents they use and produce are equally interpretative and argumentative. In that way, and if we feel comfortable with Peircean distinctions, textual criticism and editing are also indexical activities, related to analytical bibliography, which places an SE along other axes as well.

The scholarly edition as reproductive tool

To sum up, the SE is a subjective, rhetorical device. It is, moreover, both a result of and a comment on contemporary values, discussions and interests. It is situated in time, in space, in culture and in particular media ecologies (of both departure and target media). To all bibliographical genres using derivative target documents as representations of departure documents, these are factors imposing constraints on their iconic force. The situatedness limits the representational and, moreover, the remediating force of bibliographic tools, including the SE. There are no absolutes here. The SE obviously *has* representational and reproductive force – the very abundance and undisputable value of SEs throughout history testify to that truism.

15 K. Bjelland, 'The Editor as Theologian, Historian and Archaeologist: Shifting Paradigms within Editorial Theory and their Sociocultural Ramifications', *Analytical & Enumerative Bibliography* 1 (2000): 1–43.

16 P. Henrikson, 'Kampen om litteraturhistorien: romantikerna som filologer', in L. Burman and B. Ståhle Sjönell (eds), *Text och tradition. Om textedering och kanonbildning* [Text and Tradition. On Text Editing and the Creation of a Literary Canon]. Nordiskt Nätverk för Editionsfilologer. Skrifter. 4 (Stockholm: Svenska Vitterhetssamfundet, 2002), p. 56.

The interesting question is what factors are at work to limit or to enhance this force. Another important matter is what force and purpose the remediated material itself might have; that is, to what degree the SE is valuable as a laboratory, as working material for new scholarly editorial endeavours. I am not talking about the value of SEs for historians, for literary critics, for studies in the history of ideas, etc., but for the makings of new critical SEs. I should also point out that while the concept of reusability is about the degree to which fragments of an edition's texts might be imported, reused and altered by later projects (editorial or not), the concept of reproductivity catures that dimension of generating entire new critical editions. The latter but not the former signifies a change in the editions status from target to departure document.

A claim has been put forward that digital archives can be used as the platform from which to construct new critical editions of high scholarly quality that differ in scope, intended audiences, bibliographical levels and underlying editorial strategies and theoretical programmes.[17] This is an interesting claim that has a nicely pragmatic ring to it, but I think we need to address the limitations of such presumed archives. One might also generalize the question and ask in how many cases earlier, print-based editing has been able to rely, partly or even solely, on the material contained in previous SEs as the raw material for the production of new critical editions with little or no need for consulting the *fontes*, the original documents? I think the number is scarce, and I think there are several reasons for this. Obviously, the inclusivity, the simulating capacity, the modularity and the transportable flexibility of new media are considerably different from what it is possible to achieve with printed codex editions, but are the principal problems considerably different as well?

The claim of the printed edition's reproductivity is questionable. It is based on the SE's supposedly scientific nature, in that it supplies reports of the editorial labour undertaken, a conscientious inventory of the extant material of the edited work, along with reproductive tools such as the critical apparatus or the stemma, arming the users to undertake editorial research themselves based on what the SE has to report. But to what extent do printed SEs really lend themselves to being such cumulative reports and reproductive laboratories? Are they being used that way at all? One should note the distrust expressed in relation to the reproductive force of, for example, the critical apparatus, whose functionality might even be a chimera.[18] The variant notes can arguably be described as evidence-based arguments in support of the editor's claim rather than as reproductive instruments. As such, they are end points rather than starting points.

17 E.S. Ore, 'Elektronisk publisering: forskjellige utgaveformer og forholdet til grunntekst(er) og endelig(e) tekst(er)', in: L. Burman and B. Ståhle Sjönell (eds), *Vid texternas vägskäl: textkritiska uppsatser* (Nordiskt Nätverk för Editionsfilologer. Skrifter: 1) (Stockholm: Svenska Vitterhetssamfundet, 1999), pp. 138–44.

18 E. Vanhoutte, 'Where is the Editor?: Resistance in the Creation of an Electronic Critical Edition', *Human IT*, 3/1 (1999): 197–214, p. 202.

Digital editing makes use of such print-born reproductive tools, but also fosters new ideas of how to accommodate reproductivity. Such ideas are normally founded on the inclusive, simulating and hypertextual capabilities of new media, exploding the embryonic idea of synoptic and variorum editing in print media into full blown hypermedia display of several or all versions of works. There is by tradition a claim for *totality* and complete exhaustiveness within scholarly editing which is being strengthened by digital editing. The potential of digital media vastly to enhance the inclusive force of editions and archives, to enable full-text representation of many or indeed all versions of the edited work and to support the modularization of documents into movable fragments across varying contexts seems to boost the idealistic strand in editorial theory. This trend is even further supported by text encoding, where form is separated from content, and where fact is often conceived of as separable from interpretation. As a consequence, the simple replacement model and the mimetic fallacy have consolidated their positions within digital editing.

Digital scholarly editing offers the chance to organize paratexts and transmitted material in much more dynamic and complex manners than is possible within the printed edition. The modular, database logic along with the potential qualities of digital media mentioned above push the edition towards becoming an *archive*. Building a digital archive means bringing together and storing massive amounts of target documents. This is, of course, what any archive does, and we already have numerous prime examples of the beauty, force and hence the value of digital archives. But the archives and their contained material will always be situated documents themselves, dependent on the kind of situational factors we have discussed above. If such archives are to be used as laboratories for generating new scholarly representational documents such as critical editions (turning the target documents into departure documents), one would have to stay alert as to the derivative status of the archived material in the first place. An SE based primarily (if not solely) on the derivative documents of such a digital archive will always to some extent depend on the inevitable choices made by the persons building the archive, on the historical, sociocultural, cognitive and media particulars and on the pragmatic purposes and theoretic values defining and framing the final derivative documents in the archive.

A transcriptional editing approach, for example, that reduces the many textual levels of departure documents to the linguistic, alphanumerical signs and their compositional structure as interpreted by the editor sets aside McGann's bibliographical codes. This in its turn might decrease the reproductive force of the resulting edition and its text for those researchers and students primarily interested in working further with precisely such bibliographical matters. A transcriptional approach aiming for faithfulness to the text of the studied documents still faces a huge array of inevitable interpretative choices and has to make compromises and sacrifices of what to represent and what to leave behind.[19] What epistemological

---

19 Robinson, 'What Is a Critical Edition?', p. 55.

approaches we bring to the editing process, what methods we use and at what bibliographical level we position the endeavour necessarily determine the representational and laboratory strengths and weaknesses of the edition. It will be more apt for some users and the editorial ideal they subscribe to, and less apt for others. A universal aim will fail because it is rooted in an assumption that both textual material and scholarly editing are context-free phenomena.

This is true for digital imaging and the choices of parameters (such as colour, size, granularity, contrast, layers and resolution) that need to be made in the process of selection, interpretation, capture, copying, formatting and reproduction of the images. This is also the case for the seeming simplicity of transcription. Transcription involves inescapable choices of particular textual features and fixed levels of granularity at the expense of others to the degree that it becomes an argumentative statement on the constitutive components of the departure document. And encoding by markup obviously brings additional questions of hermeneutics and interpretation that add further to the subjectivity of the editing endeavour. Hypermedia archives further hypertextualize some intra-, inter- and extra-textual relations and navigation routes, and leave others dormant.

In other words, a user entering a digitization archive faces material that is encoded, manipulated, labelled, often project-specific and thereby, arguably, already interpreted. What possible bibliographic work can be done with the archive material is thus already to some degree predefined, which of course will be awkward to any archive hoping to function as reproductive laboratory fulfilling scientific ideals. In the best of archives a user is free to manipulate, recombine and rearrange some of the material, but this freedom is not without limits. A user-as-editor who within the confines of, for instance, analytical bibliography wishes to ascertain chronological relations between two or more primary documents of which there are target representations in the archive, and whose focus of interest is more oriented to the form than to the logical structure of the primary documents, probably needs access to different arrays of significant components than a linguist or a historian of ideas trying to frame the edited work in its socio-historical contexts.

I think the legitimacy of the reproductive assumption can be discussed, at least as far as we are talking about the making of new critical editions based on the target documents in previous critical editions and archives. This is not to say that such digital (or printed, for that matter) archives cannot have editorial reproductive force at all. Rather, such force will always be delimited by the inescapable fact that the archival documents are derivatives. Rockwell[20] noted that the tools in large electronic text projects 'are deployed not for general use but to make available the research of a specific project in the ways imagined by that project', and added: 'However, original research consists of asking new and unanticipated questions ...' To some degree, the edition as target document embodies the answers to the

---

20 G. Rockwell, 'What Is Text Analysis, Really?', *Literary & Linguistic Computing*, 18/2 (2003): 209–19, p. 215.

questions the editor asked him/herself. The possibility of posing the 'unanticipated questions' Rockwell refers to, and that much scholarly work is about, is reduced if we accept that every textual choice behind the edition 'inevitably reflects particular approaches to literature, and that the resulting text may be inappropriate for certain purposes'.[21]

The reproductive force of an archive will depend on many crucial factors, such as if we are dealing with the editing of works whose originals and perhaps even archetypes are long lost. Such works have come down to us only in the nth generation, each generation being a derivative translation of previous ones, possibly (but not necessarily) accumulating errors, deviations and other effects of such historical 'whispering down the lane'. I am thinking primarily of the massively versionalized classical works of antiquity. If we were discussing eighteenth- or nineteenth-century works, where we do have extant authorial manuscripts, first print editions, proofs, etc., and where the bulk of documents and versions might not be overwhelming, the perspective and the possibilities are altered, but not, I suggest, to the degree that allows for the automatic generating of tailored editions serving quite different and, more to the point, rival editorial strategies and theories.

In other words, the distance between the contained documents and the originals of which they are derivatives comes into play. With each generation of media translation, the distance is in principle increased between originals or archetypes and their derivatives, both historically and textually. The force of a laboratory for generating critical editions, then, that are based on derivative documents positioned several remedial generations from the primary documents, is affected by this circumstance. That will inevitably define what kinds of new edition one can hope to generate using such derivatives. The users of such archives will, to paraphrase Tanselle,[22] tie themselves to the historical moment in which the archive document containing the text was produced.

The reproductive force further presumes that the ambiguity inherent in the transcription, coding and encoding of the material can be disambiguated and decoded.[23] Another factor is the theoretical distance between the departure project the material was taken from, and the target editorial project in which the material is to be reused, that is whether they differ in theoretical aims and programmes, intended uses and audiences, or whether they are similar in these matters, the latter case arguably enhancing the reproductive force. And finally, there are obviously obstacles to the reproductivity claim of a more practical nature, in addition to the more principal problems discussed above. Crucial among such obstacles are issues of intellectual property (IP) and economy. Several digital scholarly

---

21 G.T. Tanselle, 'The Varieties of Scholarly Editing', in D.C. Greetham (ed.), *Scholarly Editing: A Guide to Research* (New York: MLA, 1995), p. 14.

22 Ibid.

23 L.Burnard, 'On the Hermeneutic Implications of Text Encoding', in D. Fiormonte and J. Usher (eds), *New Media and the Humanities: Research and Applications* (Oxford: HCU, 2001), p. 35.

editing projects enrol library and archive institutions as digitizers. Many such projects adhere to the 'one input – many outputs' principle, where sophisticated, information-dense computer files (such as TEI and TIFF) are being produced as archival formats, from which derivative, light and varying outputs are being produced on demand and, for example, for web delivery (such as XHTML, PDF and JPEG files). The idea is that the 'fertile' documents can be used as a raw material to research and reproduce existing documents, as well as to produce new documents, thereby saving resources. That is obviously the soundest way that mass-digitizing institutions should go about their business. Increasingly, however, digitizing libraries and archives tend to hold on to (and claim IP rights to) the thick material, tucking it away below the interface level and charging institutions and individual end-users for accessing the files, even where the works manifested in the departure documents are in the public domain. Those hoping to use the target documents in the digitized collection as departure documents for new (critical) editions will be further held back by being prevented deep access to the archival, high-resolution files.

At the end of the day, we are facing some of the core questions of philosophy of science: to what degree does the SE as genre and scholarly tool lend itself to the kind of sequential *cumulativity* of collective disciplinary knowledge that is ideal in the discourse of the sciences? Do we regard the SE as primarily a more or less *pure iconic tool*, emphasizing the versatility of the textual material in editions, or as primarily a more or less *situated text*, emphasizing its bonds to the particulars of time, culture, media and individual editorial or lectorial tastes and biases? Is the SE an autonomous or a constrained bibliographic tool? What answers we provide for these questions affect what reproductive force we ascribe to the SEs. One does not necessarily have to choose sides here, but rather discuss what we lose and gain with each perspective. Questioning the reproductive potency of digital archives is not necessarily the same as dismissing the considerable value of constructing large digital archives. While, on the one hand, I would urge libraries and archives engaging in digitization projects to use and make available the most long-term, thick and sophisticated technology they can reasonably consider as legitimate, I would, on the other, suggest they stay on a pragmatic path and not be tempted by any siren songs of universal reproductivity.

Relevance

I started this chapter by positioning the SE as a bibliographical tool, a valuable and privileged one. Such tools are governed by values, epistemologies and interests that need to be identified and formulated. I think these kinds of discussion, invigorated by the advent of new media and distribution technologies, make us better equipped at identifying the nature, strengths and weaknesses of the tools. We might be alerted not only as to what forces but also what limitations they have: for example, as iconic representations and socio-historical genres, changing with time, space, social context and media. Recognizing what interests and world-views are at stake in, for instance, the making of digital archives might reduce the risk of us expecting the wrong things from them. It might assist in avoiding the traps of mimetic fallacies and replacement models in library management when funding, engaging in and conducting digitization projects. It might make us cautious as to what we can reasonably expect from such projects.

We need to see SEs and other bibliographical tools not as neutral prolongers of the life of the works and documents but as filtering media affecting them and our way of perceiving them. This might make it easier to understand what the tools can and cannot do, where they come from, what intellectual, cultural, symbolic heritage they bring with them and where they might be going.

Chapter 3
Digital Editions and Text Processing

Dino Buzzetti

In a number of recent articles Peter Robinson[1] suggests that much of the continuing resistance of the scholarly community, both editors and readers, to supporting the adoption of digital editions can be attributed to the lack of user-friendly tools and manageable and easily available applications. The argument implies that many scholars are reluctant to devote too much time to becoming conversant with the sophisticated technologies required for the design and production of a complex and expedient digital object. This is certainly true, but in my opinion it is only one part of the truth. Another part of the truth can be elicited from the answer to this predicament that has been given, for instance, by Tito Orlandi. According to Orlandi, the main purpose of a digital edition is transferring the competence of the reader to the machine. But that goal is far from being achieved either in single editions or in general solutions. One might be tempted to say that present-day digital editions, for all their merits, are not yet fully digital, since they do not fully exploit the distinctive features of the digital form of textual representation to obtain better critical and analytical results. For a digital edition is in the first place a representation, a particular form of representation of textual information.

Recognizing this fact has two important consequences. A digital edition is, we may say, an 'image' of the text. Needless to say, the term 'image' is taken here in a figurative not a literal sense. I use the term deliberately, because it is tantamount to acknowledging the semiotic nature of the text. In fact, I take the notion of the 'image' of the text from Cesare Segre's *Introduction to the Analysis of the Literary Text*, together with a series of other basic assumptions, namely that 'the text does not have a material nature'; that 'the text is only' and 'always an image'; and that any attempt to identify it with a material witness whatsoever, even an autograph original, is 'an attempt to conceal [its] unavoidable problematic nature'.[2] For, indeed, 'the notion of an original', or of an 'autograph' for that

---

1 Cf. P. Robinson, 'Where We Are with Electronic Scholarly Editions, and Where We Want to Be', *Jahrbuch für Computerphilologie, 5 (2003)*: 125–46; P. Robinson, 'Current Issues in Making Digital Editions of Medieval Texts – or, do Electronic Scholarly Editions have a Future?', *Digital Medievalist*, 1/1 (2005). Available online at <http://www.digitalmedievalist.org/article.cfm?RecID=6>, accessed 19 June 2006.

2 C. Segre, *Avviamento all'analisi del testo letterario* (Torino: Einaudi, 1985); Engl. edn, *Introduction to the Analysis of the Literary Text*, trans. J. Meddemmen (Bloomington, IN: Indiana University Press, 1988), p. 378 and p. 376.

matter, taken 'in the sense of an authentic text, that expresses the author's will', is, in D'Arco Silvio Avalle's words, 'one of the most elusive and ambiguous notions of textual criticism'.[3] Any particular witness or any particular edition, even the most authoritative one, is only and always a representation of the text. It is in this sense, in a semiotic and not in a material sense, that a digital edition may be described as an 'image', or a manifestation of the text, that is, as that particular kind of text representation which is produced in digital form. It is primarily digital editions as representations, digital editions from a semiotic point of view, that I shall deal with in this chapter.

On the other hand, a digital representation is data, and data is processable. Data is the representation of information in a form that can be processed by a machine. And this is a point worth insisting upon; for the means of rendering a text – spoken, written, printed, digital – affords a different and distinctive approach to seizing it. In this respect, an 'image,' or representation of the text in digital form, can considerably enhance our opportunities of penetrating deeply into its discourse. But in fact, in present-day digital editions, all the foreseeable potentialities that a digital form of representation can afford are not yet fully exploited. In my opinion, the true rationale of a genuine digital edition consists precisely in taking advantage of the digital form of representation to improve our critical engagement with the text through effective computational processing. But how?

Let us start by considering some of the reasons why this goal does not seem to have been fully achieved as yet. The first reason lies with the already-mentioned reluctance of the humanities scholar to devote more than cursory attention to informatics and computer science. It is a real and in many respects justified resistance, but on the other hand, in a recent paper on markup systems that appeared in the *Jahrbuch für Computerphilologie*, Claus Huitfeldt regrets 'that many humanities scholars still regard markup as a product of computing technology and thus a purely technical tool of no interest or concern to humanities scholarship'. He makes a good point in recommending that 'textual scholars should not relate to markup technology as passive recipients of products from the computing industry, but rather should be actively involved in its development and in setting the agenda'. He aptly observes that 'the experience and expertise of textual scholars may turn out to be essential [...] as they possess insight which is essential to a successful shaping of digital text technology'.[4] This seems to be very much the case in the domain of digital editions, so that a decisive contribution to the advancement of their methods and design can be expected only from humanities scholars.

Another reason may be found in the persistence of conventional habits and practices in the production of digital editions. The edition continues to be seen chiefly as something for a human to read and only to a very limited extent for a

---

3 D'A.S. Avalle, *Principi di critica testuale* (Padova: Antenore, 1972), p. 33.

4 C. Huitfeldt, 'Scholarly Text Processing and Future Markup Systems', *Jahrbuch für Computerphilologie*, 5 (2003): 219–36. Available online at <http://www.computerphilologie. uni-muenchen.de/jg03/huitfeldt.html>, accessed 20 March 2006.

computer to process. Furthermore, transcription practices still seem to be carried out in a conventional frame of mind. In most cases descriptive markup practices consist of singling out detailed information and simply banking it for an otherwise undisclosed eventual conversion or some other remotely possible future use.

An edition in digital form, then, is considered here, alongside its conventional use, as textual data to be processed. From this point of view, our primary concern becomes that of extracting processable semantics from character data, by assigning to them a functional structure and a suitable formalism. For a humanities scholar, a reliable edition essentially serves the purpose of allowing interpretation. In this respect, visualization and string processing can be invaluable. Stylometric analysis and authorship attribution are based on processing of this kind, but apart from such special cases, the overall limitations of string manipulation are evident enough. Not much can be expected beyond what has already been obtained. The sort of results string processing can afford and their conceptual quality cannot substantially improve. As anyone can see, the Web provides an extraordinary visualization contrivance, but it does not meet the demands attended to by its content-aware counterpart, the Semantic Web. The chief concerns of text processing for interpretational purposes remain information retrieval, content management, or knowledge representation and extraction.

An example may be of use in clarifying the point. One might be tempted to equate a string of characters to the notion of a 'chain,' as defined by Louis Hjelmslev:

> The signs form *chains*, and the elements within each sign likewise form chains. We shall use the term *relation* for the function (dependence, relationship) between signs or between elements within one and the same chain: the signs, or the elements, are *related* to one another in the chain.[5]

But processing a string is not processing linguistic information, for a string of characters does not contain all the information that qualifies a chain as a linguistic unit. To that effect, representing the signs is not enough and all the functional relations between the elements of the chain should also be expressed explicitly. It is precisely that kind of information which makes up a linguistic unit out of a sequence of signs and if that information is not comprised in our textual representation, we cannot process texts as linguistic materials. Transferring the competence of the reader to the computer means processing textual data as linguistic units and implies representing all the relevant information. But the basic form of text representation as a simple string of characters does not explicitly embody it. This is a fairly obvious fact and the introduction of markup is the straight and direct answer to it. But there is a more subtle kind of confusion we should be wary of. A string of characters, or any other kind of data for that matter, is not information but an information carrier. To mistake a string for information actually means carrying

---

5 L. Hjelmslev, *Language: An Introduction* (Madison, University of Wisconsin Press, 1970), p. 32.

over into a digital environment the positivistic notion that identifies the text with a material object: the usual confusion between a witness and the text becomes the confusion between an information carrier and the information it conveys. A text has to be conceived, equally in a digital environment, as a semiotic system. A digital representation is a digital type of 'image' of the text, and a proper recognition of a digital edition as a digital representation of the text implies the recognition that text processing should be primarily concerned with the treatment of its information content and should not be mistaken for the processing of its information carrier. But, again, how might that aim be achieved?

In that respect, the problem of text representation becomes of paramount importance in order to qualify a digital edition as a properly digital one, namely as a kind of edition that makes allowance for effective processing of its information content. Now, as far as text representation is concerned, its standard form is provided by a marked-up string of characters. The introduction of 'structural markup', enabling as it does the move from simple, flat and unstructured text files to structured or semi-structured textual data, has been cheered as a decisive step 'to distinguish information and knowledge from mere "digital stuff"'.[6] One of the main motives for introducing descriptive markup has actually been the idea of processing textual data as structured information. But the mere processing of marked-up character data still falls short of adequate treatment.

Markup has been described as a 'technique for representing structure',[7] for it consists in 'the denotation of specific positions'[8] within a linear sequence of characters. But, again, we should not mistake the structure of the string for the structure of the text. Quite consistently, the ordinary notion of a text, that in a book on text processing is considered as 'literary material as originally written by an author', is clearly kept apart from the computer scientist's notion of the text, defined as 'information coded as characters or sequences of characters'.[9] For, as Michael Sperberg-McQueen has contended, 'claiming that the only essential part of a text is its sequence of graphemes' is indeed 'a misguided and inadequate theory of texts'.[10] But when it comes to its digital representation, we still find considerable uncertainty hovering around the notion of text.

---

6 R. Cover, N. Duncan and D.T. Barnard, 'The Progress of SGML (Standard Generalized Markup Language): Extracts from a Comprehensive Bibliography', *Literary and Linguistic Computing*, 6 (1981): 197–209, pp.197–8.

7 D.R. Raymond, F.W. Tompa and D. Wood, 'Markup Reconsidered', paper presented at the First International Workshop on Principles of Document Processing, Washington DC, 22–23 October 1992, Abstract available online at <http://softbase.uwaterloo.ca/~drraymon/papers/markup.ps>, accessed 14 June 2006.

8 Ibid., p. 4.

9 A.C. Day, *Text Processing* (Cambridge: Cambridge University Press, 1984), pp. 1–2.

10 C.M. Sperberg-McQueen, 'Text in the Electronic Age: Textual Study and Text Encoding, with Examples from Medieval Texts', *Literary and Linguistic Computing*, 6 (1991): 34–46, p. 35.

A lack of clarity on the semiotic nature of the digital representation of the text can be found in the very definition of markup[11] proposed by the editors of the Text Encoding Initiative (TEI),[12] the ground-breaking scholarly enterprise whose aim is 'to provide a format for data interchange in humanities research' and 'to suggest principles for the encoding of texts in the same format'.[13] If markup is defined, as it has been by the editors of the TEI *Guidelines*, as 'all the information contained in a computer *file* other than the text itself', how can it be maintained at the same time that '*any* aspect of the text of importance to a researcher' could 'be signalled by markup'?[14] For either markup is thought to be information that '*is not* part of the text'[15] and is *different* from text – and in that case the text is identified with the string of characters representing it – or markup is understood as expressing certain aspects of that information which '*is* part of the text, and is *the same as* text'[16] – and in that case the text is identified with the information content expressed by that string of characters. To overlook that difference is to overlook Hjelmslev's distinction between the 'expression' and the 'content' of a text,[17] and to ignore that 'the representation of any information content is not the information content that is represented by that representation'.[18] Clearly the structure of the representation is not the structure of what is represented. By singling out definite positions in a stream of characters, the markup assigns a structure to the expression of the text that does not necessarily coincide with the structure of its content.

---

11 L. Burnard and C.M. Sperberg-McQueen, *Living with the Guidelines: An Introduction to TEI Tagging*, Text Encoding Initiative, Document Number: TEI EDW18, 13 March 1991, p. 2.

12 Cf. D. Buzzetti and M. Rehbein, 'Textual Fluidity and Digital Editions,' in M. Dobreva (ed.), *Text Variety in the Witnesses of Medieval Texts*, Proceedings of the International Workshop (Sofia, 21–23 September 1997) (Sofia: Institute of Mathematics and Informatics of the Bulgarian Academy of Sciences, 1998), pp. 14–39; and D. Buzzetti, 'Digital Representation and the Text Model', *New Literary History*, 33/1 (2002): 61–87.

13 L. Burnard, 'An Introduction to the Text Encoding Initiative', in D. Greenstein (ed.), *Modelling Historical Data* (St. Katharinen: Max-Plank-Institut für Geschichte i.K.b. Scripta Mercaturae Verlag, 1991), p. 83.

14 Burnard and Sperberg-McQueen, *Living with the Guidelines*, p. 2 (my italics).

15 J.H. Coombs, A.H. Renear and S.J. DeRose, 'Markup Systems and the Future of Scholarly Text Processing', *Communications of the ACM*, 30 (1987): 933–47, p. 934 (my italics).

16 Buzzetti and Rehbein, 'Textual Fluidity', p. 31.

17 Cf. L. Hjelmslev, *Prolegomena to a Theory of Language*, trans. F.J. Whitfield (Madison: University of Wisconsin Press, 1961), pp. 47–70.

18 D. Buzzetti, 'Text Representation and Textual Models', in *ACH-ALLC '99 Conference Proceedings* (Charlottesville VA: University of Virginia, 1999). Available online at <http://www.iath.virginia.edu/ach-allc.99/proceedings/buzzetti.html>, accessed 14 June 2006.

In a lucid and incisive paper, John Unsworth describes humanities computing essentially as 'a practice of representation',[19] and digital textual editing is certainly no exception. So in order to establish 'the first elements of a theory of the digital text', we actually need 'to outline a semiotics of its machine-readable representation'.[20] If we consider the text as a semiotic system, there is a fundamental feature that cannot be disregarded. From a semiotic point of view the text is intrinsically and primarily an indeterminate system. To put it briefly, there are many ways of expressing the same content just as there are many ways of assigning content to the same expression. Synonymy and polysemy are two well-known and mutually related linguistic phenomena. This brings us to the conclusion, to express it in Jerome McGann's words, that 'no text is self-identical'.[21] And actually, as he observes, 'variation, in other words, is the invariant rule of the textual condition'.[22] The 'material and the conceptual "text"' are then characterized by a 'radical instability,' for 'the freedom of the reader' leads to 'interpretive differentials' and 'the ordering of the words in every text is *in fact*, at the factive level, unstable'.[23]

But such a circumstance, which is essential to the textual condition, does not compromise 'the possibility of a reliable knowledge of text'.[24] For text can also be described as an 'immutable mobile' form of representation, just as the maps and records so designed by Bruno Latour.[25] In a representation of that kind, either of its two components, the material expression or the conceptual content, may be assumed as an invariant and a mark of identity, while the other varies in an indefinite number of ways. Indetermination is thus a structural feature of textual semiotics and its basic components are related as two correlative variables in a quantum physical environment: if you determine and fix either of them with observational precision, the other remains by necessity uncertain and indeterminate. The identity of the text can then be traced in the specific form of the mutual relationship between its variation and invariance, and established in the co-dependent series of its transient and unstable manifestations.

---

19 J. Unsworth, 'What is Humanities Computing and What is Not?', in G. Braungart, K. Eibl and F. Jannidis (eds), *Jahrbuch für Computerphilologie, 4 (2002)*. Available online at <http://computerphilologie.uni-muenchen.de/jg02/unsworth.html>, accessed 14 June 2006.

20 D. Buzzetti, 'Diacritical Ambiguity and Markup,' in D. Buzzetti, G. Pancaldi and H. Short (eds), *Augmenting Comprehension: Digital Tools and the History of Ideas* (London: Office for Humanities Communication, 2004), p. 178.

21 J.J. McGann, 'Rethinking Textuality', <http://www.iath.virginia.edu/~jjm2f/old/jj2000aweb.html>, accessed 15 June 2006. For a more thorough discussion, see J.J. McGann., *Radiant Textuality: Literature after the World Wide Web* (New York: Palgrave, 2001), especially ch. 5 and the Appendix to ch. 6.

22 J.J. McGann, *The Textual Condition* (Princeton, NJ: Princeton University Press, 1991), p. 185.

23 Ibid.

24 Ibid.

25 Cf. B. Latour, 'Visualization and Cognition: Thinking with Eyes and Hands', in *Knowledge and Society: Studies in the Sociology of Culture Past and Present*, 6 (1986): 1–40.

It is important, therefore, not only to recognize the presence of the two textual components, expression and content, and not to mistake the one for the other, but also to consider the way they are mutually related. This is the core of the problem. The dominant paradigm has been that of formalization, that is translating natural language expressions into symbolic language and formulas. This was to ensure a thorough correspondence and isomorphism between the syntactic and the semantic form of linguistic expressions. Grammatical form had to be reduced to strict logical form. As Donald Davidson put it, 'to give the logical form of a sentence is [...] to describe it in terms that bring it within the scope of a semantic theory that meets clear requirements'.[26] The whole programme of artificial intelligence was committed to that ideal: according to John Haugeland's reassuring recommendation, 'If you take care of the syntax, *the semantics will take care of itself.*'[27]

But the coincidence between the syntactic and the semantic structure of textual data is by no means a condition for their automatic processing. Their disparity is, on the contrary, what essentially characterizes the textual condition. A symbolic formula is indeed a textual expression, but it constitutes only a very special case. The burden of being absolutely univocal would deprive textuality of the richness and flexibility which are continually produced by its indetermination: a symbolic calculus generates textuality only in a very impoverished and diminutive sense. In any case, textual data can be processed despite discrepancy between the syntactical structure assigned to a string of characters and the semantic model assigned to its information content. The problem is precisely how to relate the two kinds of structure in a consistent and productive way.

The discrepancy between the 'form of the expression' and the 'form of the content,' to appeal again to Hjelmslev's distinctions, is an intrinsic feature of the alphabetic form of textual representation. The ancient Stoics had already noticed that the word 'dog' does not bite, and obviously we cannot assume that the word 'ball' be round, for even in a *calligramme*, or an ideogram for that matter, it would not be three-dimensional. Incidentally, it may be observed that in an alphabetic text we read the words, and that in an ideographic text we read the meanings. More precisely, in an alphabetic text we read the meanings through the words, and in an ideographic text we read the words through the meanings. We cannot completely separate these two related aspects, for they actually concur in the concrete working of spoken and written discourse to shape the relationship between words and meanings, expression and content, the syntactic and semantic structure of the textual materials. Again, that relationship has to be properly recognized and the problem of a digital representation of the text is precisely how to implement its dynamics in a properly exhaustive and functional way.

---

26 D. Davidson, *Essays on Actions and Events* (Oxford: Oxford University Press, 1980), p. 144.

27 J. Haugeland, 'Semantic Engines: An Introduction to Mind Design', in J. Haugeland (ed.), *Mind Design: Philosophy, Psychology, Artificial Intelligence* (Montgomery VT: Bradford Books, 1981), p. 23.

It has to be observed that it is the tacit assumption of isomorphism between the syntactic and the semantic structure of the text that lies behind the assertion of the controversial OHCO model, which presumes to define 'what text really is' as 'an "ordered hierarchy of content objects" or "OHCO"'.[28] This definition relies on 'the use of SGML [Standard Generalized Markup Language] as a basic text description language'[29] and assumes that the structure assigned by markup to a string of characters is *tout court* the structure of the text. In fact, 'SGML defines a document in terms of its OHCO structure',[30] for indeed:

> one fundamental premise of SGML is that texts are composed of discrete content objects, and that supplying meaningful names for these delimited textual objects, their attributes and their hierarchical relationships independent of possible appearances is one of the most powerful means of transforming text into information units that may be addressed sensibly by knowledgeable software.[31]

One should note that here 'text' is equated throughout with 'document' or 'string of characters', and that the OHCO definition consequently identifies the 'content structure'[32] of a document with the 'hierarchical structure'[33] assigned by the SGML scheme to its representation as a sequence of characters. However, it is only on the assumption of a complete isomorphism between the syntactic and the semantic form that we may identify the structure of the expression with the structure of the content of a text.

Markup languages such as SGML and XML (eXtensible Markup Language) are data representation languages: they serve to specify data structures, but they do not provide a data model or formalism to process their information content. 'SGML explicitly declaims semantics'[34] and XML, 'just like its parent metalanguage (SGML)', 'formally governs syntax only – not semantics.'[35] It is no surprise, then, that 'the current approach for "fixing the meaning" of a data exchange/archival format', which 'is to provide an XML DTD', should be found unsatisfactory, for a DTD (Document Type Definition) is nothing but a formal

---

28 S.J. DeRose, D.D. Durand, E. Mylonas and A.H. Renear, 'What is Text, Really?', *Journal of Computing in Higher Education*, 1/2 (1990): 3–26, p. 6.

29 Ibid., p. 13.

30 Ibid., p. 12.

31 Cover et al., 'The Progress of SGML', p. 198.

32 'What is Text, Really?', p. 23.

33 Ibid., p. 22.

34 D. Raymond, F. Tompa and D. Wood, 'From Data Representation to Data Model: Meta-semantic Issues in the Evolution of SGML', *Computer Standards and Interfaces*, 10 (1995): 25–36, <http://softbase.uwaterloo.ca/~drraymon/papers/sgml.ps>, p. 2, accessed 16 June 2006; cf. C.F. Goldfarb, *The SGML Handbook* (Oxford, Oxford University Press, 1990).

35 R. Cover, 'XML and Semantic Transparency' <http://www.oasis-open.org/cover/xmlAndSemantics.html>, accessed 16 June 2006.

specification of the hierarchical structure assigned by SGML and XML to a stream of characters. 'Many communities and organizations define their own standard "community language" via DTDs', and the endorsement of the TEI DTD by the humanities computing community is no exception. But as the NARA (National Archives and Records Administration) project for the long-term preservation of digital data developed by the San Diego Supercomputer Center (SDSC) openly acknowledges, the 'shortcomings of DTDs for data modeling and validation have been widely recognized'.[36] So, the realization that 'although SGML/XML-based markup languages provide explicit rules for syntactic well-formedness and validity, they provide nothing analogous for semantic correctness',[37] or that an XML DTD cannot provide a suitable semantic model to process the information content of textual data, has led 'to a flood of extensions'[38] and attempts, such as 'XML Schema, RDF, the Semantic Web',[39] to develop a 'semantics of document markup'.[40]

The most consistent and systematic endeavour of this kind has been 'the BECHAMEL Markup Semantics project, which is developing a formal framework for the interpretation of markup, and a multi-layer knowledge representation and inferencing environment (in Prolog) with which to express theories of markup semantics'.[41] The BECHAMEL system comprises a syntactic layer to describe 'SGML/XML syntactic relations' between 'string representations';[42] an object modelling layer to describe 'the distinctive semantic relationships that they represent';[43] and a mapping layer, which 'concerns mechanisms and rules for mapping syntactic markup structures to instances of objects, properties, and

---

36 B. Ludäscher, R. Marciano and R. Moore, 'Preservation of Digital Data with Self-validating, Self-instantiating Knowledge-based Archives', *ACM SIGMOD Record*, 30/3 (2001): 54–63, p. 59. Available online at <http://users.sdsc.edu/~ludaesch/Paper/kba.pdf>, accessed 17 June 2006.

37 C.M. Sperberg-McQueen, D. Dubin, C. Huitfeldt and A. Renear, 'Drawing Inferences on the Basis of Markup', in B.T. Usdin and S.R. Newcomb (eds), *Proceedings of the Extreme Markup Languages 2002 Conference* (Montreal, Quebec, 2002), p. 1. Available online at <http://www.mulberrytech.com/Extreme/Proceedings/xslfo-pdf/2002/CMSMcQ01/EML2002CMSMcQ01.pdf>, accessed 17 June 2006.

38 Ludäscher et al., 'Preservation of Digital Data', p. 59.

39 A. Renear, D. Dubin, C.M. Sperberg-McQueen and C. Huitfeldt, 'Towards a Semantics for XML Markup', in R. Furuta, J.I. Maletic and E. Munson (eds), *Proceedings of the 2002 ACM Symposium on Document Engineering*, McLean VA, November 2002 (New York: ACM Press, 2002), p. 119.

40 Ibid., p. 123.

41 D. Dubin and D. Birnbaum, 'Interpretation Beyond Markup', in B.T. Usdin (ed.), *Proceedings of the Extreme Markup Languages 2004 Conference* (Montreal, Quebec, 2004), p. 2. Available online at <http://www.mulberrytech.com/Extreme/Proceedings/xslfo-pdf/2004/Dubin01/EML2004Dubin01.pdf>, accessed 17 June 2006.

42 Ibid., p. 6.

43 Ibid., p. 9.

relations'.[44] The identification of relevant syntactic and semantic textual structures and the invention of a bridging mechanism between them can be conceived as the basic and essential tasks of digital textual editing and processing. But it is even more important to recognize that they cannot be univocally envisaged and designed lest we should disregard text indetermination and mobility.

In a paper related to 'an ongoing project to develop a system for extracting rhyme schemes from Russian verse',[45] which illustrates 'how BECHAMEL can be used in a synthesis of different semantic models'[46] across different semantic domains, David Dubin and David Birnbaum clearly acknowledge the indeterminate relationship between the syntactic expression and the semantic content of the text, for they assume 'that the same markup can convey different meanings in different contexts' and 'that markup can communicate the same meaning in different ways using very different syntax'.[47] The recognition of this fundamental principle entails substantial consequences about markup and the role it plays in the digital representation of text:

> We don't intend to suggest that markup presents any more of an inherent problem than other methods of encoding and representing information. All the distinctions that we're able to explicate using BECHAMEL could, in principle, guide the re-tagging of documents with richer markup that would eliminate the need for an inferential step in each case. Or BECHAMEL's network of properties and relations could be serialized in the form of RDF or a topic map.[48]

In other words, the role performed by the BECHAMEL 'mapping rules'[49] could be performed either by appropriate markup at a syntactic level or by a suitable data model at a semantic one. And this leads us to our central and concluding point, for markup within a text can really be construed as a rule. To expound this assertion properly, some considerations 'on the status of markup in relation to the bibliographically coded text'[50] are given here.

---

44 D. Dubin, 'Object Mapping for Markup Semantics', in B.T. Usdin (ed.), *Proceedings of the Extreme Markup Languages 2003 Conference* (Montreal, Quebec, 2003), p. 2. Available online at <http://www.mulberrytech.com/Extreme/Proceedings/xslfo-pdf/2003/Dubin01/EML2003Dubin01.pdf>, accessed 17 June 2006.

45 Dubin and Birnbaum, 'Interpretation Beyond Markup,' p. 4.

46 Ibid., p. 2.

47 Ibid., p. 1.

48 Ibid., p. 8.

49 Ibid., p. 6.

50 D. Buzzetti and J. McGann, 'Electronic Textual Editing: Critical Editing in a Digital Horizon', in L. Burnard. K. O'Brien O'Keeffe and J. Unsworth (eds), *Electronic Textual Editing* (New York: Modern Language Association of America, 2006), p. 59.

The 'function of markup' has actually been described as that of expressing 'inference rules' about the properties it labels in a text.[51] Accordingly, as it has also been convincingly maintained, 'to describe the meaning of the markup in a document, it suffices to generate the set of inferences about the document which are licensed by the markup', and 'in some ways, we can regard the meaning of the markup as being constituted, not only described, by that set of inferences'.[52] A markup expression, then, can be regarded as an inference-licence or an 'inference-ticket', to use Gilbert Ryle's famous description, a statement which licenses us 'to move from asserting factual statements to asserting other factual statements'[53] – in our case – about 'passages in the marked-up material'.[54] But, as Ryle reminds us, inference licences and rule-statements 'belong to a different and more sophisticated level of discourse from that [...] to which belong the statements of the facts that satisfy them'.[55] So the linguistic status of markup expressions understood as rules, or inference licences, is different from the linguistic status of markup expressions construed as factual statements 'about the structure and properties of the text'.[56]

This ambivalence of markup expressions should not worry us, for as we shall see, it constitutes an essential and functional property of markup. What we may already observe, though, is that markup expressions can be construed either as the mark of a rule, or as the mark of an observed textual property – or to use a more formal language, either as the sign of an operation, or as the sign of an operation value or result. This means that markup can have both 'descriptive' and 'performative' force – or mood, to choose Searle's instead of Austin's phraseology – and as Allen Renear discerningly points out 'the recognition that markup has modality and that some of it is performative, constitutive of the text it characterizes' raises fundamental problems 'about just what markup really is, and in particular, when it is *about* a text and when it is *part* of a text ... and when, and how, it may sometimes be both'.[57] Thus, from the ambiguity between values and rules we are led to another kind of ambivalence of markup expressions, that between

---

51 C.M. Sperberg-McQueen, C. Huitfeldt and A. Renear, 'Meaning and Interpretation of Markup', *Markup Languages*, 2/3 (2000): 215–34, pp. 215 and 218.

52 Ibid., p. 231.

53 G. Ryle, *The Concept of Mind* ([1949]; 2nd edn, Harmondsworth: Penguin Books, 1963), p. 117.

54 Sperberg-McQueen et al., 'Meaning and Interpretation of Markup', p. 215.

55 Ryle, *The Concept of Mind*, p. 116.

56 Sperberg-McQueen et al., 'Meaning and Interpretation of Markup', p. 216.

57 A. Renear, 'The Descriptive/Procedural Distinction is Flawed', *Markup Languages*, 2/4 (2001): 411–20, p. 419. Cf. J.L. Austin, *How to Do Things with Words*, ed. J.O. Urmson, (Oxford: Clarendon Press, 1962); J.R. Searle, *Speech Acts: An Essay in the Philosophy of Language* (Cambridge: Cambridge University Press, 1969); and J.R. Searle, 'A Taxonomy of Illocutionary Acts', in K. Gunderson (ed.), *Language, Mind and Knowledge*, Minnesota Studies in the Philosophy of Science, 7 (Minneapolis: University of Minnesota Press, 1975), pp. 344–69, repr. in J.R. Searle, *Experience and Meaning: Studies in the Theory of Speech Acts* (Cambridge: Cambridge University Press, 1975), pp. 1–29.

expressions that are part of the text and expressions that are not – or in more formal terms, between object-language and metalinguistic expressions.

What that means in fact, is that markup may be considered either as belonging to text, 'as an extension of the expressive resources of the [...] very language constituting the text', or as an external description of the structure and properties of the text, i.e. 'as a form of metalinguistic notation'.[58] For, on the one hand, markup makes explicit some implicit feature of the text and 'as soon as something has been made explicit it has become part of the text, which has thereby changed, and acquired a new structure'. As Claus Huitfeldt aptly remarks, 'there is a similarity here to Wittgenstein's distinction in the *Tractatus* between showing and saying – the structure of the text shows itself in the text'.[59] As Wittgenstein puts it, 'that which mirrors itself in language, language cannot represent';[60] structure and logical form can only show themselves within the object-language and 'the only way to *represent* a logical form is to describe it by means of a metalanguage'. But that is also, on the other hand, what markup can actually do. So markup can both exhibit and describe a structural feature of the text, and 'it can perform both functions only by changing its logical status' and commuting between object-language and metalanguage.[61] Here is another case of markup ambiguity and we should not find it particularly disconcerting. As a matter of fact, it has been observed that markup 'is part of the text and yet it is distinct' from it,[62] and, to the same effect, markup has been described both as an external 'technique for representing structure'[63] and as that very 'structure'[64] within the text. We have to acknowledge, again, that this kind of ambiguity is another essential and functional property of markup.

All these seemingly inconsistent aspects of markup are grounded in a fundamental property of markup expressions that can be described as *diacritical*. Diacritics are special notation signs that are 'used to distinguish different sounds or values of the same letter or character',[65] and they may be considered as an expression of the 'reflexive metalinguistic nature'[66] of natural language, the capability that all natural languages possess of saying something about themselves. Whenever the notational form is ambiguous, they explicitly flag out a discriminating mark, that exhibits self-reflexively what can only be shown and cannot be said in the object-

---

58 Buzzetti, 'Diacritical Ambiguity and Markup', p. 178.

59 C. Huitfeldt, 'Multi-dimensional Texts in One-dimensional Medium', *Computers and the Humanities*, 28 (1995): 235–41, pp. 237–8.

60 L. Wittgenstein, *Tractatus Logico-philosophicus*, 4.121; see also 4.1212: 'What can be shown cannot be said.'

61 Buzzetti and McGann, 'Critical Editing in a Digital Horizon', p. 63.

62 Raymond et al., 'Markup Reconsidered', p. 3.

63 Ibid., p. 3.

64 Ibid., p. 4.

65 *Oxford English Dictionary*, s.v.

66 Cf. T. De Mauro, *Minisemantica dei linguaggi non verbali e delle lingue* (Bari: Laterza, 1982), pp. 93–4, and T. De Mauro, *Prima lezione sul linguaggio* (Bari: Laterza, 2002), pp. 89 and 91–93.

language itself. But they have themselves a 'reflexive metalinguistic nature', or a self-describing metalinguistic force, and can be converted into equivalent expressions of a genuinely metalinguistic kind. In formal terms, it can be shown that second-order object-language statements – statements based on a second-order form of predication – are equivalent to first-order metalinguistic statements – statements based on an ordinary form of predication. The notational ambiguity of markup, incapable as it is of distinguishing between the two different forms, does not prevent it from being duly construed in either of these two absolutely acceptable ways.

All this means that we can explain McGann's assertion that 'no text is self-identical'[67] through the fact that text is endowed with self-reflexive functions that allow us to discriminate and switch between different values assigned to notationally identical characters and character strings. No text is self-identical just because it is self-reflexive. To put it formally, we may say that the non-identity of the text with itself is logically equivalent to an endomorphism, or a mapping, of the text onto itself – in formula:

$$(A = A \text{ if and only if } A \neq A) \longleftrightarrow A \xrightarrow{\;markup\;} A^{68}$$

The markup can then be construed as the expression of a self-reflexive function that relates the semiotic elements of the text to other semiotic elements of the same text.

We can try to illustrate all these phenomena by means of a diagram (Figure 3.1). As we have seen, structural distinctions can refer either to the *expression* or to the *content* of the text. A markup expression can also be understood both as a *rule*, or an operation, and as a *value*, or the result of an operation. Moreover, the markup can be considered as belonging to the *object-language* of the text, or to a *metalanguage* describing it. And all these dimensions can be displayed in the diagram. To round it off, we can recall that markup structures can be 'embedded' and 'present in the data',[69] or apart as 'non-embedded structure'; accordingly, we can distinguish between *internal* structure or markup, and *external* structure or markup – 'so-called *out-of-line* markup'.[70] These two dimensions are also displayed in our diagram to complete its multi-dimensional space.

We may now try to expound the use of the diagram to represent textual mobility and build a dynamic model of textual instability. Our purpose is to show that the fundamental ambiguity of markup, due to its self-reflexive and diacritical nature, far from being 'an obstacle to an automatic processing of textual information' can actually serve that very purpose, by providing a 'formal representation of textual

---

67 Cf. note 21 above.

68 Buzzetti, 'Digital Representation and the Text Model', p. 84.

69 Raymond et al., 'Markup Reconsidered', p. 3.

70 Ibid., p. 4.

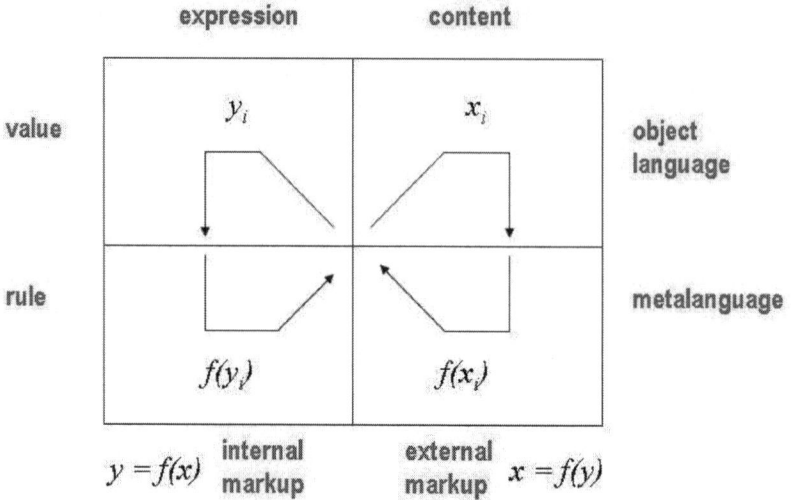

Figure 3.1   The multiple dimensions of markup

dynamics'.[71] We can refer, by way of example, to that traditional form of markup, or diacritical notation, that is represented by punctuation. For 'punctuation is not simply part of our writing system; it is a type of document markup that may vary and be replaced by other types of markup';[72] and therefore what can be said about punctuation can also be said about markup.

What a modern scholar does, for instance, by adding punctuation to a medieval text, is to mark it up. Let y_i be the result of a marking operation of this kind, which consists in inserting a punctuation mark in a certain position within the string of characters that represents the text. Our mark y_i is the *value* of the marking operation and a piece of *internal markup*. But as soon as it is drawn, it becomes part of the *expression* of the text, and a construct of its *object-language*. So we can place it in the upper left sector of our diagram. As a new component of the expression of the text it constitutes a textual variant.

But our mark can also be construed as a *rule* for mapping the syntactical phrase it belongs to onto the object domain of what it signifies. The mapping operation is a function of y_i and we may indicate it by $f(y_i)$. Considered as a function, our mark changes its linguistic status and becomes a higher-order statement in the object-language. Such a statement has metalinguistic import and can be converted into its logically equivalent statement expressed in a proper *metalanguage*. We can thus locate it in the lower left quadrant of our diagram.

---

71 Buzzetti and McGann, 'Critical Editing in a Digital Horizon', p. 64.
72 Coombs et al., 'Markup Systems and the Future of Scholarly Text Processing', p. 935.

The mapping operation $f(y_i)$ imposed by the markup expression understood as a rule assigns a structure to the content of the text. Let $x_i = f(y_i)$ be the result of that mapping. As a *value* of the mapping operation, x_i designates a structural element of the object domain signified by the text and constitutes a component of the external structure described by the text. Consequently it does not belong any more to the expression or to the internal structure of the text and it is not a part of it. It is rather to be seen as a piece of stand-off or *external markup*. As a structure assignment onto the object domain signified by the text it constitutes an interpretational variant of its *content*. It can also be denoted by an expression of a data modelling language (e.g. ERA, RDF, UML, etc.), which assigns a suitable formal model to the content of the text and which provides an *object-language* for the description of its components. Our external structure component x_i is then to be positioned in the upper right quadrant of the diagram.

The structural construct x_i that belongs to the *content* of the text can in its turn be understood as a *rule*, or as an instruction for a structuring or mapping operation onto the expression of the text. We may denote this function as $y_i = f(x_i)$. Again, understood as a function, the expression of the external structural component x_i changes its linguistic status and becomes a second-order statement in the external markup object-language, or in the data modelling language used to describe the object domain signified by the text. Such an expression, assuming as it does x_i as its argument, has a metalinguistic force and can be converted into its equivalent construct expressed in a suitable *metalanguage* referring to the text. Accordingly, we can place the functional expression $y_i = f(x_i)$ in the lower left section of the diagram. The functional expression $f(x_i)$ has y_i as its value and so the cycle is complete. External markup constructs x_i that depend on the mapping of internal markup constructs y_i can be mapped back onto internal markup constructs y_i.

The *cycle* we have described can be seen as an unfolding of textual instability and indetermination. We have described the indetermination of the text as a non-identity relation of the text with itself and this relation has been analysed into the mapping of components of the text onto other components. The non-identity relation of the text with itself is a constrained one. We can define the structure of the text as 'the set of latent relations'[73] between all its virtual parts and components, and if we conceive the structure of the text as 'the whole of all its possible variant readings and interpretations', we can also think of the text as 'a virtual unity identical with itself'.[74] Within this virtual unity we can draw a primary distinction between the expression and the content of the text and 'the variation of either component is dependent upon the invariance of its related counterpart'.[75] So the relation of the text with itself is a one-to-many-relationship and the mapping can have more than one value.

---

73 Segre, *Avviamento all'analisi del testo letterario*, p. 44; Engl. trans., p. 34.

74 Buzzetti and McGann, 'Critical Editing in a Digital Horizon,' p. 64.

75 Ibid., p. 64.

The mapping of the text onto itself can be performed by markup that gives explicit expression to implicit structural features of the text. But markup is ambiguous and can be both internal and external to the text. So markup can transform textual variants into interpretative variants and vice versa: as it happens, it can map structural components of the expression onto structural components of the content, or it can map structural constructs of the content onto structural constructs of the expression. Since the linguistic status of markup can commute between logically equivalent forms, the inversion of the mapping can be explicitly expressed and markup can provide an explicit representation of compensation constraints. Textual inner mobility can then be described as 'a permanent cycle of compensating actions between determination and indetermination of the expression and the content of the text'.[76]

What I have tried to do so far is to sketch a structural scheme for a formal representation of the semiotic working of a digital representation of a text. There may undoubtedly be better ways of doing it, but my purpose was simply to give an idea of the complexities and extent of the phenomena that must be analysed. For it is unlikely that we may ensure a suitable and efficient processing of textual information without relying on a functional and exhaustive representation of all its semiotic components and constraints. An edition can be said to be properly digital only if it affords that kind of processing. In other words, the major task seems to be that of improving the adequacy of the basic form of text representation.

The fact that texts are currently represented in computer systems as 'linear strings of atomic characters' is 'usually accepted as an immutable fact of technology';[77] but as we have seen there are reasons to think that this need not be so. Both the basic form of text representation and the current markup schemes do not afford suitable means to process a string of characters as a proper linguistic unit and so cannot ensure that the linguistic competence of the reader can be transferred to a computer. But alternative means have been proposed.

The notion of an enhanced or 'extended string' as a new data type for processing textual information was introduced some years ago by Manfred Thaller[78] and it stems from the realization that a string of characters 'is a representation of an underlying meaning with a specific information density' and that it is usually able to 'transfer only part of the meaning originally available'.[79] The extension of the data type was based on the principle that a string made up of 'information carrying

---

76 Ibid., p. 66.

77 M. Thaller, 'Strings, Texts and Meaning', in *Digital Humanities 2006*, 1st AHDO International Conference Abstracts (Paris: Université Paris-Sorbonne – Centre de Recherche Cultures Anglophones et Technologies de l'Information, 2006), p. 212.

78 Cf. M. Thaller, 'Text as a Data Type', in *ALLC-ACH'96: Conference Abstracts* (Bergen: University of Bergen, 1996), pp. 252–54. Available online at <http://gandalf.aksis. uib.no/allc/thaller.pdf >, accessed 7 August 2007.

79 Thaller, 'Strings, Texts and Meaning', p. 213.

tokens' can 'be understood to exist in an *n*-dimensional conceptual universe'[80] and that 'low level programming tools' currently used to develop text-handling applications can directly 'tackle the implications of this model'[81] – for example, by allowing the application to toggle between different ways of processing a string perhaps by sensitivity or insensitivity to a given textual feature.

The application of the 'extended string' data type 'to text critical problems' has 'proved to be a substantial step towards reaching satisfactory solutions', and 'its application to problems of analysis and interpretation looks just as promising on the same grounds'.[82] Moreover, the extension of the basic string representation from a one-dimensional to a many-dimensional case 'in turn leads to the notion, that not only the handling of information carrying tokens can be generalized', but that 'the properties of markup languages can as well'.[83] Thus, in principle, all the injunctive and performative force of markup could be transferred to effective processing and be of use in enhancing the functionality of text representation and digital editions.

The examination and testing of these new possibilities opens up a new, promising direction for research, in the conviction that only an improved form of low-level text representation can allow semantic and content-based text processing and afford an effective transfer of linguistic competence from the human reader to the machine. Without this decisive step, I fear that digital editions are doomed to fail in gaining generalized support or a discerning preference among textual scholars, and they will probably continue to lag behind in comparison or confrontation with the conventional form of text representation and transmission.

---

80 Ibid., p. 212.

81 Ibid., p. 213.

82 D. Buzzetti, 'Digital Editions: Variant Readings and Interpretations', in *ALLC-ACH'96: Conference Abstracts* (Bergen, University of Bergen, 1996), p. 256. Available online at <http://gandalf.aksis.uib.no/allc/thaller.pdf>, accessed 7 August 2007.

83 Thaller, 'Strings, Texts and Meaning', p. 213.

Chapter 4
The Book, the E-text and the 'Work-site'

Paul Eggert

Anyone preparing a scholarly edition of a classic literary work intended for print publication does so nowadays under the louring shades of the electronic edition. That the book has a future for this scholarly function is a nearly unbackable proposition. The book-based edition is apparently as dead as a dodo. That, at least, is the now widely accepted (but less widely enacted) wisdom. As someone who over the last dozen years has had a foot planted in both camps – now finding himself tending this way, now that – I believe that if the jury is not still considering the proposition it ought to retire once again. Theoretically, I find myself attracted to the possibilities of the electronic environment. Importantly for me it answers in practical form, as I shall argue, to our need to reconceptualize the nature of the *work* being edited. But speaking as a humanities scholar who lacks programming skills and ongoing access to a funded computing laboratory, the assumed advantage of the electronic environment is far less clear. This situation is worth teasing out before I go on, in this chapter, to look at ways forward in the electronic environment, both theoretical and practical.

The editor's passion: Why *not* to do electronic editions

Bringing a scholarly edition through the final stages of production involves months of work. The proofs of the volume are not just read carefully by several people but the reading text is likely to be collated orally against the original copy-text and perhaps against other versions in a loop that goes back in behind the very process that led to the proofs, and thus double or triple-checks the computer collations of the various versions of the work, on the basis of which the editing originally proceeded. Checking and rechecking the volume's several thousand internal cross-references and its hundreds of quotations in the front and end matter are also necessary. Preceding this checking in proof, but done again as part of the proofing, are the final checks to ensure that the editorial conventions – some of them quite intricate and innovative – have been used consistently; that copy-editorial conventions for expression in front and end matter have actually been followed; and that the volume's explanatory notes, its textual apparatus, both foot-of-page and end-of-volume, and any accompanying historical or biographical essays or maps have no remaining mistakes or any extraneous matter that does not support the volume as a whole. The editor wants to ensure that the edition is, in short, a unified piece of scholarship.

I describe the process impersonally, but in practice it becomes very personal. You cannot go through a process like this unaffected. You take full responsibility for the editing and production of what you know will be a once-off, expensive publication. You become obsessed with the thing, wanting desperately on the one hand, after years of work, to get it out of your life but yet knowing that its integrity depends utterly on you. You accept your fate if only because, as you go through these last grinding processes, you become increasingly aware of the sheer beauty of scholarly completeness, of having every part of the volume enlightened by every other part, all of it seamlessly interdependent and unobjectionably cross-referenced, nothing said twice, all of it as balanced as you could ever make it.

In the last few months of your labour you see these qualities taking more perfect shape daily. At last you see it finished. And then there is the final agony of separation, with you knowing that if you only had one more month, one more week, even one more day you could just do that *one* extra check, pick up perhaps a final few tiny errors whose presence, if you were to see them in print, would gall you for ever more. Now you look again, just glancing really, and you see the need for that hair space between the opening parenthesis and the lower case italic 'f'. 'Wouldn't it look better if I added it?' you ask yourself. You add it. And I bet there is another one needed on the next page ... A hair space: good God! What am I doing? Teetering on the edges of what to anyone else must seem like madness, you hand over the final Portable Document Format (PDF) files.

Then follows the sheer relief at having finally broken your bond with the yet-unborn book, releasing your surprisingly grown-up infant unto the printer and thus the world, in the knowledge that you will never again inhabit that beautifully interlocking environment as a maker, that you will never again drive or fix that robust machine of knowledge. Like every other reader you will be only a user of it.

The state of prolonged anxiety that I have described is in actual practice a productive one because of the quality of attention it brings to bear. Would we strive for such perfection if the book logic of static completion were not cracking the whip on us? In comparison, there need be no final deadline for electronic editions. They can be published electronically in instalments, and their errors corrected at any time. Not all errors can be corrected easily or safely, but in principle there is little to stop the editorial work going on in a post-publication phase. Does this mean that, for the electronic scholarly editor, without realizing it, the lack of closure will prove an invitation to drop his or her standards, excused by the fact that the errors and infelicities can be fixed as users notify them?

A second reason why not

I leave that baleful question hanging to rehearse a second argument about why adopting electronic solutions for editorial problems should not be automatic. The argument springs from a recent personal example. I am in the early stages of preparing a scholarly edition of the fifty-two short stories published in 1896 as

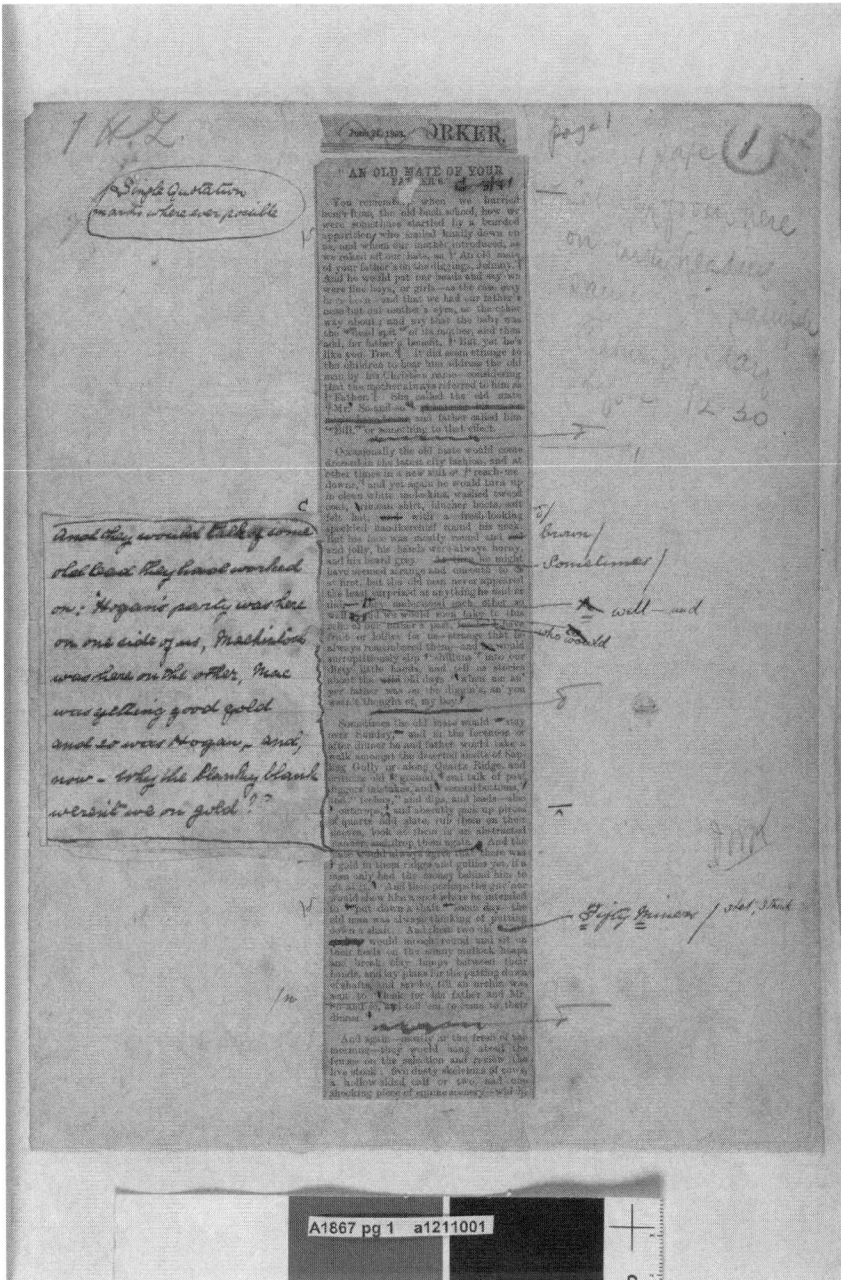

Figure 4.1 Henry Lawson, 'An Old Mate of your Father's', marked-up print clipping

Source: Mitchell Library, State Library of New South Wales, MS A1867, fol. 1.

While the Billy Boils by the Australian writer Henry Lawson.[1] Nearly every story exists in one or more newspaper printings, and in heavily revised and corrected clippings of these printings mounted on the back of large publishers' brochures. They were prepared to serve much the same function as galley proofs for Lawson, allowing him to revise the stories for book publication at will, and for the publisher's editor to copy-edit over the top. (See Figure 4.1.) In some stories the processes engendered a conversation as Lawson circled back around and had the final say.

Given that the project requires a print edition, but one that will not be able to reproduce in facsimile the 190-odd folios of marked clippings, an agreement reached with their owner, the State Library of New South Wales, was intended to provide a felicitous solution. Under the agreement, the Library would discharge its responsibilities about access for the public to its collections by digitizing and mounting the facsimiles on its website. It agreed to provide me with very high-quality (and otherwise prohibitively expensive) TIFF files for editing purposes, and I in turn would give a transcription of them to the Library so that it could discharge another of its responsibilities under State laws about providing transcriptions of web-mounted manuscript materials for the visually impaired.

This seemed a happy outcome till I turned to the business of creating a transcription of the interwoven deletions and additions in the clippings. This was not necessary for the print edition itself, which will record the alterations separately in textual apparatus entries. Was it worth learning and then teaching an assistant the routines of Text Encoding Initiative (TEI) encoding, writing the Document Type Description (DTD), devising a style sheet and then experimenting with browser or other software to present it? As a one-off requirement, the answer was clearly no. My primary aim, after all, was not to put into place a TEI-encoded transcription that might or might not be used by other scholars in the future. Such an outcome might be a noble ambition, but being only half-pregnant with it was, I decided, not a good idea.

I then spent some time looking for a less ambitious solution. I took the ASCII transcriptions of the print clippings before revision that had been made some years ago for the purposes of computer collation and tried to record the alterations in the files as clearly and simply as possible. I restricted myself to ASCII keystrokes so that the result would not be dependent on transient software or operating systems and thus would be easily reusable by someone else in the future. In addition I would be able to keep the transcription in a line-for-line relationship with the print clippings, except where there were sizeable insertions. The result was unconvincing. Ordinary readers would not be able to make sense of the symbols that I was forced to employ, no matter the ingenious simplifications that I came up with. This was a disheartening outcome.

---

1 My role is textual editor and author of the introduction. Elizabeth Webby, of the University of Sydney, is preparing the explanatory notes and a glossary of slang, idiomatic usages and Australianisms, in the use of all of which Lawson was a master.

However, my not automatically taking the electronic path soon made some positive sense when it occurred to me that the casual user of the State Library's website would, for its historical witness, be better served with a digitized facsimile of *While the Billy Boils* itself. (The revised clippings had in fact served as its printer's copy.) What differences there are between the two must have been carried out in proofs and are copy-editorial in origin, although Lawson made some. A headnote to this effect would serve ordinary users well enough. The more committed ones will be referred to the print edition.

The reader, with book in hand, will find that its material logic has been extended most usefully. The foot-of-page textual apparatus will be serving as an epitome of the whole production process, which will itself be visually available on screen at the same time. Any viewer unable to follow the series of deletions, additions and changes of mind on screen will find the whole process interpreted and recorded with exemplary economy at foot of page. And the traditional opaqueness of textual apparatus will become instantly illuminated as the reader glances back and forth between the apparatus, facsimile images and the reading text (which will be based on the text of the unrevised clippings).

Generalizing from this particular case, we may conclude that the advantages of embracing and extending the now computer-assisted logic and economies of the reference *book* can be palpable ones. If we choose instead to take the electronic route, the lesson is clear: we should embrace the working logic of its different material environment. But what does this entail, and have we achieved it yet?

The present situation with e-texts[2]

Humanities researchers comment most often upon existing texts, whether literary, documentary, filmic, biblical, legal or musical. To date, the application of IT to the humanities, particularly to the areas of literature and history, has seen a widespread emphasis on the production of digitized texts, with much of the innovation being driven by the library world. The emphasis has been on providing access to very large numbers of texts. The digitizing appeared to liberate scholarship by turning these objects into newly manipulable digital forms. Concordancing and search software has become readily available but answers only very specialized needs. Leaving aside the operations on texts performed by computational stylisticians and linguists, it is true to say that, in the main, digital texts are still serving only as surrogates for printed texts and indeed are often delivered, by preference, in that form. Existing methods of research are tacitly assumed. This is partly because the inherited consensus on what texts are and how they function has not changed with the technology.

---

2 Sections of what follows in the present chapter are reprinted from P. Eggert, 'Text-encoding, Theories of the Text and the "Work-site"', *Literary and Linguistic Computing*, 20 (2005): 425–35. Oxford University Press is thanked for granting permission to republish this material.

If in years to come historians see this as a rudimentary first stage of humanities computing they will surely trace the origins of a second stage to the growing appreciation of the problematics involved in representing pre-existing handwritten or printed documents in electronic form. The turning point will, I believe, prove to have been the recognition that every electronic representation of text is an interpretation.[3] At the moment, interpretative data is usually presented as markup within the document file itself. Interpretative data can include coding for document structure, analysis and display, and for adding annotations or links to other files. All this (with the exception of style sheets) is typically enclosed within the expanding document file, thus replicating in an essential way the paradigm of the printed book. Both for creators and for digital libraries, the logic continues to be stasis and enclosure, despite the much-heralded capacity for change. Consequently, the authenticity of the text files is potentially imperilled with every special-purpose addition of new material, and multiple efforts of use and interpretation are likely to continue in isolation from one another on different copies of the files that will then need to be separately maintained. Resources will be wasted. *Which* marked-up copy will the next interpreter–scholar use? What guarantee will there be that it has not been corrupted?

The acknowledged need for an agreed standard of text encoding has also brought its problems for the study of humanities e-texts. The TEI requirement, that documents be syntactically defined as an ordered hierarchy of content objects (OHCO) that cannot overlap, conflicts with the fact that, as many observers have pointed out, humanities texts typically require analysis involving text elements that do overlap.[4]

Electronic scholarly editions launched bravely in the early heyday of hypertext have mostly failed or lapsed through lack of thought about the consequences of dependence on proprietary software, the ease with which electronic text files may be corrupted in comparison with those in print, and the sheer amount of work that would be required to bring these large-scale editorial projects to completion. Those that did survive are mainly displaying what the medium of print could have produced anyway (textual transcriptions and printed-document facsimiles). And the much-vaunted promise of hypertext linking was scarcely an innovation for critical editions that often have, in their printed form, thousands of internal

---

3 Cf. C. Huitfeldt, 'Multi-dimensional Texts in a One-dimensional Medium', *Computers and the Humanities*, 28 (1995): 235–41: 'there are no facts about a text which are objective in the sense of not being interpretational' (p. 237). This was amply confirmed in the JITM projects (described below): see P. Berrie, P. Eggert, G. Barwell and C. Tiffin, 'Authenticating Electronic Editions', in L. Burnard, K. O'Brien O'Keefe and J. Unsworth, (eds), *Electronic Textual Editing* (New York: Modern Language Association, 2006), pp. 436–48.

4 For example, a poem can be analysed metrically or as sentences, and a novel can be analysed bibliographically in signatures, leaves and pages or in terms of narrative progression from volume to volume and chapter to chapter.

cross-references to their apparatus of variant readings and explanatory notes.[5] Concordancing, word searching and even, as in the William Blake Archive, image-component searching, once coupled to electronic editions, have lent them power. But their creators typically need to keep control of their contents in order to ensure their quality: they are, ideally, finished editions. This has meant that readers who consult them, in having to remain outside them, perpetuate the only somewhat expanded paradigm of the printed book. Is this game worth the candle?

A need for theory

We are not going to get very far with the second stage of e-texts practice unless our theoretical aims can be enunciated and our terminology defined in a way that responds to the realities of computer storage, analysis and presentation, *and* to human interaction with texts in this environment. Without this, we will continue to come unstuck or confused at every point, for we are never only dealing with technical matters. Every one of them comes to us trailing clouds of theory that we so far have not found the time to clarify. Theory, in other words, is going to have to step up to the mark. I have witnessed the term *text* used promiscuously for most of my academic career in English, and the term *work* has been shuffled ignominiously aside as embarrassingly old-fashioned. The precisions required by computer encoding, together with the passing of postmodern theory, have set the conditions and created the requirement for us to sort out more of what text means and how it functions. And there may yet be an honourable place for the work: the present chapter at least proposes one.

The standard dichotomies that have served so far by way of electronic theory are looking vulnerable now. From the late 1980s and especially after the introduction of the World Wide Web around 1992, the old-fashioned integrity of the so-called *subject* (author) and the aesthetic coherence of the work as *object* (a concept naturalized by the supposed stasis of the book) were contrasted, tellingly it was felt, with the new liberations and freedoms promised for the user by the employment of hyperlinked and distributed texts. This prospect intoxicated many minds and it reflected the postmodern moment of the technological breakthrough.[6] But matters turned out not to be so simple when the realities of textual representation and analysis were faced.

---

5 See further, P. Robinson, 'Where We Are with Scholarly Editions, and Where We Want To Be', *Jahrbuch für Computerphilologie*, 5 (2003): 126–46. Available online at <http://computerphilologie.uni-muenchen.de/jg03/robinson.html>, accessed 11 March 2008.

6 M.G. Kirschenbaum, in 'Editing the Interface: Textual Studies and First Generation Electronic Objects', *TEXT*, 14 (2002): 15–51, quotes Marie-Laure Ryan contrasting, as late as 1999, 'the characteristics of printed versus electronic media. In her first column – print – Ryan includes such words as: "durable", "unity", "order", "monologism", "sequentiality", "stolidity", and "static". In her second column – the virtual – she opposes these with: "ephemeral" (the very first item on the list), "diversity", "chaos", "dialogism",

In a paper published in 1997, Allen Renear provided a history of attitudes towards the text within the text-encoding community. The idea that 'text is a hierarchy of content objects' had been enunciated in 1990 (by De Rose et al.[7]), and it was becoming clearer that the importation of printed documents into digital media committed the encoder to giving serious thought to what a text is. Mats Dahlström lifted the stakes in pointing out that markup enacts a *theory* of what the text is, but he assumed that e-text must be considered logical rather than material.[8] And Espen Aarseth struck a related note in observing that a major difference between print and electronic texts is that the book serves as both the storage mechanism for text and is simultaneously its vehicle of delivery, whereas the computer divides up these functions. Textual ontology is changed by the practical implications of this latter fact.

The implications have been taken up more recently in various attempts to bring to bear some of the insights of bibliography and editorial theory on the so-called cybernetic theory that had grown up around the writing of creative literary works specifically for computer presentation. Commentary by Dahlström, Katherine Hayles, Peter Shillingsburg and Peter Robinson, amongst others, has been directly or indirectly pushing along this line of empirically inspired theoretical enquiry.

Observing that computer encoding forces us to retrieve our long-naturalized, and therefore mostly submerged, understandings of how physical books function as carriers of meaning, Jerome McGann has called for a general effort to articulate, for the purposes of encoding, the complete set of meanings inherent in the page and the book as physical objects: to formalize a system of what he calls the bibliographic codes. Matthew Kirschenbaum has been persuasive in calling for a theory of first-generation e-texts. With the forbidding precedent of Fredson Bowers' famous *Principles of Bibliography* (1949) behind him, Kirschenbaum has even hazarded a taxonomy of e-texts, defining concepts of layer, version and release (which three concepts he understands together), object, state, instance and copy.[9] How robust this taxonomy will prove to be remains to be seen, but that it

---

"parallelism", "fluidity", and "dynamic" … [I]t is an example of the extent to which otherwise perceptive observers of the new media have failed to take notice of the most basic lessons textual studies have to teach' (p. 24).

7 S.J. DeRose, D. Durand, E. Mylonas and A. Renear, 'What is Text, Really?', *Journal of Computing in Higher Education*, 1/2 (1990): 3–26; and see A. Renear, 'Out of Praxis: Three (Meta)Theories of Textuality', in K. Sutherland (ed.), *Electronic Text: Investigations in Method and Theory* (Oxford: Clarendon Press, 1997), pp. 107–26.

8 'Digital documents are immaterial and therefore logically defined', M, Dahlström, 'Drowning by Versions', *Human IT*, 4 (2000): 7–38, sect. 3.

9 A '*layer*' comprises all elements of an electronic work that are computationally compatible and functionally integrated … *Layers* can be distinguished by assigning them *versions*' (i.e. whole numbers for new versions and decimal numbers for refinement to layers); an *object* is a 'generic identifier for some discrete digital entity, such as a file'; a *state* 'refers to the computational composition of an *object* in some particular data format'; an *instance* 'refers to a particular *object* in a particular *state* as presented in a particular

should have been attempted at all is encouraging. The present chapter emerges from the recent debates of editorial theory and, on the practical level, from a project for producing electronic scholarly editions. The remainder of this chapter reflects on the nature of text, explores the implications for text encoding, and outlines a methodology within which text encoding may be able to respond satisfactorily to the theoretically enunciated problems.

The material e-text, readers and editorial theory

As we interact with it, e-text depends, at every point, on the various capabilities of the computing environment that convert it from a stream of binary code into a temporary visualization on screen or a printing on paper.[10] For anyone interested in the precise constitution and presentation of texts, the material basis of their generation needs to be understood, whether they be print texts or e-texts. Materiality means different things in the analogue and digital domains: in the latter it means something like complete computational specifiability. Kirschenbaum argues cogently that to insist, for e-texts, that the material be equivalent to the physical (as it is in the print world) would amount to what he names the haptic fallacy.[11] Whether the textual carrier be the physical page, a computational capacity or the sound waves that transmit orally declaimed verse, there is always a material condition for the existence of text. It will behove editors of the future to study it: they will need to be computer museologists as well, especially if they deem it important to be able to recover text in the form that early users actually saw it on screen in the mid-1980s, say.

This displacement of e-textuality onto readership on the one hand and the electronic equivalent of physical bibliography on the other might seem to be pushing us into dangerous territory for encoding, in fact towards the notion, put forward in 1995 by Alois Pichler, that: 'Our aim in transcription is not to represent as correctly as possible the originals, but rather to prepare from the original text another text so as to serve as accurately as possible certain interests in the text.' And he adds: 'what we are going to represent, and how, is determined by our research interests ... and not by a text which exists independently and which we

---

software environment'; and a *copy* 'refers to one precise and particular *instance* of one particular *state* of an *object*', rather like copies of an impression. (Kirschenbaum, 'Editing the Interface', pp. 46–9.)

10 This is Kirschenbaum's 'bibliographic' point (Kirschenbaum, 'Editing the Interface'), and see also N.K. Hayles, 'Translating Media: Why We Should Rethink Textuality', *Yale Journal of Criticism*, 16 (2003): 263–90.

11 M.G. Kirschenbaum, 'Materiality and Matter and Stuff: What Electronic Texts Are Made Of', *Electronic Book Review*, posted 1 October 2001, modified 30 November 2003 <http:// www. electronicbookreview.com>, accessed 21 April 2004.

are going to depict'.[12] In 1997 Allen Renear objected to what he called this anti-realist view of text, but his arguments seem finally to rest on the unproblematized notion that texts are or must be objective realities that encoders would do well to represent truthfully.[13]

Editorial theory has much to say here. Neoplatonic or idealist views of text amongst editors have, in recent years, been largely replaced by views of text-in-process, as fluid, and of texts as existing in relation to their publishers and readerships and not just to their authors. So there are now considered to be legitimate, alternative sources of textual authority; and texts are also seen as partially dependent, for their meaning, on their physical instantiation. Medievalists have reminded us that the usual form of publication in the Middle Ages, hand-copying in religious or professional scriptoria, necessarily meant that the normal rather than aberrant form of textual existence was one of unending variation. Manuscripts were sites of textual transaction and of social performance: they were not merely transmitters of an abstracted verbal text. Similarly, book historians observed that the serialization of a novel in a colonial newspaper transmitted different and more miscellaneous messages than its subsequent publication in a luxury three-volume novel published in London for readers who subscribed to Mudie's library. And that was different again from its subsequent life in a widely distributed sixpenny double-column printing on cheap paper, bound as a paperback that might be read to death and then discarded. Additionally, we had to confront the unignorable questions of what happens to textual meaning when the poems of self-publishing and illustrating William Blake, and the poems of Emily Dickinson that she wrote on scraps of paper with eccentric punctuation and lineation and intended only for immediate domestic consumption, were republished in new, public-bibliographical, standardizing formats.

Renear's objection to Pichler's anti-realist argument is swamped by this tide of recent editorial theory: instability in the verbal text, in physical presentation and

---

12 A. Pichler, 'Advantages of a Machine-readable Version of Wittgenstein's *Nachlass*', in K. Johannessen and T. Nordenstram (eds), *Culture and Value: Philosophy and the Cultural Sciences* (n.p.: The Austrian Ludwig Wittgenstein Society, 1995), pp. 691, 690.

13 A. Renear (in 'Theory Restored', paper presented at the Sixteenth Joint International Conference of the Association for Literary and Linguistic Computing and the Association for Computers and the Humanities, abstract in *ALLC/ACH 2004: Computing and Multilingual, Multicultural Heritage, The 16th Joint International Conference, Göteborg University, 11–16 June 2004, Conference Abstracts* (Göteborg: Göteborg University, 2004), pp. 110–12), has continued to defend the OHCO view of text against all comers, including Paul Caton's criticism at the ALLC/ACH conference in 2003 that Renear's text theory is not a scientific theory at all but only 'a set of principles that underpin a particular human practice' (p. 111). Renear's defence strikes me as sound: that theory's form will reflect the modes of thought particular to the area of study. He describes text encoding as a formal rather than an empirical science. (It strikes me, however, more as a *Wissenschaft* than a science.) Text encoding will probably always be at the intersection of scientific and humanities thinking: if so, then its theory will take different forms.

in its reception, emerges as a condition of textual existence that cannot be ignored. Texts do not have an unproblematic objective existence. They are not self-identical, even if more-or-less transparent page designs have traditionally catered to the illusion that they are. Their encoding for computer analysis and presentation is therefore doomed to remain problematic, incomplete and perspectival. In a sense, a phenomenology of texts has replaced an ontology.

In order to accommodate this shift in the understanding of textuality, I have tried elsewhere to retrieve and redefine the concept of the work so that it can serve as a container for the multiplicity of work (construed in the ordinary sense) that is done in its name. I refer to the work of the author in composition and revision, the work of editors, page designers, typesetters and, finally but crucially, of reviewers and readers – each generation of them (if the work becomes a classic) construing meanings in relation, it is likely, to newly packaged bibliographic objects, each bearing the name of the work. I conceived of the work as functioning diachronically, constituted by a dialectic of its documentary and textual dimensions – of the material or physical and the meaningful – a dialectic that (after Adorno) can be seen as a negative one, never attaining synthesis and never ending for as long as the work remains under the human eye.

The continuously unfolding nature of this dialectic enforces my observation about the perspectival nature of our knowledge of texts. The perhaps unwelcome implication of this line of argument is that totalizing conceptions of text encoding, such as those proposed by Dino Buzzetti for recording the deeper linguistic structures of texts and Jerome McGann for articulating their so-called bibliographic encoding maybe doomed to failure.[14]

A practical alternative for text encoding

Is there an alternative way forward with text encoding? Let us assume that Pichler was right: that we can only encode what our interests in the text are; or, put less controversially, that we can encode only what we know about texts. Over time there will be expansion of what we know, correction and reformulation. Perhaps we will never uncover the deeper linguistic structures or formalize the full range of possible meanings inherent in physical documentary forms, though probably we will get some way towards them. Overlapping document hierarchies are inevitable and must be catered for; and collaborative interpretation, accumulating over time, contributed by scholars and other users must be consciously allowed for and enabled. Electronic transcriptions of canonical works subjected to such encoding will become very densely marked up indeed.

---

14 For my account of the work (and its textual and documentary dimensions), see P. Eggert, 'The Work Unravelled', *TEXT*, 11 (1998): 41–60. On Buzzetti and McGann, see P. Eggert, 'What E-Textuality Has To Tell Us about Texts', unpublished paper given to the Society for Textual Scholarship conference, March 2005, New York.

The danger that I drew attention to above – the imperilling of the authenticity of such e-texts – must therefore be faced. The original scholarly editorial effort of having achieved accurate transcriptions of the verbal texts of a work needs to be guaranteed by authentication mechanisms that are themselves non-invasive and non-proprietary. We are, despite my protestations above, probably only a few years away from the day when e-publication will become the primary format of choice for scholarly editions, with print on demand, in a more sophisticated form than it exists at present, serving as the secondary format for those parts of the edition required by the reader. But no general editor can ask scholars to spend several years of their life working on an edition if the stability of the reading texts they establish cannot be guaranteed beyond the lifetime of the software company and of the public funding (almost certainly temporary) of an electronic repository. These are, or ought to be, generally recognized problems, but so far there is no generally accepted solution.

The text-encoding project in which I was involved grew out of a keen awareness of this problem. I decided to edit the famous confession or self-justification, which the notorious Australian bushranger Ned Kelly wrote in 1879, called the Jerilderie Letter (Figure 4.2). It was the stimulus for Peter Carey's novel *True History of the Kelly Gang* (2000). The challenge was how to guarantee the authenticity of the textual transcription file while allowing collaborative interpretation of it – potentially open-

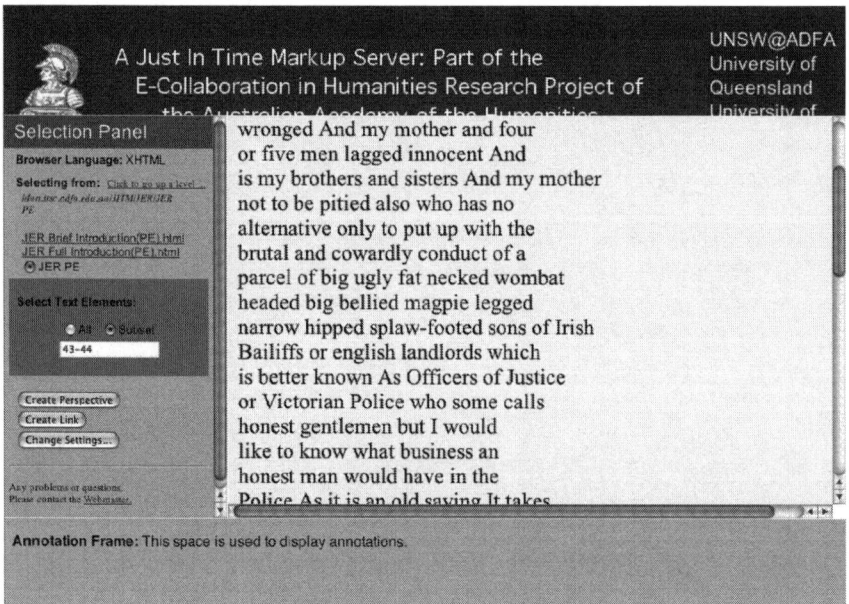

Figure 4.2   The Jerilderie Letter in a JITM environment

Source: Textual transcript courtesy of Paul Eggert. Design courtesy of Phill Berrie, Graham Barwell, Chris Tiffin and Paul Eggert.

ended collaboration. These aims had come from a previous project in which text files that were being used to create the print scholarly edition of Marcus Clarke's great convict novel from the 1870s, *His Natural Life*, were re-purposed.[15]

At first the project was envisaged as creating an electronic equivalent to the scholarly edition, only with more information: facsimiles of the early editions, transcriptions and ancillary information. If the reader did not agree with the editorial policy then at least all the information on which the edited text had been based would be readily available. Creating this textual assembly turned out to be a much bigger and more time-consuming job than we had thought. Users now had access to a preceding, much longer serialized version from which the novel itself had been adapted by the author who had much reduced it in length. This version could not be contained within the print edition. But, as user one still stood essentially outside the archive, just as one had done with the book; and we on the project team had to admit that, given sufficient volumes, we could have provided in book form what we were providing electronically anyway. This was an act of gathering, collating, organizing and making accessible electronically the related, but otherwise dispersed, materials.

By then our programmer had hit on the brilliant idea that we could guarantee the accuracy of all our text versions via a checksum algorithm if only we divided up the digital information into content on the one hand and markup on the other. This was counter-intuitive because the 1990s paradigm – into which digital text collections around the world have invested a lot of energy and money – was and still is that markup should be stored in-line within the text file.

What we realized, late in the day, once the authentication routine had been perfected, was that we had done something that might have a wider application. By splitting off text from interpretation of it we had laid the groundwork for collaborative interpretation of the text that could be stored separately from it and would not endanger its accuracy. This is what we set out to demonstrate with the Jerilderie Letter project.

In terms of presentation, the project did not achieve a fully satisfactory delivery mechanism for e-editions by the time funding ran out in 2005. Worse, ongoing availability has been interrupted and functionality diminished on two occasions since, when servers were replaced and I had no staff available to me who were capable of supporting the project files on the replacement servers. But the project did show that the basic problem of automatic authentication of texts that are undergoing continuing interpretation recorded in additional markup had been solved. And it partially addressed the theoretical problems of text definition that I have been outlining in this chapter. The technique involves the use of stand-off markup that we called Just-In-Time Markup (JITM).[16]

---

15 Published in the Academy Editions of Australian Literature series, L. Stuart, L. (ed.), *His Natural Life*, by Marcus Clarke (St Lucia: University of Queensland Press, 2001).

16 The successive JITM projects were an offshoot of the (print) Academy Editions of Australian Literature series (University of Queensland Press, 1996–2007). For the

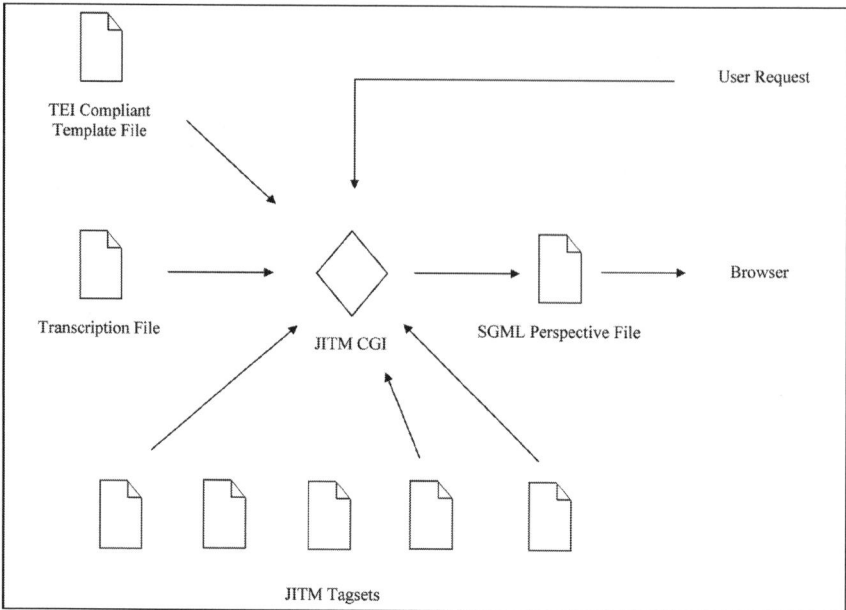

Figure 4.3   The JITM system

Source: courtesy of Phill Berrie, Graham Barwell, Chris Tiffin and Paul Eggert.

The logic of it is quite simple: see Figure 4.3. JITM uses stand-off markup stored in any number of external tagsets. The user chooses which of them will present or interpret the base transcription file. The chosen tagsets are inserted into the transcription file upon the user's call ('just in time'). The base transcription file consists only of the verbal text contained within uniquely identified text-element tags. JITM automatically authenticates the content of these text elements against a

e-editions of Marcus Clarke's 1870s convict novel *His Natural Life* and of the Jerilderie Letter go to <http://www.unsw.adfa.edu.au/JITM>, accessed 10 March 2008. For more on the authentication procedure (which also allows possible corruptions to be quarantined while leaving the rest of the text useable), see Berrie et al., 'Authenticating Electronic Editions' and other papers at <http://www.unsw.adfa.edu.au/ASEC/JITM/publications.html>, accessed 10 March 2008. JITM was originally designed on the Macintosh platform but then in Perl, so it is not Macintosh-dependent. The software works equally on desktop machines and servers using standard, non-proprietary web technologies and web browsers.

My fellow collaborators on the successive JITM projects were Phill Berrie (the programmer at the Australian Scholarly Editions Centre), Graham Barwell and Chris Tiffin. The thinking in this chapter has been stimulated by countless conversations with them and by, if anything, even more conversations on editorial theory and textual computing with Peter Shillingsburg and, to a lesser extent, with Peter Robinson, both of whom generously allowed me to read unpublished work of theirs.

stored hash value prior to and after the embedding of the markup into the text. The practical effect of this authentication is that JITM allows a base transcription file to be annotated or augmented with analytical or structural markup, in parallel and continuously, while retaining its textual integrity. Different or conflicting structural markups can be applied to the same base file in separate passes because they are in different stand-off files and can be applied to the base file selectively. In all of this, the base transcription file remains as simple as possible (thereby greatly easing its portability into future systems) and the authentication mechanism remains non-invasive. Because JITM separates the textual transcription from the markup, copyright is also simplified. Since the markup is necessarily interpretative, a copyright in it can be clearly attributed, even if the work itself is out of copyright.

JITM relies on a workable, minimalist definition of the verbal text restricted, for now, to the ISO-646 character set with the addition of entity references for characters not so accommodated.[17] The base transcription does not contain the graphic features such as italicizing that we are used to considering as an intrinsic aspect of a text, but then neither is it the textual representation that non-expert users will choose to read. They will typically read a perspective on the base transcription created by its conjunction with separate tagsets that render its page breaks, line breaks, italics, the long 's' and so on, and that will, in the act of doing so, authenticate it (see Figure 4.4). Editorially, the base transcription file is, like any other textual representation, an interpretation of the evidence. The challenge is to establish the least objectionable form of the pre-existing text that will also support authentication and ongoing collaborative interpretation. Functionally, the base transcription file may be regarded as a computer artefact that enables these results and that, amongst other things, facilitates word searches and concordancing.

For JITM there is no difference in principle between handling the rendering of italics, say, and of glosses or elucidations of difficult passages, or commentary on their editorial complications. Traditions of interpretation of canonical works are a well-known feature of humanities scholarship. In both cases JITM-like systems would seem to have an infrastructural contribution to make because ongoing collaborative interpretation of a constantly authenticated text is JITM's central feature.

---

17 Transcription of holograph manuscripts puts unacceptable pressure on the assumption that a single, stable string of characters expressed in the ISO-646 character set will be sufficient. Any change to the string of characters in a text element changes its hash value, upon whose stability JITM depends to achieve authentication. Accordingly, we began to develop a facility to allow the base transcription file to be corrected for errors *after* it has had stand-off files written specifically for it. The facility, if completed, would allow scholars to take account of ambiguous readings in holograph manuscripts. (See also the next note, on JITAM.) A further, linked development would be a tool, operating within the JITM environment, that would accommodate annotations upon annotations – a predictable outcome of a long interpretative tradition.

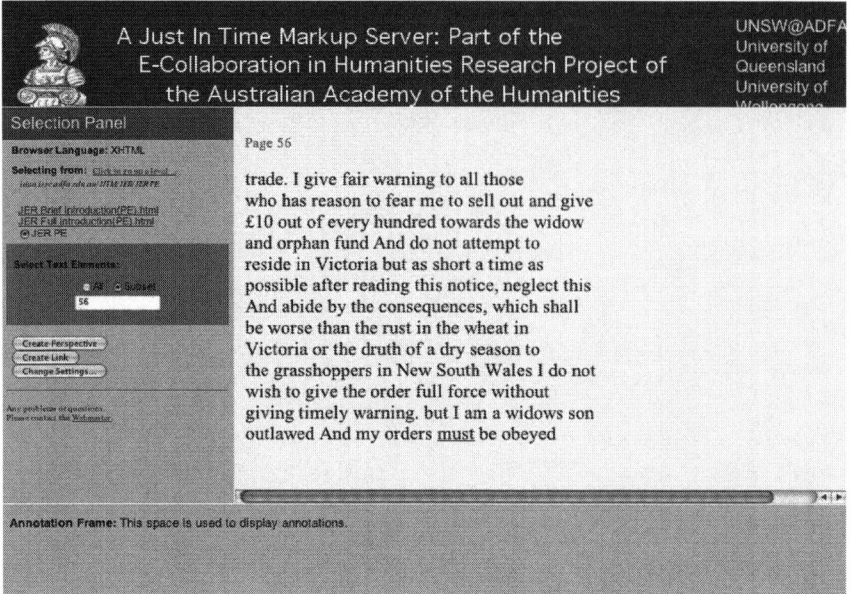

Figure 4.4   The ending of the Jerilderie Letter, with underlining rendered

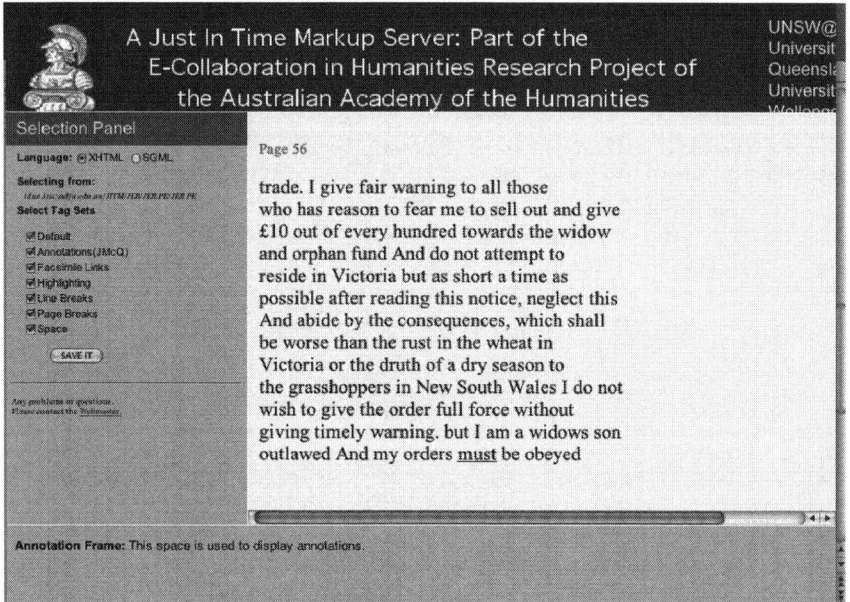

Figure 4.5   Marking the available (stand-off) tagsets for incorporation

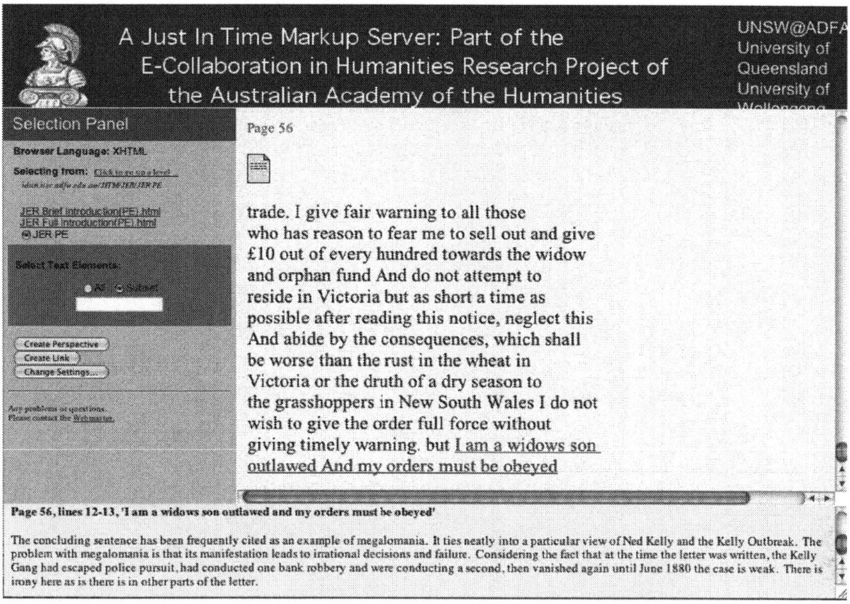

Figure 4.6   The perspective with the marked tagsets rendered

Note: The underlining signals the relevant text-span of the explanatory note.

Source: Figures 4.4–4.6: Textual transcription courtesy of Paul Eggert. Design courtesy of Phill Berrie, Graham Barwell, Chris Tiffin and Paul Eggert.

Figure 4.5 shows how a perspective on the text with annotations added is activated Just In Time. John McQuilton's social-history annotations and the facsimile icon for page 56 are marked for display, together with the other tagsets that render physical features. The following perspective on the base transcription (Figure 4.6) is the result. An automatic authentication of the transcription has been simultaneously carried out. Clicking on the page icon brings up a facsimile of the same page in the original from the holding repository's website, access to which is gained directly at the page level (Figure 4.7). User-generated perspectives on a text in JITM can also be cited in another electronic document and produced and authenticated on request, essentially as if the document were conventionally quoting one or more elements of the text. The writer creates the relevant perspective and then copies into his or her own essay the http address that generated it.

Given favourable circumstances, there could be a productive flow-on effect. Let us assume that the quoting scholar has used and benefited from the existing annotation files but realizes they lack a significant dimension. Having harvested, the scholar might also want to contribute this different interpretation of the text, or some local aspects of it, as an additional tagset that may be of use to future users of the site. JITM allows this. This collaborative adaptation of the typical publishing

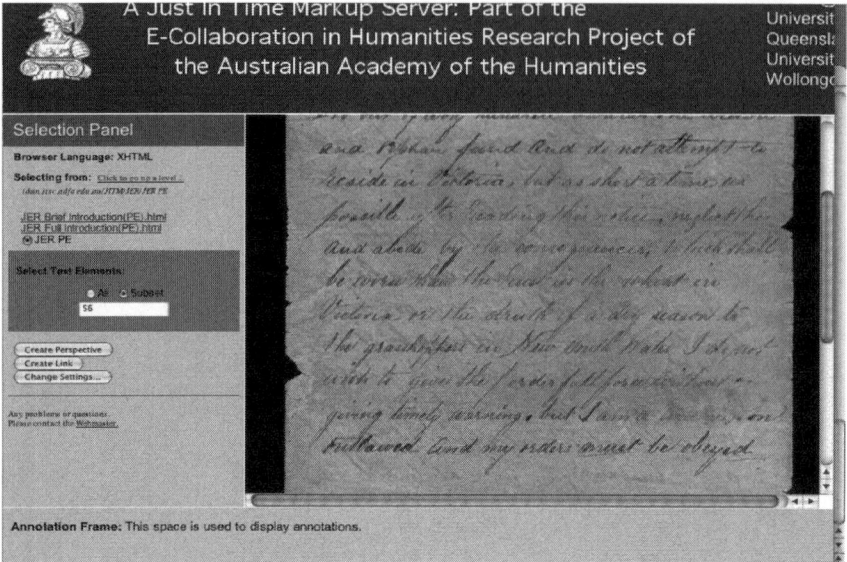

Figure 4.7   A digitized facsimile of page 56 of the Jerilderie Letter

Source: Facsimile, courtesy State Library of Victoria, MS 13361. Design courtesy Phill Berrie, Graham Barwell, Chris Tiffin and Paul Eggert.

culture in humanities research would be highly desirable, though refereeing, incentive and recognition mechanisms for humanities research would need to be adjusted accordingly.[18]

The 'work-site'

JITM-like systems also begin to address the theoretical problems outlined earlier. For a start, the base transcription files are pleasingly honest in their spareness. No one would pretend that they satisfactorily represent, by themselves, the text of a printed or handwritten document. With JITM, the creation of perspectives on the textual transcription is enabled by the selection of markup files to be applied to it. Thus JITM constantly remembers (and, in its activation by the reader, re-*members*) the editorial intervention between the source document and its textual representation, effectively interrupting any nascent naturalizing of the e-text as

---

18 JITM can be applied to existing text files that are already SGML-encoded via the use of the Just-In-Time Authentication Mechanism (JITAM) algorithm, which is character-set independent and available through a Perl scripting environment on a creative commons licence at <http://www.unsw.adfa.edu.au/ASEC/JITAM>, accessed 10 March 2008. It also allows JITM to authenticate the generated perspectives.

existing in itself without interpretation, as self-identical. And JITM incorporates the reader's participation in the textual transaction. It is integral to it. In other words, the displayed text is not *only* a machine performance, though clearly that is the enabling condition.

What we will have in practice with JITM or similar systems is what I propose we call the 'work-site'. The work-site is a text-construction site for the editor and expert reader; and it is the site of study of the work (of its finished textual versions and their annotation) for the first-time reader, as well as any position in between. Because the building of such textual and interpretative work-sites will be, if widely adopted, piece by piece, collaborative and ongoing, we are starting to look at a future for humanities, work-oriented research that is, if not scientific exactly, then more *wissenschaftlich*, in the German sense, than literary critics, historians and others are used to. JITM sets up a system where dealings with texts (enabled by emerging tools) can accumulate and be organized in relation to one another around carefully edited transcription files. And JITM facilitates subsequent research, but without imperilling the accuracy of textual resources that have been subjected to editorial scrutiny. This approach, if scaled up, may have the potential to become a building-block in a new channel of scholarly communication and publication. It is a second-stage expression of humanities computing in the literary area.

Archives vs editions

There is a temptation to use the term *archive* to describe such work-sites. But we need to remember that archival acts and editorial acts are, for good reasons, traditionally seen as performing different operations on or with texts. Editions turn documentary facts, derived from the archive, into evidence: that is, evidence within the orbit of the editorial rationale adduced to deal with the documents. The hardback edition is therefore an inherently provisional embodiment of an argument, however impressive its printed form may be.

The electronic work-site will make this clearer than it is in the print domain. The reader will be able to accept the guidance of the editor whose reading text and collations can be treated, if the reader so chooses, as the advisable pathway through the work-site. Provided the various states of the text are available in transcription and facsimile, the reader will then be at liberty to seek untrodden paths – to reject the editor's advice – and, if the reader so chooses, to leave a record of that different journey. Under JITM or similar systems, this would be a stand-off file that revises one of the available transcriptions, thus creating a new reading text. We are calling this revision file the 'tweaker'. So now *both* editions take their chances in the intellectual marketplace. The new edition 'tweaks' one of the existing text files on which the original edition was also based. The new edition, if it is persuasive, will attract in time a tradition of new interpretation, and JITM's authentication mechanism will prevent the two traditions from accidentally being applied to the wrong edition.

Both editions will now represent the work, but differently. And the term *work* will be revealed more clearly in the electronic environment as the sign under which all the textual labour has taken place in the past and under which it will take place in the future. JITM is not a totalizing text-encoding scheme, but rather an evolving, accumulative one. A work-site can grow as understanding of its textual versions, their physical embodiments and their cultural and historical meanings grow. There will be no need to appeal to a transcendental ideal. The Renear vs Pichler, realist vs anti-realist argument will resolve itself as the e-text emerges for what it is: an encoded performance of the work, one that is conditioned by its own material environment and the aims or attentiveness of its encoders. Like the scholarly edition, it does not and cannot have a simple one-to-one relationship with what it purports to represent. It will always be provisional; but some encodings, doubtless, will turn out to be more provisional than others.

If this outcome is to eventuate, editors will have to let go of that anxious, even obsessive (but definitely productive) control over their edition, which I described at the beginning. The transition will not be cost-free. It will achieve another form of productivity but only by observing a different material logic. Editors will have to be prepared to invite users into the fray as commentators and creators of competing editions using the same re-purposed materials. JITM-like systems should help this scenario to eventuate without compromising traditional standards of accuracy and rigorous reasoning.

Chapter 5

Open Source Critical Editions: A Rationale

Gabriel Bodard and Juan Garcés

In 2006 a group of scholars within the Digital Classicist[1] community began to meet, first electronically and then physically, to discuss a range of issues and strategies that they dubbed 'Open Source Critical Editions'.[2] An Open Source Critical Editions (OSCE) workshop was held on 22 September 2006 at the Centre for Computing in the Humanities, King's College London, under the auspices of the AHRC ICT Methods Network. It was also supported in part by the Perseus Project and the Digital Classicist. This workshop was set up with the aim of exploring the possibilities of, requirements for and repercussions of a new generation of digital critical editions of Greek and Latin texts where the underlying code is made available under an open licence such as Creative Commons, General Public Licence (GPL) or Apache.[3] It is our assumption, and our assertion, that these issues and protocols will apply to all humanities disciplines that deal with the publication of critical texts. Although we are a relatively homogeneous group, approaching these questions principally as Classicists, it would obviously be shortsighted and counter-productive to imagine that we do not share a great many of these concerns with scholars from other disciplines who are working toward similar protocols.

Technological questions discussed at this event included: the status of open critical editions within a repository or distributed collection of texts; the need for and requirements of a registry to bind together and provide referencing mechanisms for such texts (the Canonical Text Services protocols being an obvious candidate for such a function);[4] the authoritative status of this class of edition, whether edited by a single scholar or collaboratively; the role of e-Science and Grid applications in the

---

1 The Digital Classicist website, wiki and discussion list (sponsored by the Centre for Computing in the Humanities, King's College London and the Stoa Consortium, University of Kentucky) can all be found at <http://www.digitalclassicist.org/>. All urls valid at the time of writing, September 2007.

2 See the full Methods Network report at <http://www.methodsnetwork.ac.uk/activities/act9report.html>; contributing papers were given by (in addition to the authors): Sayeed Choudhury, Gregory Crane, Daniel Decker, Stuart Dunn, Brian Fuchs, Charlotte Roueché, Ross Scaife and Neel Smith.

3 Creative Commons licensing, see <http://www.creativecommons.org/>; GNU General Public Licence, see <http://www.gnu.org/copyleft/gpl.html>; Apache Licence, see <http://www.apache.org/licenses/>.

4 Canonical Text Services protocol, see <http://chs75.harvard.edu/projects/diginc/techpub/cts>.

creation and delivery of editions. Legal issues largely revolved around the question of copyright and licensing: what status should the data behind digital critical editions have? This group assumed that source texts should be both Open Source (with respect to the editions) and public domain (for the texts themselves), but the specifics remain to be discussed. Attribution of scholarship is clearly desirable, but the automatic granting of permission to modify and build upon scholarly work is also essential. There were also questions regarding the Classical texts upon which such editions are based: what is the copyright status of a recently published critical edition of a text or manuscript that the editor of a new edition needs to incorporate? Administrative questions posed by open critical editions included: issues of workflow, collaboration and editorial oversight (on which the examples of the Suda Online and Pleiades – to name only two prominent Classics projects with experience in this area – and of large projects like Citizendium will provide useful terms of reference);[5] protocols for publication and re-use of source data. Issues of peer review and both pre and post-publication validation of scholarship were also discussed.

Many of the arguments presented in this chapter are not new or especially startling. Our aim is to collect those elements of scholarly thinking that have some bearing on digital publication into a coherent picture that helps to define the particular assumptions within which we are working. These assumptions and arguments clearly draw upon the work of scholars both within and without the Classics,[6] and are almost always informed by the contributions of the participants in the OSCE workshop. The particular case made here is of course the work of the authors alone and should not be read as representing the opinions or arguments of any other scholar.

The interests and rationale of this active community, while relatively coherent and implicitly well understood internally, have never been fully documented. This chapter, informed by the discussions of the OSCE group yet representing the particular views of the authors, will focus on three of the core issues, all expressed in the title: (1) the sense and implications of the Open Source model; (2) the connotations of 'critical' in this context; (3) the issue of what kinds of edition should be included in such a project – literary, eclectic or individual manuscripts – and what this means for the technologies and protocols adopted. Our proposal is that Classical scholarship should recognize OSCEs as a deeper, richer and potentially different kind of publication from printed editions of texts, or even

---

5 Suda Online editorial policies, see <http://www.stoa.org/sol/policy.shtml>; Pleiades editorial workflow, see <http://icon.stoa.org/trac/pleiades/wiki/WorkFlow>; Citizendium policies, see <http://www.citizendium.org/about.html>.

6 See, for example, P. Robinson, 'Current Issues in Making Digital Editions of Medieval Texts – or, Do Electronic Scholarly Editions Have a Future?', *Digital Medievalist*, 1/1 (2005). Available online at <http://www.digitalmedievalist.org/article.cfm?RecID=6>. G. Crane, D. Bamman and A. Babeu, 'ePhilology: When the Books Talk to their Readers', in R. Siemens and S. Schreibman (eds), *Blackwell Companion to Digital Literary Studies* (Oxford: Blackwell Publishing Limited, 2007), pp. 29–64.

from digitized and open content online editions. OSCEs are more than merely the final representations of finished work; in their essence they involve the distribution of raw data, of scholarly tradition, of decision-making processes, and of the tools and applications that were used in reaching these conclusions. The protocols and technologies for this manner of publication need to be made available and comprehensible to all textual scholars if the unique advantages and opportunities afforded by digital scholarship are to become entrenched in Classical and other philological disciplines.

Open Source

The use of the term 'Open Source' in this discussion is perhaps deliberately provocative: the term is generally used in the context of software engineering projects and collaboratively authored source code. It might be argued that a term like 'Open Access' or 'Open Content' would be more appropriate to a project involving critical texts rather than algorithms. Nevertheless, we shall argue that the principles of the Open Source movement are basically those of scholarly publication, which traditionally requires full documentation of sources, references and arguments, and allows – nay demands – the re-use of these sources and reference to previous editions in future publications on the same topic.

The origins of the concept of Open Source lie in the free software movement, with operating systems like Unix and GNU, web browsing tools like Mozilla, and the large number of projects that circulate code through Open Source development sites such as SourceForge.[7] The rationale behind the Open Source movement is not that software should be free merely in the financial sense, so that it should be available at no cost, but that it should be open in the sense of free to distribute, learn from, modify and re-distribute. In other words, Open Source software is not necessarily non-commercial (although it often is), but it is software that is distributed along with its source code and with an explicit licence allowing others to modify, fix or enhance this code and circulate the improved version of the software, along with the code, under the same open licence. (Most Open Source licences prohibit the distribution of derivative software without the source code also being made available.) In the words of the GNU GPL:

> When we speak of free software, we are referring to freedom, not price. Our General Public Licenses are designed to make sure that you have the freedom to distribute copies of free software (and charge for this service if you wish), that you receive source code or can get it if you want it, that you can change the software or use pieces of it in new free programs; and that you know you can do these things.

---

7 Cf. n. 2, above; about SourceForge, see <http://sourceforge.net/docs/about>; see also Open Source Definition (from Linux Information Project) at <http://www.linfo.org/open_source.html>; Open Source Initiative at <http://www.opensource.org/docs/osd>.

To protect your rights, we need to make restrictions that forbid anyone to deny you these rights or to ask you to surrender the rights. These restrictions translate to certain responsibilities for you if you distribute copies of the software, or if you modify it.

For example, if you distribute copies of such a program, whether gratis or for a fee, you must give the recipients all the rights that you have. You must make sure that they, too, receive or can get the source code. And you must show them these terms so they know their rights.[8]

Software licensed under an Open Source agreement is not therefore wholly in the public domain: it is copyrighted, it belongs to the author, the author's rights are protected, the author will always get credit for it and there are limits on what can be done with it. But the author has prospectively given permission for the content to be reproduced under certain conditions, which vary according to the licence chosen. Open Source is not so much a business model with exclusively economic implications as a strategy based on the belief that cultural advances are made by building upon the creations and publications of those who came before us. Without full access to the raw code, the documentation and the methodological statement that makes an experiment or a solution reproducible, a given publication is a dead end; it cannot be built upon. Certain types of creation are not protected by strong copyright and patents: they are stifled by it. An Open Source licence on a software package or suite does, it is true, make it harder for a single entity to make money from a monopoly on that product, but it is equally true that in the best-case scenario it makes possible collaborative work on a scale never seen before in the programming world. It is possible for several – or several hundred – coders to work on the same problem, to take one another's scripts and improve them, build upon them, modify them, sideline or deprecate them if they are superfluous. These co-workers need never have met nor communicated with one another; they may not have the same interests or goals; but they are all, for a time, working toward the same ends.

Strict application of copyright law prevents this degree of cooperation and innovation. This is because the useful lifespan of software code is relatively short, often no more than a year or two. The limited duration of copyright and patent does nothing to reduce this stifling effect upon innovation. Open Source licences make it possible for creators of programming code voluntarily to open up their work to the possibility of such collaborative effort. Of course, many Open Source products are neglected or weak, and only the biggest projects attract the huge armies of collaborators that Mozilla, Apache and Linux can boast. This includes paid labour from employees of companies who have a vested interest of one kind or another in seeing the Open Source tools in question succeed. Companies that want to keep their secrets close and their labour in-house simply do not use Open Source licensing; indeed, in some circles Open Source is almost a dirty word.

---

8 Text of GPL from <http://www.gnu.org/copyleft/gpl.html>; cf. the legal code of the Creative Commons' Attribution-ShareAlike licence, at <http://creativecommons.org/licenses/by-sa/3.0/legalcode>.

We would argue that like software, academic research cannot afford to wait for copyright to expire.[9] In disciplines such as medicine and related sciences research more than five or ten years old is often considered, if not obsolete, then old news; in most cases it will have been tested, built upon and either superseded or rejected. Publications in the humanities do not have such short shelf-lives; it is not unknown for a work a hundred years old still to be cited in current research in the same area. Nevertheless, it is probably true that most engagement with a new piece of research, be it in a critical review, a refutation or a re-use of a theoretical model with different parameters, takes place within the first decade or so of its publication. It is essential that no legal barriers stand in the way of such free citation of and engagement with ideas.

It is recognized that critical editions are not new creations in the sense that copyright is meant to protect, but that they are, by definition, reflections and derivations of existing (usually public domain) material. Even in traditional publication media, both in printed editions such as Oxford Classical Texts and searchable corpora like the *Thesaurus Linguae Graecae*, it seems to be the assumption that verbatim reproduction of previous publications is, within certain limits, fair game. The apparatus criticus is another story: this is scholarly creation and is considered to be protected by copyright.

It is also of course clear that copyright does not prevent the ideas in a piece of scholarly literature from being cited, built upon and argued with, but only protects the actual words used in the expression of said ideas from being copied, redistributed and profited from by anyone but the author (or, more often, the publisher). In the digital age, however, there is more to scholarship than simply abstract ideas expressed in elegant rhetoric and language; sometimes the most essential part of an academic work is precisely the actual words and codes used in the expression of that work. This is true, for example, of critical editions, eclectic or supplemented texts, apparatus critici, philological commentary and text encoding, as we shall discuss below. A database or XML-encoded text is not merely an abstract idea, it is itself both the scholarly expression of research and the raw data upon which that research is based, and which must form the basis of any derivative research that attempts to reproduce or refute its conclusions.

In the case of digital editions, therefore, conventional copyright is arguably doing more to hold back research than to protect the author. We propose that a protocol for collections of digital critical editions of texts and/or manuscripts, which aims to allow for collaboration on the widest possible scale, must include the requirement (or at least the very strong recommendation) that texts are not only Open Content (allowing free access to the output itself) but also Open Source – revealing transparently the code behind the output, the research behind the text, the decisions which are part of scholarly publication.

---

9 See, for example, the discussion arising from and surrounding four articles on the value of Creative Commons licensing posted at <http://creativecommons.org/weblog/entry/7435>.

If a project were to publish digital critical editions without making the source code available, this would arguably be in conflict with the principles of scholarly editing and publication upon which the academy is based. Open Source in this context is not innovative, it is traditional.

Critical

'Critical', in this context, is a qualifier that is ostensibly clear in its denotation but betrays a more complex history and set of assumptions that will need to be elucidated, albeit briefly and selectively. Historically, 'critical' discourse in the sense we use it refers to nineteenth-century humanist scholarship, with roots reaching back to the Enlightenment and the Renaissance, to the Hellenistic librarians and earlier. In this tradition, criticism meant methodical assessment of evidence following well-founded criteria. Kant defined criticism not only as his contemporaries did, as a method of logical analysis, but more particularly as the absolute exercise of reason. In his *Critique of Pure Reason*, he called his own time the 'Zeitalter der Kritik, der sich alles unterwerfen muß'.[10] His own philosophy was aimed at establishing a firm foundation for knowledge, practice and emotion, and separating faith from knowledge.[11]

Kant's philosophy linked up with the establishment of the early-modern university, which gave criticism an institutional home. When, in 1793, the University of Halle was founded, an institutional model had been introduced that would soon spread throughout Europe and eventually, with considerable variation, all over the world. Unlike the orthodox universities in Leipzig, Wittenberg and Jena, which were controlled by the trans-territorial Lutheran church, the administrative structure of the University of Halle was reorganized by the Hohenzollern dynasty to make it accountable to the state ministry; to educate jurists, civil administrators, teachers and pastors primarily committed to the needs of civil society in the German state. As Ian Hunter puts it, the new institutional model was there to 'divorce politics from theology and to fashion a style of thought and conduct that would allow jurists and administrators to subordinate the uncompromising ideals of religion to the peace and prosperity of the state'.[12] Hence, 'critical' implies the adherence to reasonable methods and principles, the radical judgement of interpretative decisions in accordance with those methods and principles and, ideally, the civil exchange of reasonable arguments between diverging opinions. It was the role of philosophy, according to Kant, to protect the university from undue influence from outside sources, be it from the state or the church.

---

10 I. Kant, *Kritik der reinen Vernunft* ([1781]; Hamburg: Meiner Verlag, 1998), p. 7: 'the age of criticism, to which everything must conform'.

11 B. Recki, 'Kritik', *Religion in Geschichte und Gegenwart*, 4 (2001): 1781–2, p. 1781.

12 I. Hunter, 'The Regimen of Reason: Kant's Defence of the Philosophy Faculty', *Oxford Literary Review*, 17 (1995): 51–85, p. 56.

When the University of Berlin was founded 17 years later, the modernization of the university had already made its decisive breakthrough and the German idealists, from Schiller to Humboldt, had entrenched the ties between the university and the nation-state, epitomized in the idea of 'culture'. The study of culture, of course, required the interpretation of foundational texts, and Greek and Latin texts had been part of German *Bildung* for some time. In the seventeenth-century 'critical' editions had begun not only to be critical in their application of philological judgement, following the traditions of Alexandrian scholarship, but also increasingly critical in relation to the historical investigation of the sources and their relationships. It was, however, only around the person of Karl Lachmann that a set of rigorous rules was formulated in order to establish the oldest possible text from a group of manuscript witnesses. The 'Lachmann method'[13] set out the careful comparison (collation) of all extant manuscripts of a given work and the meticulous application of a series of steps that would lead not only to the constitution of an archetypal text, from which all manuscripts descended, but also the reconstruction of a genealogical family tree, which would delineate the interrelationship of all manuscripts deriving from said archetype.

Sebastiano Timpanaro described the four key traits of Lachmann's *recensio* in which he had been influenced by a number of different Classical philologists:

> [1] The rejection of the vulgate and the requirement that the manuscripts … be used as the foundation of the edition. … [2] The distrust for manuscripts of the Humanist period. … [3] The reconstruction of the history of the text and particularly of the genealogical relations that link the extant manuscripts. … [4] The formulation of criteria permitting a mechanical determination (without recourse to *iudicium*) of which reading goes back to the archetype.[14]

That an approach based on the rigorous application of rational methods could indeed reach conclusions unperturbed by, or at any rate in tension with, irrational forces outside the text can be illustrated by one of its most remarkable achievements: New Testament textual criticism initiated[15] a project, still ongoing, to establish a 'critical' text of the New Testament, that broke with the entrenched

---

13 S. Timpanaro (*The Genesis of Lachmann's Method*, ed. and trans. G.W. Most (Chicago: University of Chicago Press, 2005) and others have convincingly made the case that Karl Lachmann was probably neither the inventor nor the most consistent implementer of said method; we still retain this name out of convenience. See P. Maas, *Textual Criticism*, trans. B. Flower (Oxford: Clarendon Press, 1958) for a classic synthetic presentation of the Lachmann method.

14 Timpanaro, *Genesis*, p. 115f.

15 There were, of course, predecessors. Notably in the work of Erasmus (1516), Bengel (1734), Wettstein (1751/2) and Griesbach (1775/7), none of which fully succeeded in overcoming the text of the Textus Receptus.

Textus Receptus by strictly following the scientific rules set out by, amongst others, Karl Lachmann himself.[16]

At this point, it will be helpful to point out some central consequences of textual criticism – what makes a particular discourse 'critical' – pertinent to the argument put forward here. The critical method was drilled into generations of future scholars in seminars and closely supervised papers and theses. Later on, a system of reviews and discussions – 'peer review' – made sure that adherence to these rules was certain. The cumulative characteristic of this discourse, however, was that interaction with fellow critics – contemporary and past – had been put on the more civil basis of the exchange of rational arguments. There was no space, at least in the ideal case, for *ex cathedra* pronunciation or recourse to tradition, authority or dogmatics. Fellow critics had to be persuaded and they, furthermore, had to be persuaded solely by logical argument. Two further traits followed from this.

A crucial characteristic of critical discourse was – for obvious reasons, especially in the formative years – documentation of sources and preceding works. Many manuscripts were 'discovered' and edited by critical scholarship in the eighteenth and nineteenth centuries. Subsequent scholarship could base itself on those editions and improve them as further manuscripts were made available and improved readings of individual manuscripts and collations of a growing number of them were produced. Collecting – ideally all – preceding scholarship on particular subject matter in a bibliography and reviewing it critically became *de rigueur* in scholarly practice. One of the reasons for this was to identify clearly the contribution of an individual critical work vis-à-vis a growing body of scholarly discussion and achievement – the acknowledgement of the giants of scholarship on whose shoulders one stood. Another aspect of the relationship with antecedent work was to ensure a 'fair use' of other scholars' publications. As mentioned above, scholarly output was, subsequent to its publication, open to use according to standards established and policed by the critical community.

Critical scholarship could lead to a variety of outcomes: a new thesis in answer to a particular question; but also a new or improved edition of a manuscript or text. These outcomes needed nonetheless to be persuasive to the scholarly community. Nothing detracts more from a convincing line of argument than a detailed critical interaction with the aforementioned body of scholarship, however necessary. This was the place for the apparatus criticus, a subordinate, though no less important, text alongside and closely inter-referenced with the main text, in which this interaction could be explicitly acknowledged and developed. The apparatus criticus could comprise any of the following: a collection of variant readings or translations, elaborate textual notes and discussion, adding to the already mentioned bibliography, index or even concordance. Nothing exemplifies this established apparatus better than the footnote. Leaving the main text elegantly clean and uncluttered by distracting references and argumentation, footnotes host

---

16 Lachmann's own attempt, as Timpanaro relates it, was anything but a full success. It was for Constantine von Tischendorf to realize the first true breakthrough.

something which is fundamental to criticism. They are, as Anthony Grafton puts it, 'the humanist's rough equivalent of the scientist's report: they offer the empirical support for stories told and arguments presented'.[17] They provide the basis and infrastructure of critical discourse and thus disclose one important feature of critical practice and open up one crucial possibility. What this reveals is, of course, that criticism is fundamentally a *communal* enterprise. While the scholar's argument is presented as the erudite position of, usually, an individual critic, what makes it possible in the first place is presented explicitly or implicitly in the apparatus. But in providing the basis of the research, including all references to sources used, it creates the possibility of verification to the reader, who is now potentially able to reconstruct, double-check and critically scrutinize each critical step that forms the basis on which the argument stands or collapses.

In view of the genealogical vignette and arguments above, one major implication of the qualifier 'critical' is, we hope, more than evident: text editions should only be seen as fully critical if all interpretative decisions that led to the text (on which more below) are made as fully accessible and transparent as possible. This is not to say that this ideal is always reached or that editions that do not adhere to this definition of 'critical' are to be disregarded. We should merely like to argue that full accessibility and transparency is the ideal toward which to strive if 'critical' is understood in the way laid out above.

The realization of the ideal itself, of course, has always been constrained by the medium in which the edition is presented. Practical consideration of costs, technical possibilities, possible layout and editorial tradition will always influence the degree to which all elements that forged the edition will be displayed in front of the reader. It is quite possible that all manuscripts will be fully transcribed, including records of all graphemic idiosyncrasies. Such palaeographic insights – often important for elucidating the text – have to be sacrificed, however, when grouping variant readings in the apparatus variorum. This is in itself a valuable critical act, but the critical steps leading to the groupings of variants, after they have been heavily normalized, are, in this case, no longer available to the reader who would like to reconstruct those steps. We should like to argue that a digital edition is less constrained than paper and print, in that it is possible to be inclusive of all critical arguments. In addition, both graphemic *and* normalized transcriptions of all manuscripts that comprise the edition could and should be provided, at least as one possible scenario. This is certainly not the only example of the economy of the print medium limiting critical discourse: previous discussions are often implicitly presupposed or, at best, merely alluded to. A selective choice of arguments is made necessary, exactitude and certainty are not always spelled out. All material potentially disrupting the overall argument in a commentary is relegated to footnotes or endnotes.

---

17 A. Grafton, *The Footnote: A Curious History* (Cambridge, MA: Harvard University Press, 1997), p. viii.

This potential explicitness is desirable not only in the edition's traditional narrative medium; many – though not all – critical decisions can and should also be formalized into a machine-readable form. Making this information machine-actionable transforms a digital edition beyond a mere emulation of a print edition; it opens the edition up to further computer-assisted analysis of text features and their complex relationship, as well as making it possible to recognize complex argumentation patterns. Critical transparency, however, works in both directions: most digital editions are encoded in XML or held in a relational database. XML schemas and entity relation models, as well as transformation scripts and query algorithms, are integral parts of such a digital edition. These editions are much more than the data visible on the user interface. If they are to be 'critical' in the aforementioned sense, all these aspects may also need to be made transparent and accessible.

We argue, in sum, that 'critical', in the context of digital editions, indicates not only the presentation of texts that are the outcome of critical scholarship but, more importantly, requires transparency, to software as well as to human readers, as to the editorial interventions made and the sources, data and scholarship behind such decisions.

Editions

Critical editions – even if 'critical' is understood in the more specific sense laid out above – come in many different types and forms. In the effort to explain this variety, Martin-Dietrich Gleßgen and Lebsanft have recourse to two conflicting principles. On the one hand, there is the principle of the concrete and factual materiality of the extant documents that survive in libraries, archives and museums; on the other, is the principle of the ideal and abstract notion of a reconstructed archetype, or even Urtext.[18] Different editions are shaped by the tension between these extreme principles and are accounted for by the relative influence each principle is exerting upon the particular edition. The space between the extremes is therefore populated by a range of edition types that negotiate, mediate and compromise between these two foundational approaches. This begins with the artefact itself, and moves on to a variety of surrogates (drawn, photographed, scanned), 'diplomatic', normalized, synoptic and 'best-text' editions, until the full-on historical critical edition, complete with apparatus variorum, is reached. In order to elucidate the editorial issues raised from each pole, it might be helpful to look at two of their closest representatives in their print media incarnations: the papyrologist and the literary textual scholar.

---

18 M.-D. Gleßgen and F. Lebsanft, 'Von alter und neuer Philologie: Neuer Streit über Prinzipien und Praxis der Textkritik', in M.-D. Gleßgen and F. Lebesanft (eds), *Alte und neue Philologie*, Beihefete zu editio 8 (Tübingen: Max Niemeyer Verlag, 1997), pp. 1–14.

The papyrologist represents an editorial practice influenced by the principle of the concrete and factual materiality of ancient manuscripts. Herbert Youtie devoted his famous 1962 Russel Lecture to the more 'private' aspect of the editorial activity of the papyrologist: 'The typical product of the hours spent by the papyrologist with his papyri is the edition of one or more texts. So much is this the case that we are ready to call a scholar a papyrologist if he publishes a papyrus text now and again, no matter what else he may do.'[19] The reason that this activity is often neither appreciated nor fully discussed is, according to Youtie, owing to the fact that adjacent disciplines regularly accept published papyrus editions as 'fact': 'The general accounts can afford not to tell us what the papyrologist does, because what he does is used up in producing texts that are absorbed into literature or history. It is self-consuming labor and leaves little or no trace of itself in the editions.'[20] Papyrologists know better than to merely trust the presented readings as facts, as they 'manufactured' most of these facts during the process of transcribing. The process of transcribing and editing a papyrus is not only amongst the most demanding critical philological activities in textual scholarship, it also necessitates a particular individual and collective workflow, in order to ensure the quality of the edition.

The processes leading to an edition of a papyrus manuscript are, in all experience, doomed to fall short of full success, since they 'call for insight, ingenuity, and imagination to a degree no one man could possibly possess'. A host of factors, 'the physical state of the papyri, the nature of the handwriting on them, the "dead" languages represented by the writing', conspire to subvert the success of this endeavour.[21] Papyrologists are fully aware of this condition and have developed ways to build on their early readings, either by publishing subsequent improved editions, or in *Berichtigungslisten*, which are collections with critical presentations of corrections and supplements to such editions. While the improvement of a published edition is made via sequential publications, these publications are merely instantiations of a cyclically improved collaborative intellectual product which involves 'the laborious production of a transcript, the discovery of error, and repeated revision until all error is eliminated'.[22]

In order to open up editions to such collaborative critical scrutiny, papyrologists have developed and adopted a detailed system. This system originated at the 18th International Congress of Orientalists (Leiden, September 1932) – the Leiden Convention.[23] It allows readers of such transcriptions, via a variety of marks

---

19 H. Youtie, 'The Papyrologist: Artificer of Fact', *Greek, Roman & Byzantine Studies*, 4 (1963): 19–32, p. 22.

20 Ibid., p. 21.

21 Ibid., p. 23.

22 Ibid., p. 29.

23 On the congress, see especially B.A. van Groningen, 'Projet d'unification des systèmes de signes critiques', *Chronique d'Égypte*, 7 (1932): 262–9; A.S. Hunt, 'A Note on the Transliteration of Papyri', *Chronique d'Égypte*, 7 (1932): 272–4.

on the text such as brackets and other sigla and diacritical signs, to reconstruct which letters have been added, corrected or expanded by the editor, as well as the layout of the text on the original support: 'From all [these] signs a practised eye can visualize the actual shape of the original text, locate its holes and tears, and perhaps even imagine its folds.'[24] Turner is, however, quick to add some of the shortcomings of the 'Leiden system', one of which is that 'it is not possible to be so confident that what is stated to be there is there'. This shortcoming led to an alternative approach – the diplomatic transcription – being established alongside the application of the 'Leiden system'. Turner describes this approach as follows:

> This transcription does not separate words, and follows exactly the layout of the original for spacings and interlinear additions, accents, critical marks, etc. It shows no letter as read which cannot be guaranteed. Ambiguous traces are described in the critical note.
> … One purpose of making such a transcript is to force the transcriber to discriminate between what he sees and what he would like to see, to call his attention to the subjective factor in decipherment, and to make him devise verifications for his readings.[25]

In order to prepare a critical print edition, the papyrologist usually has to decide beforehand – unless working with a particularly generous publisher – what kind of edition will be presented: how much of the text to normalize, add and correct, and how much of the decision-making process to make explicit.

While the papyrologist edits a text still bearing the traces of its physical appearance on the actual manuscript, textual scholars seek to construct an altogether more disembodied work. As Paul Maas formulated it in the very first pages of his classic textbook, 'the business of textual criticism is to produce a text as close as possible to the original (*constitutio textus*)'.[26] But this formulation begs at least two questions: that of how close one can get to the original; and, more fundamentally, how safe it is to assume that there was such a thing as an 'original'. Martin West, established Classical scholar and editor of the Teubner *Iliad* edition, admits this difficulty in his editorial work on Homer: 'The Homeric poems, because of their oral background and the special nature of their early transmission, pose peculiar problems to the editor and textual critic. To begin with, there is the problem of defining what the text is exactly that they are aiming to establish.'[27] The problem with the Homeric poems is that they have 'grown' considerably over the time of their transmission. There was neither a definable Urtext, nor a single 'Athenian' text, as quoted by Hipparchus, Thucydides and Plato. Not even Alexandrian

---

24 E. Turner, *Greek Papyri: An Introduction* (Oxford: Oxford University Press, 1980), p. 70.

25 Ibid., p. 71.

26 Maas, *Textual Criticism*, p. 1.

27 M.L. West, 'The Textual Criticism and Editing of Homer', in G.W. Most (ed.), *Editing Texts: Texte edieren*, Aporemata 2 (Göttingen: Vandenhoeck & Ruprecht, 1998), p. 94.

scholarship, which probably established some agreement about its *Versbestand*, determined a single circumspect text. In view of this circumstance, West proposes a compromise: 'Let us state our aim to be the establishment, so far as our means allow, of the pristine text of the poems in the form they attained following the last phase of creative effort.' In other words, we must concede that, as the tradition has passed through several centuries of 'wildness', it may be impossible to establish exactly what lies on the far side.

In the reconstructions of the New Testament, on the other hand, proximity to the autographs is an ideological demand, since it is traditionally seen as the authoritative text written by divinely inspired authors. Any deviation from the original necessarily represents a corruption of the canonical text. In 1882, editors Brook Westcott and Fenton Hort could still give their critical edition of the New Testament the ambitious title *The New Testament in the Original Greek*. After the collation of numerous additional manuscripts and copious scholarly discussions, the Institute for New Testament Textual Research in Münster, responsible for the standard critical edition, has adopted the more realistic aim of reconstructing the *Ausgangstext* ('Initial text'), i.e. 'the text that precedes [the] process of copying', adding: 'Between the text of the author and the initial text there may be developments that have left no traces in any of the surviving manuscripts.'[28]

Critical editions of texts with multiple manuscript witnesses have tended to present the reconstructed text as the lemma and a summary of agreements and disagreements with the individual manuscripts or manuscript groups in the apparatus variorum. But even though the aim of reconstructing the oldest possible text has been widely accepted as the core critical task, how to present it has remained an incompletely resolved issue. The classic representative criticizing the presentation of an eclectic text as lemma remains Joseph Bédier.[29] His disagreement with the Lachmann method demonstrated a profound uneasiness about offering a reconstructed text that is not attested in its wording in any concrete manuscript. His suggestion was to choose the text of a concrete manuscript that is deemed by the editor to most closely represent the archetype of the text tradition – the 'Best Text'. 'Best' was still defined by Bédier as coming closest to the notional source text from which all other witnesses depart. However, what if a textual tradition is more complex than a tree model could explain? What if the transmission of the text implied not only copying but continuous creative rewriting leading to chronic instability within the text – variance. Bernard Cerquiglini in his 1989 essay *Eloge de la variante*[30] is chief instigator of a

---

28 Institute for New Testament Textual Research in Münster, available at <http://www.uni-muenster.de/INTF/>.

29 Famously discussed by Bédier in 'La tradition manuscrite de Lai de l'ombre', *Romania*, 54 (1928).

30 B. Cerquiglini, *In Praise of the Variant: A Critical History of Philology*, trans. B. Wing (Baltimore: The Johns Hopkins University Press, 1999).

re-orientation of the philological perspective. Basically, the 'new philology' can be seen as embracing the concrete and factual materiality of texts.

Digital editions may stimulate our critical engagement with such crucial textual debate. They may push the classic definition of the 'edition' by not only offering a presentational publication layer but also by allowing access to the underlying encoding of the repository or database beneath. Indeed, an editor need not make any authoritative decisions that supersede all alternative readings if all possibilities can be unambiguously reconstructed from the base manuscript data, although most would in practice probably want to privilege their favoured readings in some way.[31] The critical edition, with sources fully incorporated, would potentially provide an interactive resource that assists the user in creating virtual research environments. Responses to a richer variety of analytical perspectives would be made possible and this would feed into future editions. This model should enable a more holistic notion of what is understood by a text as well as which sources can be represented by a modern edition.

Concluding remarks

To summarize, the model we are proposing here is for digital critical editions to be recognized as a deeper, richer and potentially very different kind of publication from printed editions of texts, even if such editions are digitized and made available in open content form. Open Source Critical Editions are more than merely presentations of finished work; they involve an essential distribution of the raw data, the scholarly tradition, the decision-making process, and the tools and applications that were used in reaching these conclusions. The Open Content model is an extremely important new movement in publication; the OSCE proposal is for a potentially new approach to research itself.

In theory the editorial and even publication implications of the Open Source Critical Editions discussion allow for a wide range of approaches, from a traditional one-editor text published in static form to a free-for-all wiki that can be contributed to concurrently and without restriction by any number of editors.[32] However, as we have stressed above, our model calls very clearly for all editorial contributions, modifications and decisions to be transparent and explicit, to be attributed and citable, and to be stable and permanent. We do not have space in this chapter to

---

31 An example of such a radically 'agnostic' editorial policy is that of the *Online Critical Pseudepigrapha*, available at <http://www.purl.org/net/ocp>; all witnesses (including scholarly emendations) are transcribed, and eclectic editions can be generated from combinations of these at the presentational stage.

32 See, for example, Peter Robinson's abstract titled 'A New Paradigm for Electronic Scholarly Editions' (2006) <http://www.methodsnetwork.ac.uk/activities/es03abstracts. html>, which seems to imply a relatively unstructured approach to scholarly editing of digital editions.

discuss all the protocol and workflow issues that editors of this sort of edition need to address, but we should like to stress that openness and critical method require both robust citation and versioning protocols, and for whatever editorial control is in place to be documented and fully attributed.

Clearly there are issues of technology, protocol and academic workflow that arise from the model proposed in this chapter. All of these issues are being explored and will continue to be explored both within the digital Classicist community and the much wider world that is digital academia. In particular there are two sets of issues that interest us, and which we feel warrant further exploration and discussion. The first of these is the need for the development of technologies, protocols and methodologies to make the OSCE model possible. Many of these may be adapted from those used in other disciplines. The second issue is the relationship between published OSCEs and large collections of less deeply marked-up but Open Content texts. It will be essential to ensure not only that the larger collections have the capacity to include the richer texts, but also that the protocols adopted by both movements allow the wealth of the smaller, deeply encoded body of editions to be used to enrich the collection as a whole and educate the technologies that query, organize and deliver it.

We should also stress that, as Crane has been arguing for years,[33] it should not be Classicists, or even perhaps digital humanists, who are inventing completely new technologies and protocols and workflow methodologies as our intellectual and academic world evolves. Many of these issues will have been addressed by other disciplines, in particular (but not only) the sciences, and where possible we should adopt or (if they are Open Source, for example) adapt the tools of these better-funded fields. There are gaps in the resources available, and some of our needs are either unique or as yet unmet, but these gaps are better filled by adapting from and contributing to the wider academic community than by inventing new methods from scratch, just as the EpiDoc Guidelines for publication and interchange of Greek and Latin epigraphic documents in XML built upon the solid groundwork provided by the venerable Text Encoding Initiative rather than creating their own schema from nothing.[34] It will not always be possible to borrow wholesale from other disciplines, but Classicists should take advantage of models, tools and systems developed in other fields, without underestimating the extent to which the approaches designed or improved within their own framework might be fed back successfully to the lively exchange of cross-disciplinary ideas and experiences.[35]

33 G. Crane, 'Classics and the Computer: An End of the History', in S. Schreibman, R. Siemens and J. Unsworth (eds), *A Companion to Digital Humanities* (Oxford: Blackwell Publishing Limited, 2004), pp. 46–55.

34 All EpiDoc materials, including guidelines and documentation, accessible via <http://epidoc.sourceforge.net/>; history and current publications of the Text Encoding Initiative at <http://www.tei-c.org/>.

35 The Canonical Text Services (originally 'Classical') is an excellent example of such a technology created specifically by and for the Classical field, but which draws from

We hope that presenting the rationale of the OSCEs by way of unpacking three of its core concepts will provide a summary of a vigorous discussion of these issues, open these arguments up to a wider audience, and lay the foundation for future projects and discussions.

---

information science principles (e.g. FRBR), and should be taken up by scholars with a concern for text repositories from all backgrounds; see Christopher Blackwell and Neel Smith, 'A guide to version 1.1 of the Canonical Text Services Protocol', available at <http://chs75.harvard.edu/projects/diginc/techpub/cts-overview>.

Chapter 6

Every Reader his own Bibliographer
– An Absurdity?[1]

Edward Vanhoutte

Unheilbar Blinde sind nicht sehend zu machen;
aber verschlossene Augen lassen sich mit geübter,
feinfühliger Hand öffnen.[2]

Introduction

The primary subject of textual scholarship is the study of the different phases
in the creative process of an author through the focus on their complete oeuvre
or on one title only, and/or the study of the transmissional history of the text.
The final objective of textual scholarship is the application of the results of that
research to the scholarly editing of texts.[3] Scholarly editions provide students of

1 The title of this paper is a quotation by Fredson Bowers who, in a lecture before
the Bibliographical Society in London on 23 January 1958, defended the scholarly
editor's scholarly integrity by disapproving of the fashion to provide 'evidence for further
bibliographical investigation' since this bibliographical research is an essential part of the
scholarly editor's task and is thus completed at the moment of publication of the edition.
He also warned against a possible inflation of the scholarly quality of the editorial practice
when the editor uses 'the printed evidence which enables the critic to do the job himself if
he wishes' with the aim to excuse 'his own weakness of analysis'. Bowers crisply concludes
his defence of the scholarly editor with the following sentences: 'It is an anomaly for an
editor proposing to establish a text to expect wiser heads to carry forward and then to apply
the basic bibliographical examination of the document on which the very details of the
establishment should have rested. "Every reader his own bibliographer" is an absurdity.'
(F. Bowers, 'Principle and Practice in the Editing of Early Dramatic Texts', in *Textual and
Literary Criticism: The Sandars Lectures in Bibliography 1957–1958* (Cambridge, 1966),
p. 146.)

2 G. Witkowski, *Textkritik und Editionstechnik neuerer Schriftwerke. Ein
methodologischer Versuch* (Leipzig: H. Haessel Verlag, 1924), p. 131.

3 Cf. Scheibe: 'Le but véritable des études textuelles est de mettre en lumière le travail
de l'écrivain aux différentes étapes du processus de la création littéraire. [...] L'objectif
final de la textologie réside toujours dans l'application du faisceau complet de ses résultats
à une édition de textes, singulièrement lorsque celle-ci porte sur l'ensemble d'un oeuvre

the text with the foundational data for any sensible statement about these texts. By extrapolation, textual scholarship lays down the fundamental basis for all text-based humanities activities and disciplines.

As Dirk Van Hulle has reiterated, '[l]iterary critics tend to take the text for granted by assuming that the words on which they base their interpretations are an unproblematic starting point.'[4] Scholarly editing as a product-generating activity can react to this observation in two extreme ways. The first possibility is not to contest the literary critics' assumptions about the definite singularity of the text and provide them with the result of scholarly editing, namely an established text preferably accompanied by annotations. The second option is to confront them with their wrong assumption and draw their attention to the multiplicity of the fluid text caused by its genetic and transmissional history. This can be done by introducing them to the results of textual scholarship.

The first option is a function of the reading edition, the second option of the historical-critical or variorum edition. In this essay I use the term *minimal edition* for the former and *maximal edition* for the latter. The minimal edition is a cultural product that is produced by the scholarly editor acting as a curator or guardian of the text, whereas the maximal edition is an academic product in which the scholarly editor demonstrates his/her scholarly accuracy and scrutiny. To be clear, I define a reading edition here as the presentation of a scholarly established text, possibly but not necessarily accompanied by explanatory textual notes.

The literary critic is in the first place a reader, possibly an academic, and exceptionally a textual critic or a scholarly editor. In addition, the commercial reality of scholarly editions of the minimal and the maximal type should be taken into consideration when theorizing about their essential function and audiences. In this chapter I formulate six propositions about the audience, nature, function and status of the scholarly edition that lead to a seventh proposition about the electronic edition as the ideal maximal medium for the inclusion of the minimal edition, even in printable form.

Audience

The audience for scholarly editions of any kind is ill-defined and generally overestimated. The reception of the text-critical edition[5] of Hendrik Conscience's

---

et permet d'en faire revivre le déploiement.' (S. Scheibe, 'Quelles éditions pour quels lecteurs?', in L. Hay (ed.), *La Naissance du Texte* (n.p.: José Corti, 1989), p. 78.)

4 D. Van Hulle, *Textual Awareness: A Genetic Study of Late Works by Joyce, Proust & Mann* (Ann Arbor: University of Michigan Press, 2004), p. 2.

5 The *text-critical edition* presents itself explicitly as a reading edition but contains elements which are traditionally found in a study edition (e.g. annotations and a textual essay containing chapters on the genetic history of the text, on the transmission of the text and the bibliographic description of the extant witnesses, on the editorial principles). The

De Leeuw van Vlaenderen[6] (The Lion of Flanders)[7] illustrates this. This edition provides a critically established non-modernized and 'clear' reading text; a contextualizing essay by a leading scholar other than the editor; a bibliographic description of the witnesses; a genetic essay; an explication of the editorial principles; a list of emendations in the reading text with references to the corresponding readings in the most important witnesses; a glossary; and short biographies of the historical figures mentioned in the novel and in the commentary section. The edition does not contain an apparatus variorum and is specifically aimed at both the advanced reader and a wider audience of interested book buyers. The book contains 535 pages, is hardbound with dust jacket and ribbon bookmarker and at time of writing costs €39.35. The reviews in scholarly journals, quality newspapers and lifestyle magazines were unanimously positive and praised the book for its design and finish, its choice of the unmodernized version of the rare first printed edition as base text and the scholarly quality of the critically established reading text and the commentary. The book sold 900 copies in four years, and 25 per cent of the print run is still available.

In the same year this edition was published, the popular Flemish newspaper *Het Laatste Nieuws* gave away 500,000 copies of a modernized version of *The Lion of Flanders*. The book reproduces a modernized text from a 1984 reading edition (including printing errors), without any explanation of the editorial principles or contextualizing commentary. The book is 368 pages long and hardbound, and free copies could be collected from newsagents in exchange for a voucher published in the newspaper. The book was not reviewed in any media worth mentioning. Their version of *The Lion* was the first of a series of 35 (translated) reprints from world literature of which 3,332,000 copies sold at €4.90 a piece[8] in less than 35 weeks. The generated sales are equivalent to almost 61 per cent of the total turnover of fiction, tourism, cartography and reference book titles realized by the 90 members of the Flemish Publishers Association (Vlaamse Uitgevers Vereniging) in 2002.[9]

---

purpose of the edition is to inform the interested reader rather than provide a forum for the textual scholar to demonstrate the results of their research. The method used by the editor is based on an eclectic application of Anglo-American, German and French theories.

6 *De Leeuw van Vlaenderen* appeared in 1838 as the first novel in Flanders written in Dutch. As such it promoted the use of Dutch instead of French as a literary language and it marks the beginning of modern Flemish literature.

7 H. Conscience, *De Leeuw van Vlaenderen of de Slag der Gulden Sporen. Tekstkritische editie door Edward Vanhoutte, met een uitleiding door Karel Wauters* (Tielt: Lannoo, 2002).

8 *Jaarverslag boek.be 2004*, p. 33 <http://www.boek.be/files/bestanden/Jaarverslag_2004.pdf>. All urls valid at the time of writing, September 2007.

9 The fiction, tourism, cartography and reference book market represented c. €26,788,900 or 10 per cent of the total book market in Flanders in 2002. Figures based on the sales figures of the Vlaamse Uitgevers Vereniging 2003 <http://www.boek.be/files/bestanden/VUV_Verslag_omzetcijfers_2003.pdf>.

The average market for scholarly reading editions of modern poetry and prose in a minor language like Dutch is about 600 copies.[10] With 900 sold copies, the text-critical edition of *The Lion of Flanders* did remarkably well. However, the 500,000 copies of the same title distributed by the newspaper disclose an enormous market of so-called 'readers' – or, more exactly, acquirers of books. This brings me to my first two propositions:

1. Buyers of books are not interested in literature, they are interested in books as physical objects.[11]
2. Buyers of literature are not interested in a reliable text specifically, but in any easily acquirable text.

These two characteristics distinguish book buyers from buyers of scholarly editions. The latter group represents but a fraction of the group of buyers of literature and consists almost exclusively of three distinctive categories: academic libraries, advanced readers – both academics and non-academics – and students. The motivations within these three categories for buying scholarly editions range from collection pressure for libraries and collectors, and curriculum obligations for students to peer assessment and scholarly interest and use in the case of the academic buyer and the non-academic advanced amateur. Whereas the institutional purchases establish a basic and solid revenue for almost any scholarly edition which is within their scope of collection and acquisition, those in the latter two categories will only consider buying the edition when the specific text that is the object of the editorial enterprise is of any concern to them. In other words, it would be naive to think that the sales potential of a specific edition includes all literary scholars of its language and period. Hence my two further propositions:[12]

3. The audience for scholarly editions is small, specialized and mainly undefined.
4. The audience for a particular scholarly edition exclusive of reading editions will rarely outnumber the active scholarly community engaged with the specific edited title.

---

10 Average based on the sales figures of the scholarly reading editions of modern poetry and prose produced by the Centre for Scholarly Editing and Document Studies of the Royal Academy of Dutch Language and Literature in Belgium.

11 All leading newspapers and magazines in Flanders nowadays publish their own series of classical titles or thematic libraries for their readers.

12 Whereas these four propositions sketch the reality against which we have to assess our debates and discussions about the acceptance and success or failure of scholarly editions and their audience, they say nothing about the success of scholarly editing and textual scholarship as an academic field.

However, this last proposition needs some further refinement, for not all professional academics are interested in the full capabilities of the scholarly edition. Frankly, even advanced readers are very rarely interested in the genesis of a text, variant states, the chronology of an author's work or manuscript facsimiles. These are the four lowest scoring reasons given by 91 academic readers of the departments of Germanic and English philology of the University of Regensburg in Germany when asked to vote for their three most important reasons (out of a given list of ten) for using a scholarly edition. Of the responding group 12.1 per cent were students in their first year, 57.1 per cent were advanced students, and 30.8 per cent were graduates, lecturers and professors.[13] This is an acceptable representation of what we generally consider the professional audience for scholarly editions. The primary reason for consulting a scholarly edition, voted for by 80.2 per cent of the participants, was the 'need for a reliable textual basis'. In second place was for 'commentary and annotations to support understanding' (62.6 per cent). 'Search for bibliographic data on a text or an author' occupied the third position (51.6 per cent), and 'checking of a quote of primary data' (34.1 per cent) was the fourth most important reason given by the participants of this survey. Amongst them, these four reasons got a convincing 76.2 per cent of all votes, the first two even got 47.6 per cent of all votes. At the bottom of the ranking we find interest in manuscript facsimiles voted for by only 2.2 per cent of the participants and interest in the chronology of the author's work with a score of 5.5 per cent. An interest in variants and stages of development was mentioned by 15.4 per cent of the people and interest in the genesis of a text by 14.3 per cent.[14] Even combining the votes for the latter two reasons would not rank them within the top four. It must be acknowledged, however, that the people who did express a genetic interest considered it rather important.[15]

Nature

Where the scholarliness of an edition according to the theoretical models is measured by the extent of the full genetic documentation of a text and/or its transmissional history, conventionally expressed in scholarly constructs such as the apparatus variorum, the scholarly community – the primary audience for scholarly editions – surprisingly seems only vaguely interested in textual variants and genetic details. This conclusion is corroborated by another question in Steding's survey which shows that the commentary, the recent status of the edition and the reliability of the text are the three most important reasons for choosing one scholarly edition of a text over another, with the critical apparatus showing a relatively low influence on

---

13 S.A. Steding, *Computer-based Scholarly Editions: Context – Concept – Creation – Clientele* (Berlin: Logos Verlag, 2002), p. 234.

14 Ibid., p. 243.

15 Ibid., p. 244.

the scholar's choice.[16] No wonder that the historical-critical edition, the showpiece of the German editorial tradition, is a commercial disaster with sales figures easily dropping below the threshold of the 100 copies that are normally sold to libraries. My fifth proposition then is the following:

5. Scholarly editing as a scholarly discipline is in disharmony with the importance of the scholarly edition as a cultural product.

Phrased differently and more clearly: we are creating the wrong types of editions even for the obvious supporters inside the scholarly community. How did that happen? I argue that the diverse theories of the various editorial traditions have resulted in ambiguous and ambidextrous scholarly editions that are estranged from their primary users. Further, the rigid opinion about what constitutes a scholarly edition has caused its sublimation as the exponent of textual scholarship – or science. As an academic product the scholarly edition is of inestimable value; as a cultural product it is valueless. A closer look at the theories of the German school of *Editionswissenschaft* (often translated as 'edition science' or 'textology') may illustrate my point.

Function

Since the earliest beginnings of the history of textual criticism in the sixth or the fourth centuries BCE,[17] the fundamental distrust towards texts has been the foundation of and the argument for all scholarly editorial practice. Indeed, the social reality of the production process of texts and the subsequent mechanics of their transmission through time urge any student of the text to be alert to the status of the text at hand – at least, this is what we teach, have taught, and should keep on teaching our students in the arts and the humanities. Scholarly editions serve

---

16 'Most useful commentary' and 'latest edition of the text' was mentioned by 52.7 per cent of the respondents, and 'most reliable text' by 49.5 per cent. Only 20 per cent voted for 'most useful critical apparatus' (ibid.).

17 In the sixth-century BCE, an unknown Greek scholar provided a text of the Homeric epics by removing the errors that had corrupted it in the course of oral transmission: D.C. Greetham, *Textual Scholarship: An Introduction* (New York & London: Garland Publishing, 1994), p. 297. More frequently quoted as the origin of textual criticism is the fourth-century BCE when scholars in Alexandria, realizing that the transmission of texts through history resulted in several textual versions, attempted to reconstruct the Homeric texts: G.T. Tanselle, *The Life and Work of Fredson Bowers* (Charlottesville: Bibliographical Society of the University of Virginia, 1993), p. 21; D. Van Hulle, *Textual Awareness: A Genetic Approach to the Late Works of James Joyce, Marcel Proust and Thomas Mann*, PhD thesis (Antwerp: University of Antwerp, 1999), p. 345; W.P. Williams and C.S. Abbot, *An Introduction to Bibliographical and Textual Studies*, 2nd edn (New York: Modern Language Association of America, 1989), p. 1.

the purpose of taking away this distrust by offering a scholarly established – or reliable – text that is the basis for any further textual research and interpretation. But it is a paradox of textual scholarship that this distrust is also applied to the scholarly edition itself that wants to dissolve this distrust by proposing a scholarly established reading text, especially by scholarly editors. Theoretically, the edited text constitutes the latest phase in the textual history at the moment of publication and is thus perceived as yet another version to be distrusted by the student of the text. Psychologically, the scholarly editor who is aware of their own editorial practice transfers the basic rule never to trust the author when studying their texts to the textual scholar and their editions.

In the Anglo-American tradition, the acknowledgement of the scholarly editors' subjective critical judgements and the articulation of the editors' freedom to apply their theory of the text in editing has referred the concept of the *definitive* text to the annals of scholarly editing and introduced different editorial or formal orientations.[18] G. Thomas Tanselle and Peter Shillingsburg have demonstrated that this concept of definiteness in the writings of Fredson Bowers and the Center for Editions of American Authors (CEAA) guidelines must be read rhetorically rather than literally. According to Tanselle, the word 'definitive' was for Bowers 'rhetorically effective in helping him emphasize the rigor, discipline, and thoroughness of the bibliographical way'.[19] That is why

---

18 In *Scholarly Editing in the Computer Age: Theory and Practice*, 3rd edn (Ann Arbor: University of Michigan Press, 1996), Peter Shillingsburg defines formal orientation as 'a perspective on forms that leads to the selection of one set of formal requirements over another' (p. 16); and he distinguishes five such orientations: documentary, aesthetic, authorial, sociological and bibliographic (pp. 15–27). The main difference between the documentary orientation and the others listed is the strict adherence to the historical appearance of the text as the argument for authority, which results in the publication of a non-critical text. In the two earlier editions of this book this was called the *historical* orientation. The four other formal orientations of scholarly editing use textual criticism to constitute a critical text which is freed from errors and corruptions. This results in an eclectic text which is as a construct non-historical.

19 Tanselle, *The Life and Work of Fredson Bowers*, p. 129. On Bowers' frequent use of the word 'definitive' in connection with critical editing, G.T. Tanselle explains that '[T]hose who already understood the nature of critical editing recognized that he was employing "definitive" in a special sense and that the word was rhetorically effective in helping him emphasize the rigor, discipline, and thoroughness of the bibliographical way. They knew, and realized he knew, that no product of critical judgement can ever be definitive' (ibid., p. 129). In his essay 'Critical Editions, Hypertexts, and Genetic Criticism', *The Romanic Review*, 86/3 (1995): 581–93, Tanselle proves his case by bringing to mind that even the supporters of the CEAA's guidelines recognized that 'it was not the only responsible way to produce a scholarly text.' (p. 582) Cf. 'One indication of this recognition was the decision to use the phrase "An Approved Edition," not "The Approved Edition," on the CEAA emblem; the scholars responsible for this wording wished to make the point that the editions formally approved by the CEAA were not the only responsible editions of those works that could be produced' (ibid., p. 582, n. 3). See also Shillingsburg, *Scholarly Editing in the Computer*

Bowers did not consider it a function of the critical edition to reproduce the textual evidence 'since the editor should have exhausted their significance in the preparation of the definitive text'.[20]

In the historical-critical or variorum edition, this call for confidence in the theory and practice of what was then called critical bibliography has been replaced by a call for the discipline's movement towards a true science. The cornerstone of true science is the principle of external replication. This means that the scientific results or data obtained under conditions that are the same each time should be reproducible by peers in order to be valid. Further, the report on the research should contain sufficient information to enable peers to assess observations and to evaluate intellectual processes.[21] This is exactly what historical-critical or variorum editions do in the presentation of their formalized and formulized apparatuses – apart from providing the data for a more or less correct assessment of the genetic and transmissional history of the text. The scientific reflex in editorial theory could hence be interpreted as the recognition that the function of the maximal edition is not to inform the reader but to protect the editor. That is why I call these maximal editions ambiguous and ambidextrous. Ambiguous because the presentation of the genetic and transmissional variants subverts the stability of the reliable textual basis the literary critic is looking for; but at the same time, the presentation of an established reading text may be too speculative for geneticists and scholars interested in the variant stages of the work. Ambidextrous because a maximal edition logically contains a minimal edition and presents the textual archive alongside.

This is a conceptual problem that the rigid typological models of the German school of *Editionswissenschaft* sidestep, since in this tradition the scholarly quality which is attributed to the presentation of the maximal edition does not automatically apply to the presentation of the minimal edition, as can be deduced from the typology of three influential theorists. Georg Witkowski based his distinction between scholarly editions ('Wissenschaftliche Ausgaben') and non-scholarly editions – either with or without commentary (respectively 'Erläuterte nichtwissenschaftliche Ausgaben' and 'Nichtwissenschaftliche Ausgaben ohne Erläuterung') – on the edition's function. A scholarly edition facilitates research ('allseitige Erforschung'), a non-scholarly edition promotes the enjoyment of

---

Age: 'No one seriously claims that editing can be done definitively' (p. 95). It is interesting, however, to observe that the term 'definitive' appears again in Peter Robinson's negative attitude towards too much editorial interference in an electronic archive/edition: 'This does not mean that we will eventually impose our own text on the Tales and call it definitive', P. Robinson, 'Is There a Text in These Variants?', in R. Finneran (ed.), *The Literary Text in the Digital Age* (Ann Arbor: University of Michigan Press, 1996), p. 111.

20 Bowers, *Textual and Literary Criticism*, p. 185.

21 Council of Biology Editors, *Scientific Style and Format: The CBE Manual for Authors, Editors, and Publishers* (Cambridge:Cambridge Univeristy Press, 1994).

reading ('Genießen des Kunstwerks').[22] Witkowski makes clear, however, that the text in any type of edition should always be based on a critically established text ('kritisch gesicherte Text'), no matter what audience the edition is aimed at. Witkowski's non-scholarly edition with commentary therefore corresponds with Klaus Kanzog's study edition ('Studienausgabe'), which is one of the four types he distinguishes in his *Prolegomena zu einer historisch-kritischen Ausgabe der Werke Heinrich von Kleists* (1970). Kanzog ordered his four types in a hierarchical classification with the archive edition ('Archiv-Ausgabe') on top, respectively followed by the historical-critical edition ('Historisch-Kritische Ausgabe'), the study edition ('Studienausgabe') and the reading edition ('Leseausgabe') on the lowest level.[23] The reading edition, according to Kanzog, is intended for a general reading public and can, depending on the choice of the reading text, the editorial principles and the facultative commentary, be a critical or a non-critical edition, and can thus qualify as scholarly or not. Around the same time that Kanzog published his typology, Siefried Scheibe separated reading editions from different types of scholarly editions ('verschiedene Formen wissenschaftlicher editionen').[24] When he refined his model ten years later he explicitly stated that the concept of a scholarly edition should not be used to indicate a specific function ('Tätigkeit'), but to indicate a specific type of edition ('Ausgabentyp') that excluded the reading edition.[25] Although Scheibe prescribed the presentation of a critically established text for the reading edition, he did realize, mainly by analysing the publication practices of the publishers, that this type of edition has no critical ambitions whatsoever, and thus he categorizes it as non-scholarly.[26]

---

22 Witkowski, *Textkritik und Editionstechnik neuerer Schriftwerke,* p. 67. Here Witkowski presents the first coherent and theoretically based typology in German modern editorial theory. His model distinguishes among twelve types of edition ('Ausgabe').

23 The archive edition provides the exact documentation in a useful system of all witnesses and textual phenomena including all genetic and transmissional variants. The historical-critical edition assesses this material, provides an established text and orders the variants from the perspective of that text. In doing so, it offers a genetic documentation of the history of the text. The study edition provides a scholarly established text, ideally derived from the historical-critical edition, together with a commentary section that does not only treat the critical and historical status of the text but also its interpretation. It does not concern the documentation of the variants and is intended for a scholarly public. K. Kanzog, *Prolegomena zu einer historisch-kritischen Ausgabe der Werke Heinrich von Kleists. Theorie und Praxis einer modernen Klassiker-Edition* (München: Carl Hanser Verlag, 1970), pp. 9–38.

24 S. Scheibe, 'Zu einigen Grundprinzipien einer historisch-kritischen Ausgabe', in G. Martens and H. Zeller (eds), *Texte und Varianten* (München: Beck, 1971), p. 1.

25 S. Scheibe, 'Diskussion zu Theorie und Praxis der Edition. Aufgaben der germanistischen Textologie in DDR', *Zeitschrift für Germanistik*, 4 (1981): 453–63, pp. 454–5.

26 '[…] la diffusion la plus large est celle des éditions courantes que les maisons d'édition produisent en dehors de toute ambition critique.' Scheibe, 'Quelles éditions pour quels lecteurs?' p. 84.

Whereas Witkowski is categorical about the need for a critically edited text in a reading edition, but calls such an edition non-scholarly, Kanzog distinguishes between a scholarly reading edition whose text is critically established and a non-scholarly reading edition without such a text. Scheibe ultimately decided that a reading edition is never a scholarly edition because it does not demonstrate the correlations of the one text with the many texts. Further, whether an edition is scholarly or not depends in Witkowski's view on its function, for Kanzog it depends on the presentation of contextualizing materials such as commentary and editorial principles, and for Scheibe it depends on the method: every edition that has not been produced according to the methodology for historical-critical or study editions is non-scholarly. An extreme application of Scheibe's theory would mean that the edited text of a historical-critical edition, when published in isolation as a reading edition, constitutes a non-scholarly edition.

Status

With my sixth proposition I deliberately move away from a functional, presentational or methodological distinction between the scholarly and non-scholarly edition as suggested by German editorial theories:

6. The qualifying characteristic of an edition is the scholarly status of its text, not its function, form of appearance or method.

This means that Kanzog's archive edition as well as Scheibe's reading edition qualify as scholarly as long as the text they represent is the result of scholarly editorial practice, independent of whether it is arrived at by critical or non-critical editing or transcription, or whether it is presented as a sequential or a non-sequential text.[27] A reading edition, (re)presenting only one version of a text with no or almost no additional information can therefore be as scholarly or non-scholarly as a full historical-critical edition representing every single variant in every single witness of that text independently of the degree of articulation or documentation of its scholarly method. This stance creates room for the publication of scholarly minimal editions which can attract wider audiences of buyers of literature (proposition 4) and can provide a reliable textual basis to literary critics.

---

27 It is tempting to take Kanzog's basic criterion – whether the text is critically established or not – as the real distinctive feature of a scholarly edition but this is in contradiction with my views on non-critical editing as explained elsewhere. Whether the edition presents additional con-text-ualizing materials gathered and researched according to articulated methodological principles and presented in one or other typological model is in my opinion not decisive. Neither is its orientation towards a scholarly or a non-scholarly audience.

Electronic editions

The electronic paradigm in scholarly editing has almost exclusively focused on the advantages of the size and economics of available storage capacity, the democratizing possibilities of providing access to full-colour representations of documentary witnesses and the non-sequentiality of hypertext. The digital archive as expanded text has in some cases jostled the one text away in favour of the multitude of many texts. Scholarly assessment of electronic editions is mainly based on the incorporation of the digital archive representing the textual history and the presence of collational evidence; thus on its appearance as a maximal edition. But the presentation of the digital archive does not discharge the editor from a responsibility to serve the text and support its function in society. Therefore, electronic scholarly editing is in need of the reintegration of the minimal edition without any compromise to its scholarly status. A major challenge for the electronic edition is to combine the maximal and the minimal editions in one product and to free textual scholarship from the layout economics invented for the printed page.

The electronic edition of *De trein der traagheid*[28] offers a model to do all this and to reintegrate the printed edition beyond the electronic product. The edition currently presents a critically established reading text and 19 versions of the novella from its print history. The result of the collation of all versions is documented according to the TEI parallel segmentation method inside a master XML file that also contains all editorial annotations. This guarantees the completely equal treatment of each version of the text in the generating processes invoked by the user. Through the interface of the edition, the user can exploit the underlying TEI encoding by selecting any version and can generate three possible views of the texts: XML for analysis, XHTML for consultation on the screen and PDF for printing out as a reading edition. Any version can also be combined with any combination of any number of witnesses whereby the initial version functions as orientation text and the other selected versions are displayed in a lemmatized apparatus variorum. From within this apparatus, the generated edition can be reoriented from the point of view of any included witness. The model applied to this specific textual history allows the user to generate 10,485,760 possible editions of the complete text of the novella; when it is taken into account that editions for each separate chapter can be generated as well, this figure is multiplied by 35, giving a total of 367,001,600 possible editions.[29] Any one of these editions can again be exported to XML, XHTML or PDF. Any number of versions, depending on the dimension and resolution of the user's screen, can also be displayed in parallel and

---

28 R. Van den Branden, E. Vanhoutte and X. Roelens, *Johan Daisne. De trein der traagheid op CD-ROM. Elektronische editie* (Gent: KANTL, 2008).

29 The formula to calculate the possible editions one can generate from *n* number of witnesses, given that there is always one witness that functions as the orientation text and that the orientation text can never be collated against itself, is $n \times 2^{n-1}$.

the respective lists of variants can be generated on the fly.[30] The minimal and the maximal editions are fully searchable, and the search results can be displayed in a KWIC concordance format.

This model considers the electronic edition as a maximal edition that logically contains a minimal edition. An essential function of this maximal edition is that it fulfils the user's need for a reliable textual basis through the inclusion of a critically established reading text. Rather than providing a valuable supplement to a print edition, as is often the reduced function of an electronic edition in an editorial project, this model empowers the user to check upon the choices made in the critical establishment of the text by way of access to the textual archive. At the same time, the model allows the user to ignore the editors' suggestions and to develop their own perspective on the maximal edition, or to generate a minimal edition of their choice. The reproducability of the thus generated minimal edition is guaranteed by a record of the choices that informed it. This documentary feature of the electronic edition facilitates the scholarly debate on any one of the many texts and provides any reader with a clear statement on the status of the minimal edition generated and printed for distribution or reading. Because of the scholarly basis of the electronic edition as a whole, even the most plain reading text with no additional information generated qualifies as a scholarly edition. By emphasizing the on-the-fly generation of user-defined printable editions as a central feature in our system, together with the documentation of its definition, we strive towards the re-evaluation of scholarly editions as cultural products.

My final and concluding proposition, therefore, is as follows:

7. The electronic edition is the medium par excellence for the promotion of the scholarly reading edition and the recentering of the printed edition.

---

30 The edition is powered by MORKEL, a dedicated suite of Open Source XML-aware parsers, processors and engines combined with appropriate XSLT and XSLFO scripts.

PART II
In Practice

Chapter 7

'… they hid their books underground'[1]

Espen S. Ore

Introduction

This chapter considers a number of different forms an electronic edition may take and suggests that such editions can span a broadly defined field ranging from the critical scholarly edition, where a large amount of work at an academic level is performed on relatively small amounts of data, to the large-scale, more or less automated, digitization of considerable amounts of data. It will claim that, since tools are now available that make it possible for users to exploit electronic data in a variety of ways, straightforward digitization that makes data available quickly is preferable to a critical edition which is never finished, even if less scholarly value is added. In what follows, I will use as examples scholarly critical editions, diplomatic editions, editions in the form of digital facsimiles and editions making document content available through databases linked with digital facsimiles. I use the term 'edition' here in a broad sense, to refer to any published version of a text (or a document). The examples used are from projects carried out – or being carried out – in Norway, but the experiences and views arising from them should be generally applicable.

I begin with two contrasting stories. In the second century BCE the citizens of the town of Scepsis in the Troad (modern Turkey) buried books, including the manuscripts of Aristotle and Theophrastus, underground, fearing they might otherwise be stolen and included in the library of Pergamum, where King Eumenes wanted to outdo the great library in Alexandria. The end result after almost a hundred years of underground storage was that, when they were dug up and sold to Apellicon of Teos,[2] the scrolls were suffering from mildew and other sorts of damage. Apellicon was a bibliophile rather than a philosopher. He was also no philologist and, according to Strabo, he introduced much erroneous material to fill in lacunae, lacunae which mainly came from the damage caused by the books' burial. By contrast, in another story Ptolemaius III let the Athenians keep the money deposited against the return of books he had borrowed (Attic tragedies) rather than return them. Having acquired surreptitiously, he added them to the Library in

---

1 H.L. Jones (trans.), *The Geography of Strabo* (Loeb Edition, Cambridge, MA: Harvard University Press, 1924), 13.54.

2 Apellicon, a rich book collector who died around 85 BCE, is known from Strabo's Geography and from Plutarch's *Life of Sulla*.

Alexandria.[3] Unlike the buried depository, the Library in Alexandria was not a dead end for books. Scholars working at Alexandria produced new and corrected editions of the classics which could be considered early instances of critical editions. They developed markup to show which lines the editor considered suspicious or copied from somewhere else; other markup pointed outside the physical copy or edition into separate commentaries. And this work has not been forgotten. The commentaries of the Alexandrian philologists was included as marginalia in medieval manuscripts; their canonical texts became the basis for most or all of the medieval manuscript traditions. This material continues to serve modern editors of classical texts.

Modern edition projects, ranging from scholarly critical editions at one extreme to those making available facsimiles of manuscripts at the other, ideally produce something which can be built upon by philologists of the future. Although there has been recent discussion as to the extent to which a new editorial project can build on existing digital archives, there are examples one can cite of projects which have further exploited such work done by others, and there is no reason to believe that the digital medium will prove an exception.[4] It remains important that previously unpublished texts and manuscripts be made widely available in digital form as rapidly as possible so that scholars can benefit fully from them, however raw a form in which these are presented. At a conference organized in April 2001 by the Editing Medieval Manuscripts Research Group at the Centre for Advanced Study at the Norwegian Academy of Science and Letters,[5] Már Jónsson referred to a state that he described as 'editorial impotence' (Már 2001).[6] He claimed that one of the reasons the annual number of published editions of Norse medieval texts is reduced over time is the high requirement for scholarly work expected in the critical apparatus. According to Már this creates a problem: not only are the texts not available with additional scholarly content until they are published, but they are just not available outside the archives or libraries where the originals are stored. One does not have to consider only Norse medieval manuscripts to find examples of texts that are difficult to access. This can also be the case for rare and out-of-print books; hence the scholarly appeal of projects like Google Book Search.[7]

---

3 Galen XVII.i as quoted in E.R. Bevan, *The House of Ptolemy* (London: Methuen, 1927), p. 125. Available online at <http://penelope.uchicago.edu/Thayer/E/Gazetteer/Places/Africa/Egypt/_Texts/BEVHOP/4F*.html>, accessed 24 September 2007.

4 See for instance M. Dahlström, 'How Reproductive is a Scholarly Edition', *Literary and Linguistic Computing*, 19/1 (2004): 17–33; and E.S. Ore, 'Monkey Business–or What is an Edition?', *Literary and Linguistic Computing*, 19/1 (2004): 35–44.

5 Editing Medieval Manuscripts, Centre for Advanced Study 2000–2001, <http://www.cas.uio.no/Groups/EdMa2000/index.html>, accessed 24 September 2007.

6 I have used a manuscript version of the paper as it was given at the conference: M. Jónsson, 'Utgiverisk impotens', *Nordiske middelaldertekster – Utgivere & brukere,* Oslo, Centre for Advanced Studies at the Norwegian Academy of Sciences and Letters, 27–29 April 2001. A revised version was published in Icelandic in 'Getuleysi útgefenda?', *Skírnir*, 175 (2001): 510–29.

7 Google Books <http://books.google.com>, accessed June 2007.

In a traditional critical edition the individual scholar starts out with a set of manuscripts and works towards an end result, either a printed or an electronic edition intended as a finished product. This is of course serious scholarly work, but I wish to argue in favour of various levels of editorial projects with different aims, some of which may not only support a product to be given in its finished state to a reader or user, but may also benefit the next generation of editors or current editors with different goals. Those who, for instance, produce a set of facsimiles are providing both an edition and a basis for further work. I have earlier suggested a model for these separate aspects of editorial work.[8] A slightly revised version of this model is shown in Figure 7.1. The main ideas are that (1) the archive of texts (including facsimiles) is what will be carried into the future and what can be used for future editions; and (2) different scholars and/or institutions can be responsible for different modules or versions/editions. An institution such as a national library would need to take responsibility for the long-term preservation of an archive deriving from its own holdings, the benefit being that it would be able to supply instant facsimiles in digital or print form for users. But scholarly philological work may just as naturally be done outside the context of a national library, and the input into and output from a text archive may be something as simple as facsimiles of the pages from a printed book and the necessary metadata to perform some kind of searching and identification, or it may be a full-scale critical edition of an author's opus.

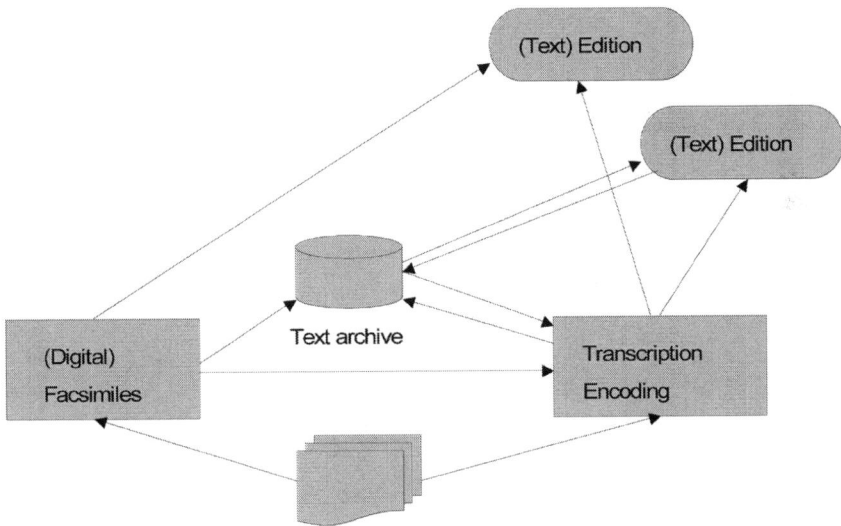

Figure 7.1   **Editions, archives and more: An abstract model**

---

8 Ore, 'Monkey Business', p. 37.

Some Norwegian digital edition projects

This section presents some Norwegian edition projects which aim wholly or partly at the creation of digital editions spanning the range from critical scholarly editions to non-critical non-scholarly editions.

Wittgenstein's Nachlass

One project not easily classifiable on the critical/non-critical scale is the Bergen Electronic Edition of Wittgenstein's *Nachlass* (BEE).[9] This project has produced a set of CDs which were published by Oxford University Press between 1998 and 2000, and which comprise encoded texts and high-resolution digital facsimiles of the 20,000 pages of the *Nachlass*. These materials are presented within a proprietary delivery system which, even if the CDs themselves are preserved, makes it impossible to guarantee their longevity. But the underlying text and image files from which this edition was published are stored as documented and encoded text files and can thus be preserved. Should this archive be considered an edition? There is no overall editorial voice presented with the CD materials, which would seem to suggest it is not an edition, but at the same time enough information has been stored in the archive to allow for automatic generation of a diplomatic and a normalized text: there are tags which make it possible to generate indexes of names and places, while batch conversion of the facsimiles produced the image files available in the published version. In this case, the serious scholarly work was done when the archive was produced, and the files as presented on CD are mainly generated computationally. Wittgenstein's *Nachlass* is an interesting case for an electronic edition, as its complex structure means it is probably uneditable by any conventional editorial method.

Henrik Ibsen's Writings (HIW)

The year 2006 was the hundredth anniversary of the death of Heinrik Ibsen. It was also the year when the first volumes of a new complete critical scholarly edition of Ibsen's writings were published.[10] This is a large project by Norwegian standards, with members from three Norwegian universities and the National Library of Norway (hereafter NL), and financial support from the Norwegian Research Council. The project's overall budget is almost US $10 million. Despite this, the partners are currently seeking funding for the production of a digital edition which had been envisioned, but not funded, from the start. There is digital

---

9 E.S. Ore and P. Cripps, 'The Electronic Publication of Wittgenstein's *Nachlass*' in L. Burnard, M. Deegan and H. Short (eds), *The Digital Demotic* (London: Office for Humanities Communication, King's College, 1997).

10 See the website <http://www.ibsen.uio.no/his/hjemmeside/tekster.html#B1> (in Norwegian), accessed March 2006.

content available, though only for a few specialists; as yet no widely accessible digital edition exists. But since the underlying content has been encoded according to robust international standards (TEI), this may prove to be the most enduring legacy of the project.

To further complicate matters, the digital Ibsen draws extensively on earlier digitization work. In 1977 the Norwegian Computing Centre for the Humanities (NCCH) in Bergen started work on a concordance to Henrik Ibsen's dramas and poems.[11] The concordance was eventually produced – probably one of the last large concordances ever to be printed in Norway – but the project was especially valuable because of its contingent benefits. The Ibsen texts were entered from an earlier scholarly critical edition, and subsequently the text was grammatically tagged. This corpus is still available for searching in Bergen. (One of the search engines used in Bergen is still TACT which was originally developed in Toronto in 1989; so this is both long-lasting data and long-lasting software use.) When the work on the new Ibsen edition began, the project received the text files from Bergen and thus had a flying start, with material that often required only minimal editing to provide the texts that were to be the base texts for the new edition. Another Ibsen-related project ran from 1998 to 2000: the Centre for Ibsen Studies at the University of Oslo received external financial support for the large-scale digitization of all Ibsen manuscripts, letters, etc. This included material from the main collection of Ibsen material at the NL and from the extensive collection at the Royal Library in Copenhagen, Denmark. (The NL is responsible for updating the facsimile collection and editing the metadata.) This collection of digital facsimiles is available on the web,[12] and has been used and is still used by the Ibsen project.

I suggest that it is reasonable to consider the products from the two earlier Ibsen projects, which are both generally available and can be delivered in special formats (complete tagged text files or high-quality TIFF respectively), as editions (published versions of texts) and as archives simultaneously. This does not mean that I wish to make the term 'edition' meaningless by calling everything an edition. In all these examples we have products where documents and/or text have been processed and transferred into a new form, usually with some added information and in ways that make the documents more available than they were formerly – for some purposes at least.

The new edition of *Henrik Ibsen's Writings* has so far been manifested in two books of texts and two books of commentaries. The new text – that is, the edited text with its emendations and results of choices between variant readings – is to be placed in the archive, along with the annotations and commentaries (see Figure 7.2). The digital edition will of course reflect the current status of hardware and software, and current ideas on the organization of information; we might,

---

11 See the University of Bergen web pages on the Heinrik Ibsen materials, <http://gandalf.aksis.uib.no/ibsen/ibs-man2.htm> (in Norwegian), accessed March 2006.

12 See the Centre for Ibsen Studies web pages for these materials at <http://www.dokpro.uio.no/litteratur/ibsen/ms/indexe.html>, accessed September 2007.

for instance, include an implementation of topic maps which are a useful way of visualizing information and seeing connections in an archive. In just a few years, however, much of this will be obsolete, especially the hardware and software solutions. Special care will have to be taken both to preserve the digital edition itself and to maintain its accessibility. If we just keep the CDs or whatever medium the edition is stored on, we will have done more or less the same as the people of Scepsis did with Aristotle's library; or perhaps worse, since there may be nothing left except lacunae, given the unknown lifespan of a CD. The paper edition, on the other hand, will survive just by being stored in a moderate physical climate for thousands of years. But a printed book, however significant, is from one point of view a dead thing. It cannot easily be modified. I would argue that the most important product from this editorial project is the digital archive that can serve as a starting point for future editions of many kinds.

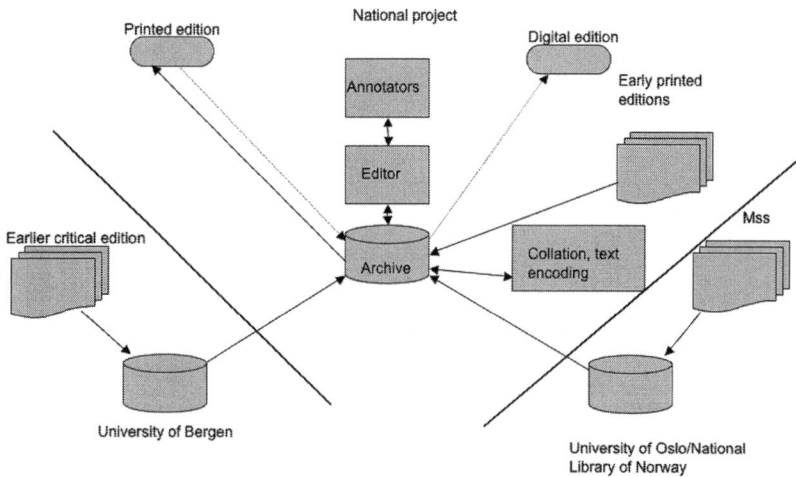

Figure 7.2   *Henrik Ibsen's Writings*: **Many institutions, many roles**

In the library

In the library of Alexandria there was no sharp division between library and document science, on the one hand, and philology and textual criticism, on the other, as there is today. A somewhat simplified model of current conventional scholarship is that the philological and textual critical work is generally done by academics, while the library provides primary and secondary source materials. This still largely holds true for traditional editions produced by one single scholar, but the boundaries are becoming increasingly blurred as teams of scholars, technical specialists and librarians engage in editorial and digitization projects large and small, exploiting the connective and transformative power of the new technologies. Projects like the BEE or HIW are examples of large, team-based editorial projects: in HIW, for example, the NL has supplied a bibliographical stylebook as well as codicological and paleographical expertise from the NL's manuscript department. Other initiatives may be developed by libraries themselves, and libraries such as the NL may hold material that they themselves wish to digitize, publish or even edit. The NL is engaged in a number of projects discussed below, and these include critical and scholarly editions, as well as digital facsimiles of a range of documents of many kinds.

The Diriks scrapbooks

The NL's manuscript collection includes documents with a more complex structure than, for example, the relatively straightforward manuscripts sent to the publishers for printing by Henrik Ibsen. One item of note is a set of scrapbooks with material covering almost a hundred years of the Norwegian family Diriks. The Diriks family was related to the Munch family, and the scrapbooks hold original work by both Edvard Munch and Pablo Picasso. The scrapbooks are important not so much for the objects made by world-famous artists (though these are of great interest), but because they have a mass of objects and information related to Norwegian culture and national and local history from the first half of the nineteenth to the early twentieth centuries (see Figure 7.3).

The scrapbooks are now disintegrating and need to be conserved. The conservation work requires that the books be taken apart, which gives an excellent opportunity for digitization. In order to preserve the complete scrapbooks as the complex objects they are, a virtual version has been constructed from static HTML pages with JPEG images linked in. The data structures of these volumes are complex: for example, there may be multi-page objects which can include other objects which in their turn can also be multi-page and have other objects attached to them. But even when it is possible to page through a digital surrogate of an

Figure 7.3   A double page from a virtual Diriks album

Source: National Library, Norway.

album or a multi-page object, this is not the only or even the most effective way of organizing information on a computer screen. A click on an object in a virtual Diriks album will display an information page with metadata from a database where information about all the objects is stored. It is also possible to go directly to the database and search for pages or names or other types of stored information and to move from there to metadata and an image of an object. But the overall structure of the complex scrapbooks is not lost, so that when a single object is displayed there is always a link to the virtual album page that holds the object.[13] (See Figure 7.4.)

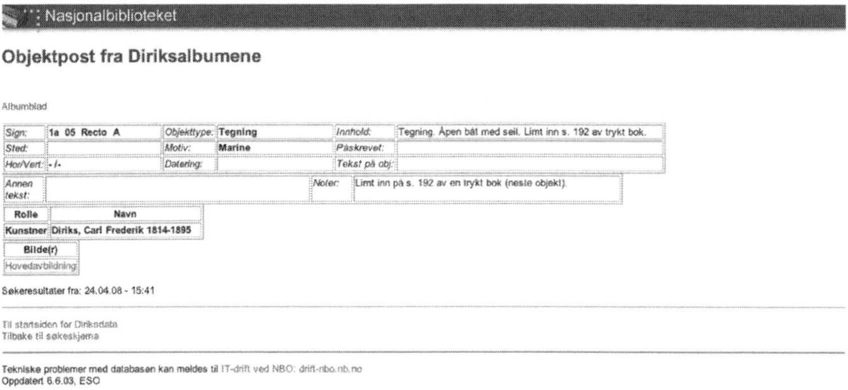
Nasjonalbiblioteket

Objektpost fra Diriksalbumene

Albumblad

Sign:	**1a 05 Recto A**	*Objekttype:*	**Tegning**	*Innhold:*	Tegning. Åpen båt med seil. Limt inn s. 192 av trykt bok.
Sted:		*Motiv:*	**Marine**	*Påskrevet:*	
Hor/Vert:	- / -	*Datering:*		*Tekst på obj:*	
Annen tekst:		*Noter:*	Limt inn på s. 192 av en trykt bok (neste objekt).		

Rolle	**Navn**
Kunstner	**Diriks, Carl Frederik 1814-1895**

Bilde(r)
Hovedavbildning

Søkeresultater fra: 24.04.08 - 15:41

Til startsiden for Diriksdata
Tilbake til søkeskjema

Tekniske problemer med databasen kan meldes til IT-drift ved NBO: drift-nbo.nb.no
Oppdatert 6.6.03, ESO

Figure 7.4 A Diriks album object in the database

Project 1905

In 1905 Norway broke away from a 91-year-old union with Sweden, an event which was marked in a number of different ways in 2005. One was a joint Norwegian–Swedish historical project which produced a website developed at the NL. This displays contents from the NL, the Swedish Royal Library, the Norwegian and Swedish National Archives and, as a special favour to the project, the Swedish royal family's private archives. The NL's first item on the 1905-related website was a searchable bibliography, appropriately for a library. Then special texts written by historians were added, with links to digitized Norwegian and Swedish newspapers: the complete 1905 run of six publications. The Library also organized the presentation or publication of some thousands of documents from the

13 See the Diriks Family web pages at the NL at <http://www.nb.no/baser/diriks/>, accessed September 2007.

national archives and the Swedish Royal Library. The documents comprise texts (manuscripts, typescripts and printed material), photographs, drawings and maps. The digitized newspapers were made available using newspaper-specific software; other documents were recorded with metadata including full-text descriptions of the contents in a database. This means that it is possible to search and get a list of found items, and then have an object displayed. This is not exactly an image database, given that some of the objects are facsimiles of readable text documents; rather, it can be considered to be simultaneously an image database, a source text presentation system – and perhaps an edition.[14]

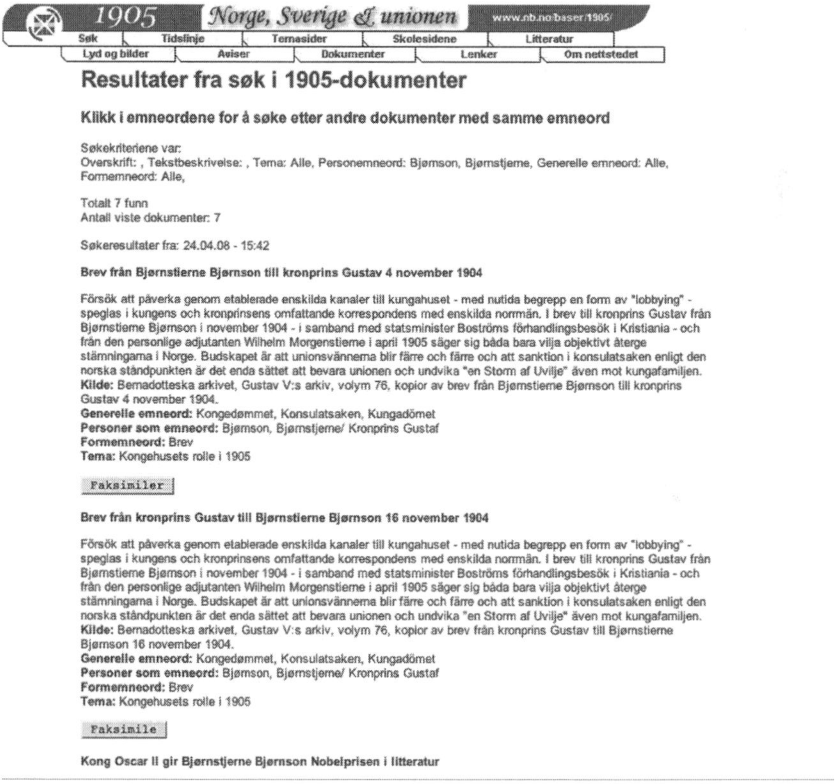

Figure 7.5   From the Swedish royal family archives

---

14 See the 1905 Project website <http://www.nb.no/baser/1905/index.html>, accessed September 2007.

Digitization and facsimile projects (non-critical editions)

Since Ibsen is one of Norway's greatest authors, it is not surprising that there is other activity in the NL to digitize and distribute his works. In 2006 we began scanning the printed first editions in the collections. The HIW project has collated multiple copies of the same edition and, interestingly, found there are differences between copies – especially when it comes to the oldest works. A selection of these Ibsen facsimiles has been made available in a prototype Ibsen resource for use in secondary schools in Norway.[15] The first editions have also been chosen as the base texts for the new edition of Ibsen to be produced by HIW. When the digital editions are published, there will be links on a page-by-page basis to the digital facsimiles provided by the NL.

The NL is the Norwegian deposit library, and as such it is mandated by law to acquire and keep more or less everything published in Norway, which includes digital material. The NL has over some years developed digital security storage with the data servers stored physically inside a mountain, though, unlike the scrolls buried at Scepsis, this underground store will not be allowed to rot away. Care is taken that the data are copied as new media are introduced. These data also hold time-based media, including radio and TV programmes from the national Norwegian Broadcasting Company, as well as all the web pages from the .no domain, harvested at regular intervals.

As of 2006, the NL has embarked on a major programme to digitize its complete collections. Books are being scanned, then the scanned pages are converted to searchable text by OCR. This allows for free text searching of the contents, and permits the correct page to be displayed when a word is found. Work has also started on the digitization of other non-book content: newspapers, journals, etc. Eventually the digital collections will include complex objects such as maps, sound and movies/videos, as well as images: photos, drawings, etc.

How non-critical and one-directional can an edition be?

The work we now do at the NL generally provides users with individual pages (and, in the future, with articles from newspapers) shown as facsimiles, with some tools for browsing but with no additional information (see Figure 7.6). This presentation format is similar to that of Google Book Search.[16] In a recent paper in *Prosa*, the journal for Norwegian non-fiction writers and translators, Eirik Newth

---

15 See the Heinrik Ibsen Project website at the NL <http://www.nb.no/tilgjengelig/>, accessed June 2007, or the report *Digitalisering og tilgjengeliggjøring for kultur og læring*, Prosjektrapport (Oslo: ABM-Utvikling, 2006).

16 Google Books <http://books.google.com/>, accessed June 2007.

argues that this is too little, given the opportunities the electronic medium offers.[17] Newth especially marks as weaknesses the following:

- There are no pointers to information about the book or other external relevant sources.
- There is no user interaction.

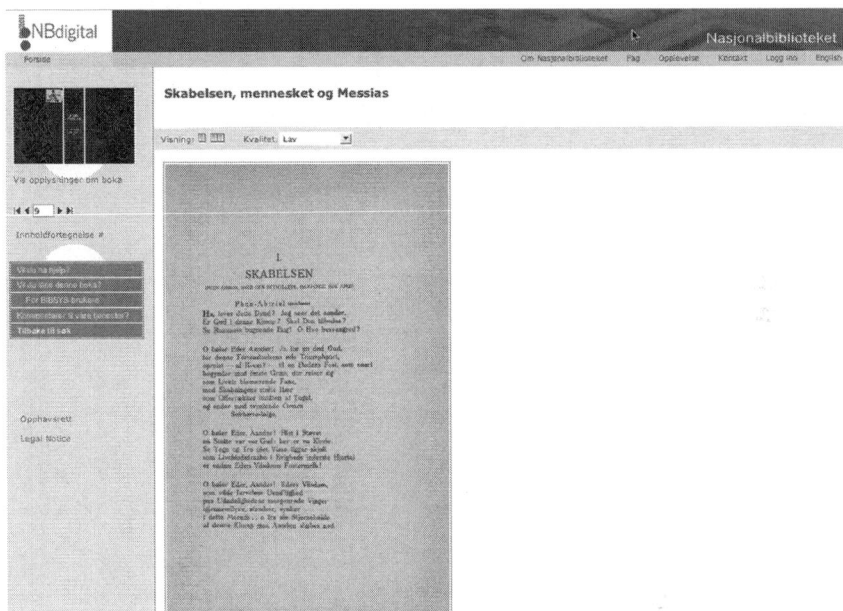

Figure 7.6   Presentation of a printed book page

Source: National Library, Norway.

The NL holds 450,000 Norwegian books and the number is growing. There are 850,000 journal issues and 4,700,000 newspaper issues. And there is more: 4,000,000 manuscripts, 1,300,000 photographs. In addition, we have music, radio programmes, video and more. Given this number of objects it is impossible to find the necessary resources for complex presentation of every item or for individually linking them to external sources. There may, however, be solutions to this, and Newth suggests three possible approaches for producing and distributing information on the web:

---

17 E. Newth, 'All litteratur til folket nå! Om Nasjonalbibliotekets digitalisering, Google Book Search og brukerne', *Prosa*, 3 (2007): 6–12.

- Top down: the NL would do all the linking, writing of comments, etc. on its own. This is unrealistic in terms of resource needs.
- Bottom up: this would be something similar to Wikipedia. The NL would produce digitized material and a Wikipedia-like mechanism would be used to invite comments and links. Although this would be a cheap solution it would not be satisfactory without quality control.
- The middle way: input in a way similar to Wikipedia but with clear editorial responsibility and quality control at the NL. In addition, the NL could select certain key documents and groups of documents and produce additional material connected to these.

Future uses of digital content

If the third strategy suggested above were to be adopted, this would open up some exciting new possibilities for exploitation of digital content supplied by the NL, possibilities that might at last fulfil the long-awaited promise of hypertext. For a number of reasons, the theoretical potential of hypertext, much vaunted at the end of the 1980s and beginning of the 1990s, has not been realized in actual systems that create complex linking of multimedia content.[18] Some of the features proposed in theorizing about hypertext, such as links from one place to another, are available in a simplified form in, for instance, web document markup (HTML) and web protocols (HTTP), but with the disadvantage that the linking information is usually hard-coded as part of a text's markup and this markup is usually embedded as part of a document. If we look back to some of the early descriptions of hypertext or similar ways of organizing information,[19] one of the main aspects of the proposed systems is that the user should be able to add his or her own links to selected parts of the same or other documents, creating personalized hypertexts that might also be shared with others. There has recently been experimentation with markup that lies outside digital data as overlays or even parallel documents, known as 'off-set' or 'stand-off' markup. One such system is described elsewhere in this volume (see chapter 4). We can confidently expect that tools will be developed to permit users to create nets of tags, either private or public, which can operate on sets of multimedia data. The underlying data will maintain its integrity for long-term preservation purposes, while the nets will exist as 'views' on the data, and in some cases the combination of well-formed data and complex editorial views might be seen to constitute new kinds of edition.

---

18 Some commercial software systems such as Panorama and before that Dynabook could store notes and comments as external texts with links to the text commented upon. But these and other serious SGML presentation tools did not survive the move to XML and there does not seem to be any company currently developing such software.

19 V. Bush, 'As We Might Think', *Atlantic Monthly*, August (1945); T.H. Nelson, *Literary Machines* (privately published, 1986).

But texts are still buried. Once digital facsimiles are made of documents, copies of these facsimiles can be made at no loss to the original or to the facsimiles. Yet personal and anecdotal evidence suggests that some institutions holding, for example, medieval manuscripts or papyri continue to show some reluctance to make available copies of digital facsimiles of unpublished texts. This can also extend to photographs of objects in archaeological collections. This may be nothing more than a matter of unrevised official policy at the holding institutions, and we must hope that the texts have not been harmed while they have been kept hidden away. It is difficult to see any good reason for not making digital facsimiles available, while there are contrary examples showing that delayed publication has resulted in informal editions, such as was the case with the Derveni papyrus.[20] One hopes that texts will not stay buried and that, at the very least, digital facsimile editions of as many unpublished or inaccessible works as possible may be made generally available.

---

20 R. Janko, review of T. Kouremenos, G.M. Parássoglou and K. Tsantsanoglou (eds with intro. and comm.), *The Derveni Papyrus*, Studi e testi per il 'Corpus dei papiri filosofici greci e latini', vol. 13, Florence: Casa Editrice Leo S. Olschki, 2006, *Bryn Mawr Classical Review*, 29 October (2006). Available online at <http://ccat.sas.upenn.edu/bmcr/2006/2006-10-29.html#n9>, accessed August 2007.

Chapter 8

The Cambridge Edition of the Works of Jonathan Swift and the Future of the Scholarly Edition

Linda Bree and James McLaverty

In setting up a scholarly edition in the twenty-first century new questions arise which scholars of previous generations would not have had to consider: in particular the vital question as to whether the edition is to exist in electronic or print form only, or in some combination of the two. The choice is an important one in itself, and it is also vital in that it defines the parameters of all sorts of other decisions that have to be made about the content and presentation of the edition concerned.

If the edition is to be an electronic one, many restrictions determined by the publishing requirements of print volumes become much less relevant. Most obviously, the constraint upon content, arising from the need to keep within the length that can be accommodated by the publisher of a printed book, no longer has much force. Instead the boundaries of what is to be done are determined more by the limits of technology, the energy and expertise of those contributing to the edition, and/or the funds available to support the project in its formative and its ongoing stages. Under some forms of electronic presentation, the question of which text to use as copy text – perhaps the most important question of all for print editions – may no longer matter, since it is quite feasible for any number of different versions of the text to be included in electronic form, and they can be compared using any one of the texts as a control for the others; it may even be possible for the reader to create a new eclectic text by mixing and matching from the different versions on offer.

On the other hand, in an electronic edition, issues of inputting, formatting and presentation – the equivalent, in some ways, of matters which in a traditional print edition would generally be the responsibility of the publisher once the creative process of scholarly editing was more or less complete – now help determine the project from the outset. Technical expertise becomes as important as academic endeavour; and even if dedicated technicians are available to work on the project from the outset, the scholar is also likely to have to acquire skills which may well be useful and interesting in themselves but which stray a long way from what could be regarded as making a direct contribution to scholarly research. Electronic editions inevitably involve expenditure, in technology and associated expertise, and so financial matters also have to be attended to, in detail, at the outset: many such projects could not even be contemplated without the assistance of substantial outside funding.

The balance of attractions between a print and an electronic edition are changing all the time, as technological innovation in the academic area advances and the relationship between print and electronic forms of publishing evolves. We are still in a transitional stage as far as technology is concerned – or perhaps in a new condition where flux will become the norm – and it is still not clear in what form scholars and students will wish to work with material in, say, 20 years' time. However scholars are already very used to working online not only with primary material from databases such as Early English Books Online (EEBO) and Eighteenth Century Collections Online (ECCO) but also with the kind of reference material available from the *Oxford English Dictionary* and the *Oxford Dictionary of National Biography*, as well as a wide range of other electronic resources. It is already clear, therefore, that to choose a print-only edition for a project beginning in the first decade of the twenty-first century not only means excluding some features which only an electronic edition could provide, but may be so restrictive as to limit the use and usability of the work in the short and medium as well as the longer term. At the very least, the kind of searchability which on-screen text almost always allows renders a print-only index a very inadequate substitute (though a good index still has a value in listing topics not much amenable to simple word-recognition). However, this is one aspect of a print-only project which should not cause much problem, since it is not difficult for a publisher to offer print books in some searchable electronic form, however basic, by coding the material during the production process.

As far as the Cambridge Edition of the Works of Jonathan Swift is concerned, we are in the very fortunate position of having substantial grant support for the Swift archive, which can produce electronic, searchable versions of the wide range of texts produced by Swift (or which are reliably thought to be by Swift), in all the lifetime editions that survive. But we still had the decision to take as to whether to produce the whole edition in electronic form, or to follow the traditional route of offering a scholarly print edition of the works themselves. In fact this decision proved a very straightforward one, since we felt strongly that – even taking into account the enormous resource offered by the electronic medium – a print edition had significant advantages over electronic texts that we did not wish to sacrifice.

Partly these advantages were practical. The first is that the project is, frankly, more manageable if considered in a traditional way, volume by volume, rather than as a huge 'Swift database': Swift's texts are going to appear in 18 print volumes, each is in the hands of a volume editor responsible to the General Editors and the Press for its contents and for presenting them in the required format, and the General Editors are able to carry out the job of thoroughly checking the volumes one by one as they come in. The second is that the traditional publisher–scholar partnership for specialist academic work in print form, where the scholars provide the material, the scholar and publisher discuss how it can be published, and the publisher publishes it, seemed to us to remain both valid and useful in practical terms; and it has the added advantage of ensuring that the project did not risk delays caused by technical problems which might have very little to do with the academic resources devoted to the project. The third is that print volumes offer a tried and tested financial model for preparation, publication, marketing and sale: once the volumes have been published they will be sold – in hardback and possibly in paperback form, individually and eventually as a set – in order to cover the costs of the enterprise, and if reprinting of new editions is required they will be published in the usual way, while the General Editors and volume editors will receive a modest royalty for their labour, and, throughout, the work carried out by the Press and the editors will be protected by copyright law.

The question of finance is a particularly important one in connection with the question of whether to publish in print or electronic form. Electronic editions are generally more expensive to produce than print editions – they may offer more, but they also require more technological and scholarly input. So far they have been resourced in two ways: by means of substantial (and sometimes massive) grant support, and/or by the diligent and extensive unpaid labour of academics, involving not only academic endeavour but technological expertise and quite possibly marketing skills too. Because so many electronic projects have been carried out in this way it becomes almost impossible to estimate the 'worth' or 'value' of any individual project of this kind. Of course this does not matter much if the project is to be made freely available on the web (which some grants require and which some scholars prefer); but if investment has to be recovered the situation becomes very complex. In this respect the very inclusiveness of electronic editions can begin to dilute what might be regarded as their value, since inevitably they contain material readily available elsewhere. After all, if a high proportion of the relevant information is available free on Google, why should readers pay substantial sums of money, essentially, for a small percentage of the whole? In any case, in practice, as patterns of production and dissemination of electronic material are established, it is becoming clear that electronic databases, scholarly editions among the rest, are unlikely to be sold, like books, as individual items: they will either be made freely available, or they will become small parts of large 'bundling' arrangements that commercial organizations – and perhaps some of the larger academic publishers – offer to financial institutions for substantial bulk fees. In either form they will need a level of ongoing maintenance which someone who has published a book does not have to be concerned with; the author of a book might offer a small number of corrections in case of reprinting, and the publisher, as well as reprinting to meet demand, will replace defective copies, but once a book is published effectively no further substantial input is required just to keep it in a state in which it can be consulted, which is not the case with electronic data.

All these are the practical factors we took into account in making the decision to produce our edition primarily in print-version format. But we took academic and scholarly concerns firmly into account too, addressing central questions about the aims and desires of the scholars editing the texts, and the needs of the scholars and advanced students who would be the most likely readers of any scholarly edition of this kind. What do such readers want from a scholarly edition in the first decades of the twenty-first century? What would they go to a scholarly edition for? What is most important to them, and how do they want it presented? And as far as the editors of the volumes are concerned (whose needs and wishes are also relevant), on what kind of scholarship do they wish – or need, for professional purposes – to be concentrating their energies?

The roots of the modern scholarly edition lie somewhere between the detailed editing treatment given to the works of a small group of elite writers, notably Shakespeare, in the eighteenth-century, and the 'Collected Works' of writers which began to proliferate in the eighteenth and nineteenth centuries. Initially these multi-volume editions, sometimes overseen by the author in his (or, much more rarely, her) own lifetime, mostly provided no more than a text of the works concerned, which might well differ from any previously published version. If the edition was published by others after the author's death it might be accompanied by a more or less brief, more or less accurate, biographical sketch of the author concerned: Rowe set the biographical pattern with his Shakespeare (1709), and the biographical essay by Arthur Murphy which introduced Henry Fielding's *Works* (1762) helped open up the practice to near-contemporary authors, while the whole tradition was reinforced in a powerful way by Johnson's *Lives of the English Poets* (1779). Still texts were often either 'improved' or simply produced in a careless way, so that they diverged considerably from the originals, and no attempt was made to produce a textual 'history'. Only in the twentieth-century, as a more systematic approach developed for addressing the works of 'great' writers in the context of academic study, did the modern contents of the 'scholarly edition' come to be settled. First and foremost was the provision of an authoritative text, according to stated principles: probably the most usual aim was to achieve a representation of the author's last lifetime treatment of the text while trying to differentiate between author's and publisher's interventions, though sometimes the first printed edition has been used as copy text. In either case variations from the copy text are traced and tabulated through a detailed textual apparatus (often compressed into a series of codes and symbols very hostile to ready interpretation). Also important to a scholarly edition has been the need to provide a context for the text: by convention straightforward literary criticism has been excluded from the contents of a scholarly edition, which – with the exception of its choice and justification of copy text – generally claims to be giving information rather than opinion in introduction and notes; but the edition will usually contain a detailed introduction explaining the pre- and often post-publication history of the work, and explanatory notes drawing attention to matters such as literary borrowings, factual references and meanings of words, knowledge of which may well have been obvious at least to some of the author's original readers, but which even professional scholars can no longer be relied on to understand.[1] Emphasis is given to the meticulous sourcing of information, to enable readers to follow up the references provided by the editor. And all has to be distilled and selected so that it can be presented comprehensively and coherently within the finite number of pages of a book. All these components require massive scholarly skill, expertise and energy; as a result, a good volume in a scholarly edition may well take years, even decades, to come to fruition, and will represent the fruits of very extended, sustained work by a specialist editor or editors.

We decided that this model, far from being outdated by technological possibilities, still had an enormous amount to offer in scholarly terms. We still see the value of printed volumes, in each of which a scholar, or pair of scholars, who have spent years working in a dedicated way with the text and its contextual information are able to present the fruits of that study in a form which enables the scholarly reader to find, within the pages of a book, a reliable text produced on principles clearly explained and with detail of variants from the chosen copy text, information on how the work was produced and with which large or small variants, and informed explanation of historical, cultural, literary and linguistic issues. And there is, after all, at the very least, something appropriate about reproducing in printed form a work originally intended and designed as a printed book or pamphlet.

The Cambridge edition of Swift will, therefore, aim to play a major role in provoking and sustaining debate about its author. It will claim authority for its texts, its contextual essays and its annotations. Those claims will be open to dispute, but they are essential to the shaping of scholarly study of an author. The edition will define a canon of Swift texts, with an accompanying rationale. It will have to decide whether to print, for example, *A Letter to a Young Poet*, or 'The Gentleman at Large's Litany', and, more dramatically, it will have to decide in the case of *Tale of a Tub*, whether to include 'The History of Martin', first published in 1720. In this last case, Marcus Walsh's careful weighing of the evidence will conclude with a decisive rejection:

> The satire on the Church of England is of course out of line with Swift's sentiments as expressed in the Apology. It is hard to believe that Jonathan Swift could have dropped 'the former Martin' and made him signify instead 'Lady *Besses* Institution'. It is harder still to think of the Martin who runs mad in his opposition to '*Jack*'s children' as a creation of the Jonathan Swift who so firmly insisted on the greater urgency of the Presbyterian threat.

The definition of the canon in this way is a vital function of the modern scholarly edition.

---

1 For a powerful defence of explanatory material in editing, see R.D. Hume, 'The Aims and Uses of "Textual Studies"', *Papers of the Bibliographical Society of America*, 99 (2005): 197–230.

For the texts that the Cambridge Swift decides are canonical, it will present reading texts with a justification both of the choice of version and of any eclecticism and correction, serving the scholarly community by providing a text that can be cited, interpreted and disputed. The choice of reading text is essential to provide stability in critical discourse but also to provoke and sustain textual analysis and debate; where all variant texts are recommended for reading (an unhelpful state of affairs) the need for editorial analysis disappears. In addition, Swift's are often typographically complex texts, and the print edition forces the editor, in collaboration with the Press, to discriminate for the reader between significant and insignificant features in the knowledge that the choices made will be permanently realized. Once again, it is the necessity of choosing that provokes the analysis.

Introductions will also claim authority by presenting a literary and intellectual context in which the work should be read. Although their aim is not to be deliberately contentious, the issues they raise – that of Jacobitism in *The Conduct of the Allies*, for example – are central to contemporary understanding of Swift. In the case of *Conduct of the Allies*, Bertrand Goldgar devotes several pages to the passage in which Swift says that if a foreign power is called in to guarantee the succession of the crown as stipulated in the Barrier Treaty 'we put it out of the Power of our own Legislature to change our Succession, without the Consent of that Prince or State who is Guarantee, how much soever the Necessities of the Kingdom may require it'. Goldgar explains the precise legislation Swift might have been thought to offend against, the nature of the attack on him for making room for the Pretender, and the various modern interpretations of Swift's motivation and that of his advisers. In conclusion he summarizes the controversy generated by *The Conduct of the Allies*, reversing the characterization of one of the pamphlets by demonstrating that it is an ironic Tory defence of the government position. His introduction to the material revivifies a controversy, enabling the reader to make an informed decision about it, but it also places this Jacobite debate within a broader picture of the pamphlet's purposes. His introduction, like others, adds to contextual explanations a historical perspective on its own operation by affording some account of reception of Swift's works.

The authority of the print volumes, their assumption of a strong voice in contemporary scholarly debate, goes along with their longevity, expressed through their presence on library shelves. Whereas the continuing availability of an electronic edition, unless it is supported by a system of subscription (and possibly even then), will often be in doubt and access to it is likely to be subject to continuing adaptation, print culture has developed ways of ensuring continuing access to its products. Even the edition that is out of print is available in a copyright library, and for the foreseeable future scholars will know how to access it and use it. The future of the print edition is secure, as that of the electronic edition cannot be at present.

Although the choices represented in a print edition seem to us important and the analysis and evaluation they provoke essential to scholarly editing, the print edition is limited in space and cannot present the full range of the evidence on which its judgements are based. In particular it cannot hope to represent the degree of variation in accidentals (punctuation, capitalization and other typography) between editions at a time when the significance of these features is being recognized as important.[2] For this reason the electronic archive will prove a particularly valuable supplement to the Cambridge Swift. Only one version of a particular Swift text will be presented in print (and readers benefit from the consequent debates over the choice of reading text), but we recognize that other texts have their own validity. It is possible to value one version above others, without disputing the worth of its rivals. The print volumes of the Swift edition will list emendations and provide historical collations of substantives, but the archive will supplement that by providing access to all authoritative texts, while accepting a responsibility to analyse and explain them. Taking its lead from the edition, the archive will avoid a 'hands-off' approach or editorial neutrality, in the belief that providing users with a very wide range of options with no guidance deprives them of real choice. Although claims have been made for the democratizing effects of electronic text – and possibilities of free access are real – there is a danger of bewildering the inexperienced user and declining an opportunity to educate. Discussions which treat texts as persons with equal rights obscure the danger that real persons who are empowered by traditional editions will be disempowered by electronic ones. The aim of the archive, therefore, is to provide informed access to different and authoritative texts. The creation of menus will be central to the enterprise, with detailed introductions that we hope may be subject to summary: 'the first edition of Gulliver's Travels, censored by Andrew Tooke and served raw'; 'the first Irish *Gulliver's Travels*, with some new ingredients'; 'a reheated *Gulliver's Travels*, with a new Lindalanian sauce, on a bed of revised capitals and italics'. Each text will have an essay detailing its place in the sequence of composition and revision; its date, its printer, its revisions, if any, their nature and significance; its readership; its print number or survival rate; the quality of its printing; its illustrations; and its texture of accidentals. Users will be told why they might want to read this text and what its disadvantages and limitations are.

The archive, which will be under the direction of David Womersley at Oxford and James McLaverty at Keele, two of the general editors of the print edition, will be of prose texts only.[3] It is designed as a companion to the Swift Poems Project, which has been the work of James Woolley and John Fischer for over 25 years.[4]

---

2 For an important recent study, including an analysis of the frontispieces of *Gulliver's Travels*, see J. Barchas, *Graphic Design, Print Culture and the Eighteenth-Century Novel* (Cambridge: Cambridge University Press, 2003).

3 In 2004 a grant from the AHRB of £533,661 over five years provided research assistants for the print edition and the archive, and paid for reprographics and electronic typesetting. Access to the archive will be through the sponsoring universities, Keele and Oxford. The researchers are currently Dr Paddy Bullard, at St Catherine's, Oxford, and Dr Adam Rounce, at Keele.

4 Professors Woolley and Fischer initially worked on the project with Dr A.C. Elias, and they have recently been joined by Professor Stephen Karian.

The Poems Project will include transcriptions of all authoritative versions of Swift's poems and extensive bibliographical lists, with commentaries, for locating the poems in their publication contexts. It is hoped that in the long term it will be possible to make the poetry and prose archives compatible, or at least to create very strong links between them.

The Swift electronic archive will not be strictly canonical like the print edition. It will include texts that have been disattributed there and texts that have been rejected after careful consideration of claims for their inclusion. The volumes of the edition will continue to print in appendices texts that are judged doubtful, but the electronic archive opens up the possibility of making rejected texts available without embarrassing the print edition with material that, once it has been rejected by the editor, only a few specialist scholars will want to read. The print volumes can remain 'clean', presenting the work of Swift, in so far as we can determine it, while the archive can provide a level of information about such texts that makes their claims intelligible without endorsing them.

As the print edition will not include parallel texts or alternative versions as appendices, as has become the practice with, for example, Wordsworth's *The Prelude* or Pope's *The Rape of the Lock*, the major role of the archive will be to present versions that might have had a strong claim to be the reading text. So, for example, the Cambridge edition will print the edition of *Gulliver's Travels* that formed volume III of Faulkner's *Works* in 1735, rather than the first edition of 1726. As the first edition was to some degree censored by Revd Andrew Tooke, and Swift clearly attempted to secure the fullest and most correct text possible for Faulkner, the 1735 edition clearly has independent authority and represents something between a restoration and revision of the text. It contains a letter from Gulliver to 'his Cousin Sympson', dated 2 April 1727, complaining in an eccentric and dramatized fashion about the first edition, which, while it may not be wholly serious, encourages the editor to use the 1735 rather than the 1726 text.[5] Nevertheless, the first edition retains its interest, both as a representation of Swift's earlier, and less directly politically coloured, thoughts, and as the text that many of his contemporaries responded to. The archive will, therefore, provide the first edition, as well as Faulkner's, and it will also include the Dublin edition with corrected readings produced by John Hyde in 1726, and eleven other editions of the *Travels* with a claim to some authority.

The textual situation of *Gulliver's Travels* echoes that of Swift's other substantial masterpiece, *A Tale of Tub*. In this case the first edition of 1704 was not censored, but the fifth edition of 1710 provided important supplementary materials. Swift supplied a new 'Apology' to preface the volume, and added footnotes to the text,

---

5 Claude Rawson gives a characteristically nuanced view of Sympson's letter in the World Classics edition, edited with Ian Higgins (Oxford: Oxford University Press, 2005), pp. xv–xxiii. See also M. Treadwell, 'Benjamin Motte, Andrew Tooke and *Gulliver's Travels*', in H. Real and H.J. Vienken (eds), *Proceedings of the First Münster Symposium on Jonathan Swift* (München: Fink, 1985).

many of them copied from William Wotton's *Observations upon the Tale of a Tub*, thereby converting a hostile critique into a helpful commentary. Once again, the choice of the late edition as reading text is justified by the care Swift took over it (though the central text is largely unamended from the fourth edition), but the first edition retains its importance as the expression of Swift's first thoughts and as the text many of his contemporaries, including, of course, Wotton, responded to. All five early editions, and the first incorporation of *Tale of a Tub* in the Faulkner edition, in 1755, will be provided by the archive.[6]

The situation with many of Swift's political writings differs from that of *Gulliver's Travels* and *Tale of a Tub*, in that he never revisited them in a serious way and the right choice for reading text seems to lie with the first edition or one of its near contemporaries. That can still leave plenty of work for the archive to do because of the extent of early revision. *The Publick Spirit of the Whigs*, for example, appeared in eight quarto versions published by John Morphew in 1714, some of them expurgated and some of them not. The clear choice for the Cambridge Swift is of one of the unexpurgated editions, but the substitutions made by Swift's printer, John Barber, using material provided by Bolingbroke make the other early issues of intense interest.[7] Again, the archive will allow them to be read complete.

Although substantive variation provides an important justification for the archive, the basic information on such variation is already provided in the historical collation of the print edition. These collations, however, provoke general hostility in literary critics, and assertions of their value by their advocates (among whom we number ourselves) have proved powerless against the prevailing revulsion. Literary critics are much more likely to be willing to read the variant text independently or against a narrative account, or even against the historical collation itself, and that is what the archive will encourage them to do. Consulting the variant text will, of course, enable the reader to take the whole range of variation, accidental and substantive, into account, and that is where the great strength of an archive with a collational facility lies. In a seminal essay over 30 years ago Morse Peckham pointed out the inadequacy of the traditional historical collation because it failed to give a full account of accidental changes.[8] Such changes, he believed, might reflect great historical shifts and help provide information for researchers. The very division between accidentals and substantive is, of course, problematic. A revising author, such as Pope, might devote more attention to accidentals than he does to substantives, and a change in punctuation, italics or even capitals, might

---

6 For a guide to editions, see D. Woolley, 'The Textual History of *A Tale of a Tub*', *Swift Studies*, 21 (2006): 7–26.

7 Ian Gadd will argue in the print edition that it is probable that Barber was willing to leave type standing for relatively short periods and that this standing type lies behind the many variants. It could be that he was uncertain of demand or he may have wanted to avoid storing copies of a controversial work on the premises.

8 'Reflections on the Foundations of Modern Textual Editing', *Proof*, 1 (1971): 122–55.

have as much impact on the meaning of a text as a change in wording.[9] Such effects, if they were particular, might be identified and recorded in the collation, but more general effects are much more difficult to deal with.

Swift takes an active interest in accidentals and variation may well be indicative of authorial intervention, but the interpretation of variations is difficult working by single cases and must depend on an accumulation of evidence. For example, sometimes it seems that key words in an argument become italicized (such as *wit, sublime* or *praise* in *Tale of a Tub*), or a technical term will be acknowledged in the same way (*fee-simple* in the same work), or a saying is mocked (*I speak without Vanity*). Parts of the body that might be thought 'rude' are fairly routinely italicized. Sometimes italic is used expressively (*furious zeal* in *Gulliver's Travels*) or to hold a word at arm's length through revulsion (as when the Chief Minister is called 'the *Ablest Dog in the Pack*'). In the 1735 *Gulliver's Travels*, italic is added quite extensively, with the purpose, we suspect, of drawing attention to the party-political nature of some of the satire. In order for such effects to be properly appreciated the reader needs to have the extensive contact with the text that through-reading allows, but it is also necessary, if the archive is to have its full usefulness, for there to be commentary which draws attention to these effects.

Access to the archive will be free and will include search and collation facilities. It will not include the corrected reading texts available in the print edition or the introductions and explanatory notes. After the current stage of the project, we would like to see the development of the archive to include visual materials, chiefly illustrations and images of the text. Such illustration would be selective because ECCO provides access to textual images in a large number of cases. The archive was due to be deposited with the Arts and Humanities Data Service (AHDS) at the end of the period of the grant, 2010, but, with the withdrawal of Arts and Humanities Research Council (AHRC) funding from the AHDS, it now seems most likely that the archive will be maintained at Oxford or Keele.[10] This change seems symptomatic of the uncertainties besetting the publication of electronic texts at present and encourages us in the view that the future of the scholarly edition may lie in a combination of stable printed volumes embodying carefully weighed value judgements and an electronic archive that provides both the evidence for those judgements and the opportunity to challenge them.

---

9 For the alleged importance of a single comma, see J. McLaverty, 'Warburton's False Comma: Reason and Virtue in Pope's *Essay on Man*', *Modern Philology*, 99 (2002): 379–92.

10 The AHRC requires deposit for a minimum period of three years. For such a period costs would be minimal; the long-term costs of maintaining the archive as a publicly available facility are another matter.

Chapter 9

Editions and Archives: Textual Editing and the Nineteenth-century Serials Edition (ncse)

James Mussell and Suzanne Paylor

Introduction: Editing periodicals in the digital domain

Critical editions of periodicals are extremely rare in paper form: not only are runs often lengthy and so necessitate large, expensive editions, but their diverse contents, predominantly written with an eye to the passing moment and their position within the market, sit uneasily alongside the well-structured, single-authored works that are by convention deemed worthy of republication and preservation. One of the few to be published is the recent edition of *Blackwood's Magazine* published by Pickering and Chatto.[1] With 163 years' worth of issues to choose from, the editors opted to make selections from the journal's first eight years of publication. This is the period in which the magazine lampooned the 'Cockney School' of poetry and, by dividing the contents into volumes dedicated to verse, prose, the 'Noctes Ambrosianae' and criticism, the editors stress Blackwood's role as a vehicle for literature in this early period.[2] By including rare material such as the 'Chaldee Manuscript', excised from the second printing of the journal, the edition anthologizes the periodical to make persuasive arguments for *Blackwood's* as an active participant in early nineteenth-century literary culture.[3]

Periodicals, through their associations with the ephemeral print of journalism, are often considered vehicles for texts before their memorialization in more stable form elsewhere. Consequently, editors today who publish digests of journalism, or who harvest the archive for the choice works of a single writer, are often following in the footsteps of those periodical authors who preceded

---

1 N. Mason et al. (eds), *Blackwood's Magazine 1817–1825: Selections from Maga's Infancy*, 6 vols (London: Pickering and Chatto, 2006).

2 The 'Cockney School' was a derisory term aimed at a group of poets and intellectuals who gathered in London in the early nineteenth-century. For a recent overview see J.N. Cox, *Poetry and Politics in the Cockney School: Keats, Shelley, Hunt and their Circle* (Cambridge: Cambridge University Press, 1998).

3 For the 'Chaldee Manuscript' see A.L. Strout, 'James Hogg's "Chaldee Manuscript"', *PMLA*, 65 (1950): 695–718; Flynn, P., 'Beginning *Blackwood's*: The Right Mix of Dulce and Utilité', *Victorian Periodicals Review*, 39 (2006): 136–57.

them.[4] However, this preference for the more stable form of the book over that of the periodical risks severely misrepresenting the culture of the past. As recent work in nineteenth-century studies has revealed, not only was the periodical press the predominant source of print in the period, but studies of the press provide a much more nuanced understanding of the market for print and the diversity of writing that sustained it.[5] Although the periodical press has been used as a source for background to the nineteenth-century, it is increasingly evident that it was the medium through which the nineteenth-century made sense of both itself and the world.

The marginalization of the nineteenth-century periodical has been enforced by its inaccessibility. As multi-authored texts, often pitched at certain configurations of readers at certain moments, periodicals demand twenty-first century readers who are knowledgeable in a variety of disciplines and the minutiae of nineteenth-century life. Perhaps a more significant barrier, however, is the condition of the archive. The fragile and decomposing remains of the nineteenth-century periodical press are scattered across institutions around the world. Even those runs archived in leading libraries are marked by their conservation and use, whether this is through the choices made by the original archivists of what material to keep, or the state of the surviving pages after years of handling. Digitization directly addresses these difficulties. Not only is it possible to digitize large tracts of material – reconstituting runs from disparate sources and making available durable copies – but the latitude permitted in the digital environment allows us to create alternative models of the critical edition that are not derived from our encounters with books. Indeed, there are already a wide variety of digital projects underway that attempt to address the limitations of scholarship derived solely from books.[6] While such

---

4 For one of the few digests of nineteenth-century periodicals, see A. King and J. Plunkett (eds), *Victorian Print Media: A Reader* (Oxford: Oxford University Press, 2005).

5 John North, the editor of the *Waterloo Directory of English Newspapers and Periodicals, 1800–1900* has estimated that there were up to 125,000 individual titles published in the period. J.S. North (ed.), *Waterloo Directory of English Newspapers and Periodicals: 1800–1900*, 2nd series (20 vols) (Waterloo, ON: North Waterloo Academic Press, 2003) and <http://www.victorianperiodicals.com>. For some of the key recent works on the nineteenth-century press, see M. Beetham, *A Magazine of Her Own? Domesticity and Desire in the Woman's Magazine, 1800–1914* (London: Routledge, 1996); L. Brake, *Subjugated Knowledges: Journalism, Gender and Literature1837–1907* (New York: Macmillan, 1994), *Print in Transition, 1850–1910: Studies in Media and Book History* (Basingstoke: Palgrave, 2001); L. Brake, A. Jones and L. Madden (eds), *Investigating Victorian Journalism* (Basingstoke: Macmillan, 1990); J. Shattock and M. Wolff (eds), *The Victorian Periodical Press: Samplings and Soundings* (Leicester: Leicester University Press, 1982); M. Turner, *Trollope and the Magazines: Gendered Issues in Mid-Victorian Britain* (Basingstoke: Macmillan, 2000). (Throughout this chapter, URLs not otherwise dated are correct as of 1 September 2008.)

6 J.J. McGann, *Radiant Textuality: Literature after the World Wide Web* (New York: Palgrave, 2001), pp. 18–19. For some examples of projects that are resolutely un-booklike,

activity underscores the necessity for models of editing capable of managing such disparate projects, it also reminds us that the current model – derived from the archetype of the book – is at best a limited, institutionally ratified starting point, and at worst an unnecessary discursive constraint.

The intellectual interest and cultural importance of the nineteenth-century archive, coupled with its amenable copyright status and demonstrable commercial potential, has prompted a number of large-scale digitization projects focusing on periodicals.[7] These have largely been facilitated by the existence of large tracts of microfilm – a result of previous attempts to address preservation issues and distribute surviving runs of important titles – that can be digitized with a minimum of editorial intervention. However, most of these projects employ an unreflexive organizational structure that does not respond to the seriality of their contents. Rather than produce critical editions of nineteenth-century periodicals, these projects tend to provide archives of nineteenth-century content.

Although such projects are likely to transform the way in which scholars view the period simply by rendering their contents searchable, we suggest that there is another way to present this type of material. All acts of republishing involve some degree of editing. Whereas many archives present themselves as simply providing user-friendly access to types of content, they do so by eliding the labour necessary to create and order digital objects. In the case of periodicals, such archival strategies are doubly inappropriate as much of their historical importance lies in their form. In this chapter we outline the generic features of the periodical press and demonstrate their constitutive role in structuring content and conveying it to readers. Drawing on the *Nineteenth-Century Serials Edition* (ncse) as a case study, we argue that it is possible to design and implement digital tools that can translate the form of the genre into the digital domain.[8] ncse is a scholarly edition of six nineteenth-century periodicals: the *Monthly Repository* (1806–38); *Northern Star* (1837–52); *Leader* (1850–60); *English Woman's Journal* (1858–64); *Tomahawk* (1867–70); and *Publishers' Circular* (1880–90). While they are significant journals in their own right, together they demonstrate the remarkable diversity of the nineteenth-century periodical press. By publishing them as an edition, we explore this diversity through recognizing what it is that connects them. It is only by paying close attention to periodical form, we suggest, that we can prevent the marginalization of genre once again in the production and reproduction of content.

---

see the Blake Archive <http://www.blakearchive.org>; Corpus Vitrearum Medii Aevi <http://www.cvma.ac.uk/>; the explorer at the Monticello site <http://www.monticello.org/>.

7 See for instance Proquest's *British Periodicals*; Thomson Gale's *19th Century UK Periodicals Online*; and the British Library's *British Newspapers, 1800–1900*.

8 The *Nineteenth-Century Serials Edition* (ncse) is an AHRC-funded research project based at Birkbeck College in collaboration with the British Library, the Centre for Computing in the Humanities, King's College, London, and Olive Software. See <http://www.ncse.ac.uk>.

The periodical as genre

Periodicals are habitually considered as books that happen to have been published serially. The very practice of binding periodicals into volumes emulates this latent desire, embodied in the book, for permanence and coherence. However, such an approach misrepresents the open-ended nature of periodical publication, and the relationship that a single number has to a specific moment. Serial novels have a coherence predicated by their genre and warranted by a single author. Whereas a serial novel has a definite end-point, even if unknown by the author at the time of writing, a periodical, on the whole, attempts to exist for as long as possible. This, of course, can result in runs far longer than the average book and the sheer number of pages alone often prevents republication in paper. The contents of periodicals are necessarily contextual: different combinations of content are arranged in each number in order to appeal to certain configurations of readers at specific moments. In other words, the meaning of a particular article cannot be separated from either the other articles on the page and in the number, or the historical moment in which it was conceived and published.

Very few periodicals are authored by a single individual. Even the well-known quarterly reviews such as the *Edinburgh* and the *Quarterly Review* were recognized as having a team of contributors despite concealing their activities behind the editorial 'we'. Indeed, the editorial persona is often used as a substitute authorial figure, providing a focal point for the title as a whole. However, the assumption that the editor is the most important person risks relegating the input of individual authors, and elides the complex negotiations necessary to bring each number to publication. For instance, the editor is not necessarily the proprietor of a specific title, and what appears on the page is likely to be the result of collaboration between printers, artists, engravers and authors. Depending on the editorial priorities of a specific project, it is feasible to use any of these people as an organizing principle through which to edit the periodical.

The existence of a title over time produces complex bibliographical histories. As proprietors sell titles and editors move on, fall out with contributors or reconceive of their audience and the appearance and identity of the periodical, so the text accordingly changes. Figure 9.1 represents a period in the life of the *Monthly Repository* between 1805 and 1835. Over this period the journal was known by a range of names, and even produced a supplement that eventually became a title in its own right. Indeed, it is difficult to define precisely what the *Monthly Repository* actually is. Although the title 'Monthly Repository' was first used when the *Unitarian Theological Magazine* was renamed the *Monthly Repository of Theology and General Literature*, the earlier journal still constitutes part of the history of the title. Equally, the various qualifications and subtitles that were added to 'Monthly Repository' over its run posit both a continuity (they are versions of the *Monthly Repository*) and a discontinuity (it is, for instance, the *Monthly Repository and Review* in 1828). The *Unitarian Chronicle* might appear to be a separate publication but it was initially published in February 1832 as the *Unitarian Chronicle and Companion to the*

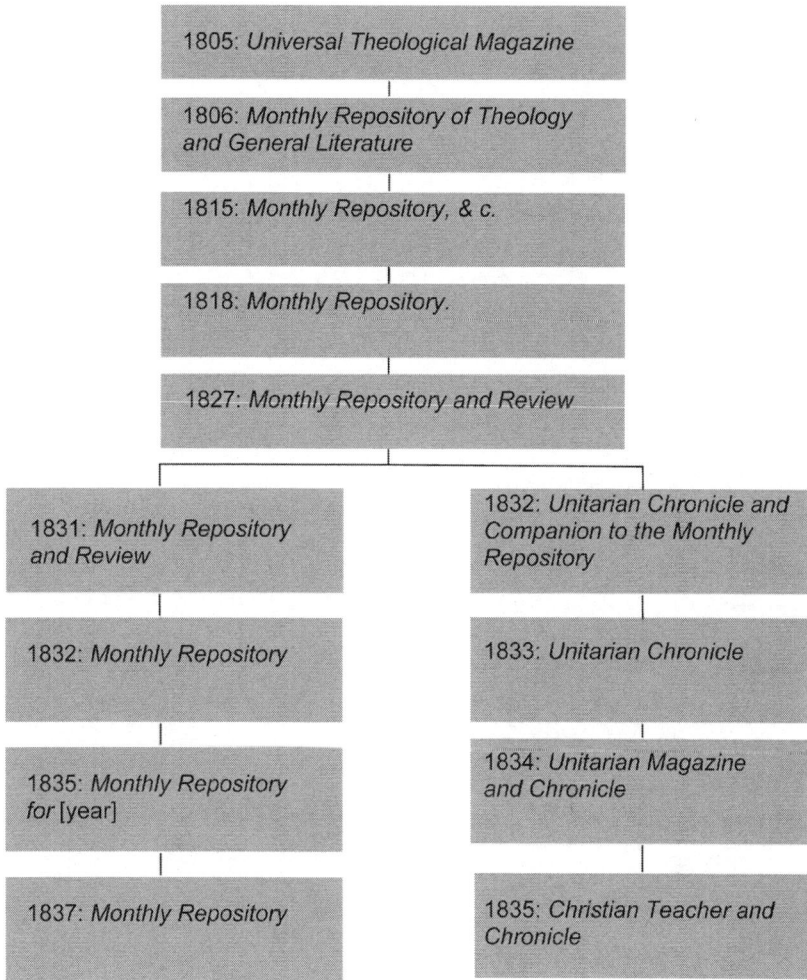

Figure 9.1   Family tree showing the various incarnations of the *Monthly Repository* according to the mastheads of issues

Monthly Repository and formatted so that readers could bind it up with the *Monthly Repository*.[9] By April 1833, however, it had become simply *Unitarian Chronicle* and officially divested itself of its ties to the older journal. The now independent *Unitarian Chronicle* continued on under this title until January 1834 when it became *Unitarian Magazine and Chronicle*, lasting a further two years until it was merged and became

9 Anon., 'Address', *Unitarian Chronicle and Companion to the Monthly Repository* (1832), 2.

the *Christian Teacher and Chronicle* in January 1836. The *Unitarian Chronicle* was clearly part of the *Monthly Repository* until at least April 1833, when its ties were dissolved. However, according to its title, the post-April 1833 *Unitarian Chronicle* is part of the same publication as the pre-April 1833 *Unitarian Chronicle*: if one were to include the *Unitarian Chronicle* as part of an edition of the *Monthly Repository*, dividing it at April 1833 would involve separating two halves of a single title.

As the examples from the *Monthly Repository* and *Unitarian Chronicle* demonstrate, beginnings and endings in periodical culture are always provisional. Often new periodicals will appear under the title of periodicals thought extinct, positing a continuity with their predecessor even if they bear no other relationship than their shared name. It is also common for periodicals to change their name in line with changes in personnel, ownership or contents. This makes it difficult to identify when a journal becomes something else, and makes it impossible to consider any particular title completely 'finished.' Although it is easy to imagine periodicals being archived as rows of volumes, all with the same name, on library shelves, their shifting identities and unresolved endpoints require substantial decision-making before this order can be imposed.

Seriality seems to imply linear publishing models, but the actual state of the periodical press more closely resembles family trees, in which new branches (and indeed offspring – sometimes illegitimate) are constantly being discovered. Whereas it is difficult to build such an architecture for paper editions of periodicals, in digital form not only are such structures relatively easy to design and implement, but they can also be repurposed according to user needs. It is this flexibility that is important in conceiving of the periodical press. By contrast, the shape of the surviving archive is largely the result of interventions that did not consider the periodical as periodical. A well-known example of this is the lack of surviving advertising and supplementary materials in bound volumes of periodicals. Although such components were integral features of the press – providing income streams, enticing subscribers, and differentiating titles from one another – traditionally they have not been considered worth preserving. A less familiar example is the lack of multiple editions of single numbers that survive. Many periodicals – especially those weeklies that are closer to the model of the newspaper – published more than one edition on any particular date. For instance the *Leader* published an edition on the advertised date, a Saturday, for readers in the town, but preceded this with an edition published on a Friday for its country readers. As there were last-minute additions to the town edition, country readers were in effect a week behind, even though their edition was published a day earlier. The *Northern Star*, a radical weekly connected with the Chartist movement, published editions according to current events. In the run held at the British Library there are usually three editions, but sometimes this increases to nine. It was officially published on a Saturday: however, in 1842 printing began on Wednesday and was completed on Thursday to make the first edition published on Friday; while printing began on Friday to make the second edition published on Saturday morning; and a third edition was published on Saturday afternoon. Rather than thinking of the *Northern*

Star as a Saturday weekly, it is also possible to consider it a Wednesday, Thursday or Friday weekly, depending on which edition you are reading.

Unlike a paper edition, which forces issues into linear groupings of sequential numbers, a digital edition offers the potential for a more dynamic organization of the material. For instance, it is possible to present all the various editions of a number, or let the user decide which edition (for instance all the town editions, or all the third editions) he or she wants to read. The periodical archive contains material that has been produced over a period of time, and then been subjected to the archival strategies of a particular institution. Runs of journals therefore both represent their precise moments of publication, while also bearing marks of their transformation into stable retrievable forms. These two transformations – publishing and preservation – produce sets of categories that correspond to specific moments in the bibliographical history of the journal. For instance, whereas some users might be interested in specific numbers of a title, others might want to read it according to a specific year; equally, some might be interested in certain articles or types of article, and others might wish to read whole volumes. It is quite feasible to imagine user interfaces that delimit content according to such criteria: however, without the structural relationships that underpin different levels of content, the history of the periodical itself is overlooked.

The location of an article within a number structures what it means. For instance, each number of the *Leader* is divided into two broad sections, the first dealing with contemporary events, and the second with the arts. There are some articles that could feasibly appear in either section, but the actual location might reveal whether it was the newsworthiness of the event or its contents that were deemed relevant by the editor. Similar inferences can be drawn from the location of numbers within bound volumes. For instance, many journals were bound in volumes that correspond to calendar years: the *Publishers Circular*, a fortnightly trade journal for the book trade, not only published a special Christmas number, full of illustrations from contemporary magazines, but its advertising columns trace the changes in the publishing market according to the season. Even the fact that a number belongs to a specific volume is important: the allocation of volume numbers to individual issues identifies them as part of a set, a relationship that is enacted materially if they are then bound together.

There are also generic and thematic relationships running across the archive. For instance, correspondence is a recurring feature throughout the press. In the *Nineteenth-Century Serials Edition* alone, printed correspondence is a feature of four of its six titles, and two of those include correspondence in a department called 'Open Council'. Different types of content appear in different types of journal – letters are rare in quarterlies or literary monthlies; reflective essays are rare in weeklies – and are often geared towards certain types of reader. While it is important to recognize the recurrence of such generic forms across titles, it is also possible to find types of content that fall outside of them. For instance, even though correspondence columns are common, letters can also appear in other parts of a number: as part of a department of news, as part of a broader essay, or – in the case of the *Monthly*

Repository – as the main form of contribution in all sections. Although they are still letters, their significance is connected to where they function in the text.

The signals that indicate structure on the page are visual. Such features are often unique to specific titles, allowing them to compete in the crowded marketplace, but they also share certain generic features. Mastheads, for instance, combine text and images to provide a logo that both says what a journal is called, and often also indicates something about it. Figure 9.2 shows how the *Northern Star* substituted a relatively unadorned masthead in 1839 for a much more elaborate one with the words clustered around a symbolic printing press, radiating light into the world.

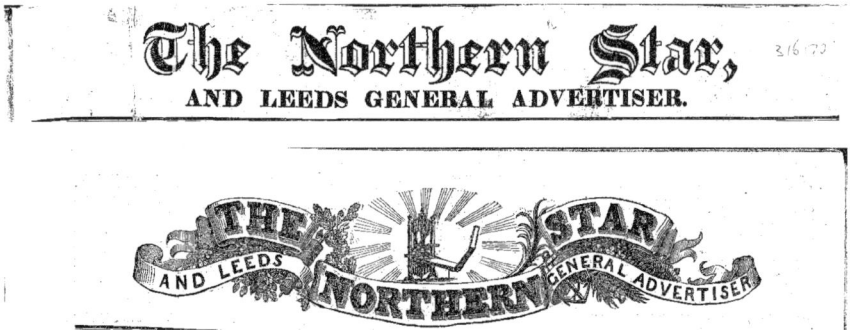

Figure 9.2   Mastheads of the *Northern Star* from 5 January 1839 and 12 January 1839

Source: Images from the *Nineteenth-Century Serials Edition* <www.ncse.ac.uk> [accessed 7 August 2007].

However, the identity of a periodical is bound up in much more than its masthead. Not only do the types of articles that appear determine its character, but so does the way in which they look, whether this is through the interposition of images, or the type in which they are set. The layout of articles on the page and the order in which they come are further ways in which a periodical posits an identity over numbers, despite necessarily changing its contents. Typographical marks, such as different text sizes or founts, distinguish between the headings of departments and the articles they contain. Equally, the size of type and the width of columns bear important cultural meanings: not only are text-rich pages difficult to read, but in the nineteenth-century (as today) they signal a serious, often masculine, readership. Consequently, editors have to reconcile the practical demands of both contributors and readers with the wider semiotic codes of presentation associated with certain types of periodical. Careful editorial attention must be paid to these non-textual marks: not only are they essential to the genre (demarcating levels of structure and, through components such as mastheads and date/volume information, allowing titles to appear as serials), but they also distinguish titles from one another while at the same time linking them with certain periodical sub-genres.

The formal features of the periodical press are not only essential components of its meaning, they also contain information that is not in its textual content. For instance, paper size bears important social connotations but decisions to change the size of a page are rarely discussed in print by the editors of journals.[10] The *Northern Star* and the *Leader* were both weeklies, but the *Northern Star* was printed on eight large pages whereas the *Leader* had 24 smaller pages. The *Leader* was primarily aimed at a middle-class, metropolitan, intellectual elite, whereas the *Northern Star* imagined its readers as working class and mainly from the north of England. The *Northern Star* was explicitly a newspaper, numbering its pages one to eight in each number, and not including paratextual material such as indices and volume title-pages. The *Leader*, however, presented a more book-like form, and provided readers with the materials to bind numbers into volumes. However, despite its initial differences, the *Northern Star* was gradually modified over its run until it resembled the form of the *Leader* (Figure 9.3). By August 1852 both titles shared the same size, number of columns, and the practice of publishing a town and country edition each week. Readers were forewarned about this change by the editor and proprietor of the *Northern Star*, George Julian Harney, in the number for 7 August 1852. He announced that the title would increase from eight to 16 pages, but maintained this would provide more columns despite a reduction in page size. He writes:

> Among other advantages this change will admit of each department having its appropriate page or pages. And as it is designed to make the paper of more than passing interest, its more compact form will with many be an additional inducement to preserve each consecutive number for binding in half-yearly volumes.[11]

By promoting the journal's smaller size and recommending readers preserve the numbers as they are published, Harney severs the title's link with the ephemerality of the newspaper and aligns it with review-type periodicals such as the *Leader*. Although we have commentary from the *Northern Star* about its formal changes, their significance can only be drawn through comparison with other titles. In addition, not all periodicals print self-reflexive material – there is little, for instance, in the *Leader* – and so it is only through such comparisons that conclusions as to the cultural significance of form can be drawn. Representing the formal features of periodicals provides crucial evidence as to intended readerships, evidence that, in turn, reflexively guides us in interpreting the content they contain.

---

10 For a recent exception to this, see the voluminous self-reflexive material that accompanied the *Guardian's* transformation into Berliner format in 2005. For instance, see Jane Martinson, 'Berliner Launch Hits Profits at Guardian', *Guardian*, 5 August 2005 <http://business.guardian.co.uk/story/0,,1542977,00.html>.

11 [G.J. Harney], 'To the Readers and Friends of the "Star of Freedom"', *The Star of Freedom*, 1, 7 August (1852), p. 1.

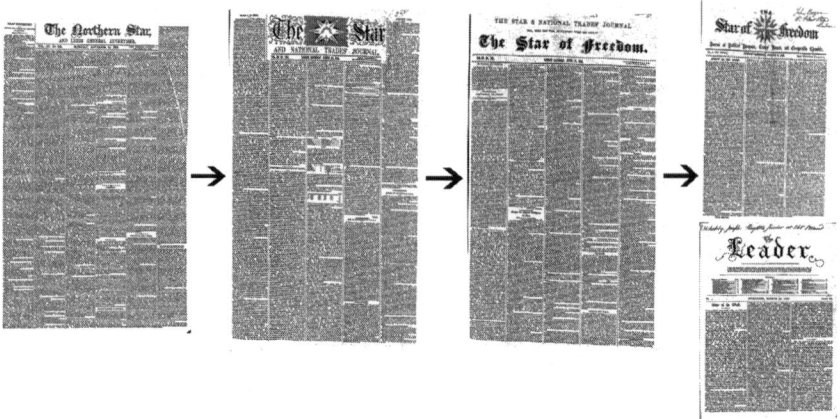

Figure 9.3   The *Northern Star* increasingly resembles the *Leader* over its run

Source: Images from the *Nineteenth-Century Serials Edition* <www.ncse.ac.uk> [accessed 7 August 2007].

Although these important contextual features are often overlooked when reading the periodical press, whether in print or digital form, the prosopographical relationships that inform the personnel who produce the periodical have been given substantial attention. Established projects such as the well-known *Wellesley Index* and *Waterloo Directory* have produced major reference tools that list the people associated with the nineteenth-century periodical press.[12] This research has been supplemented by a growing secondary literature that considers how various figures from the period contributed to the press, and includes key reference works such as the *Dictionary of Nineteenth-Century Journalism*.[13] The common practice of anonymity in the journalism of the period meant that it was possible to combine a number of roles simultaneously, with individuals often contributing to journals or editing them without the knowledge of either colleagues or peers. As a result, these relationships were often predicated on personal grounds as much as professional ones and any attempt to trace the activities of those involved must take into account aspects of their lives beyond their careers in journalism.

---

12 North (ed.), *Waterloo Directory*; W.E. Houghton (ed.), *Wellesley Index to Victorian Periodicals, 1824–1900*, 5 vols (Toronto: University of Toronto Press, 1966–79).

13 See for instance Turner, *Trollope and the Magazines*; K. Jackson, *George Newnes and the New Journalism in Britain, 1880–1910* (Aldershot: Ashgate, 2001); V. Grey, *Charles Knight: Educator, Publisher, Writer* (Aldershot: Ashgate, 2006); L. Brake and M. Demoor (eds), *Dictionary of Nineteenth-century Journalism* (London and Ghent, British Library and Academia Press, forthcoming).

Formal features, in particular, cause problems for reproduction as they tend to be the very things that differentiate periodicals from books. Although typography is important in both genres, the preference for abstract text over its actual appearance as print warrants e-Texts such as Project Gutenberg that produce transcripts of books rather than facsimile pages. It is, of course, equally possible to abstract the text from periodicals. However, their multi-faceted pages are structured on the basis of the contextual links between components, and extracting individual articles or altering their appearance elides this fundamental principle underpinning content. Equally, the misattribution of the author as sole creative agent in the production of literature permits the elision of the other people who play a role in producing literary works. But it is difficult to reify the author in the multi-authored periodical press: rather, authors become contributors, part of a network of actors who work under the direction of an editor. Critical editions of periodicals that either imagine them as series of books or as repositories of single-authored articles impose order by transforming periodical content into something more book-like. However, with freedom from the practical constraints of paper, we argue that now is the time to start designing critical editions of periodicals that enact discursive structures that are derived from periodicals rather than other print genres. To do this, we must foreground form.

Conserving periodical form in the digital domain

Conservation is particularly pressing for the periodical press as the archive is rapidly deteriorating. The ephemerality of periodicals – both in terms of their original projected life and their actual material condition – means that digitization is allied to preservation for the periodical press in a way that it is not for, say, classic literary works. The difficulties of preserving such material in paper (there are many of them; they are often printed on poor-quality paper; they take up a great deal of space) requires preservation of not just what periodicals say, but also of what they look like. Unlike the previous move to shift paper archives into microfilm, digital preservation provides a versatile medium in which we can minimize the loss of information that results from such radical transformations of material form.

Recent digitizations of periodicals have tended to adopt an archive model that attempts to retain formal features through the use of facsimile pages. Although this foregrounds the visual components of the page, such strategies are clearly limited if they do not incorporate the other relational structures into their edition architecture. For instance, the British Library's *Penny Illustrated Paper*, part of their Collect Britain suite of projects, provides easy access to the whole run of the journal from a single search screen (see Figure 9.4). By giving users a simple keyword search option, with date and article-type qualifying criteria, access to the newspaper resembles familiar interfaces such as Google. Search results are displayed in a list, with a small image taken from the page displaying the hit (see Figure 9.5). This avoids problems with displaying potentially inaccurate text generated by Optical Character Recognition (OCR), while also foregrounding

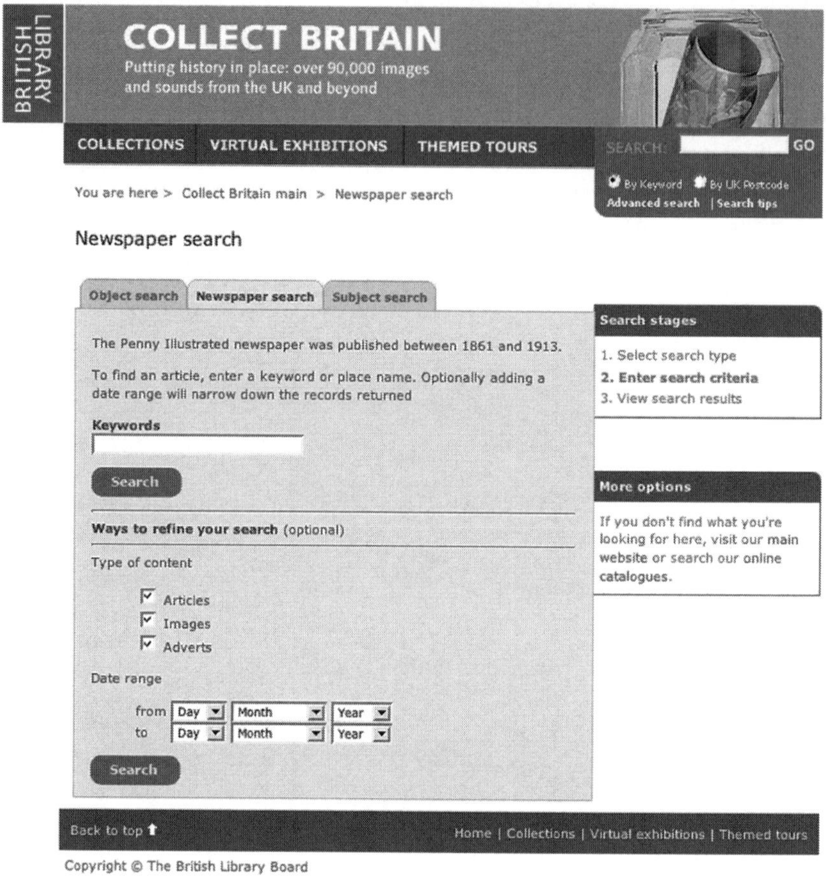

Figure 9.4   Collect Britain search screen for the *Penny Illustrated Newspaper*

Source: <http://www.collectbritain.co.uk/system/paper/index.cfm>, accessed 30 May 2007.
© British Library Board. All Rights Reserved.

the visual aspect of print. Clicking on a hit takes you directly to the full article, extracted from the page (see Figure 9.6). From this screen users can repurpose the image by saving it into their own collections or emailing it to themselves. There is also an option to view the whole page that allows users to view the extract in the context of the articles that surround it. As Figure 9.7 shows, it also compensates for the occasional errors that can occur as a result of the segmentation process.

The British Library's *Penny Illustrated Paper* provides ready access to articles, but in doing so it privileges users who know what they are looking for. As the only way to access the newspaper is through a search term, it is almost impossible to browse it. Equally, the decision to take users straight to the article, rather than to the page the article is on, suggests that articles are self-contained units of information

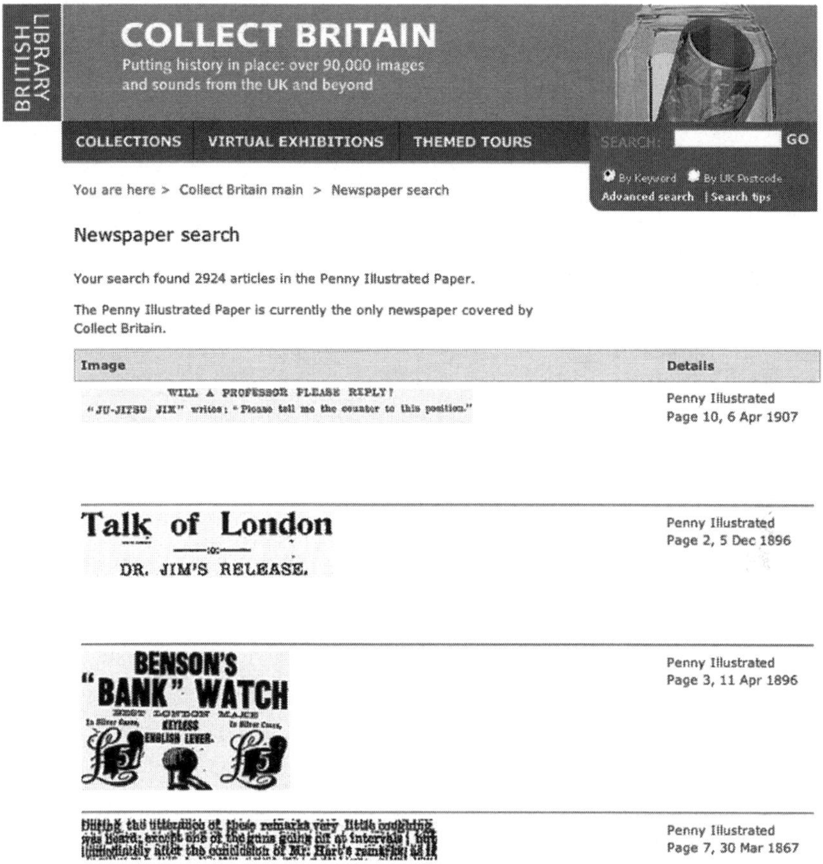

Figure 9.5   Search results screen for the *Penny Illustrated Newspaper*

Source: <http://www.collectbritain.co.uk/system/paper/index.cfm?fuseaction=paper.search>, accessed 30 May 2007. © British Library Board. All Rights Reserved.

that exist independently of their surroundings. This is further reiterated by the disparity between the page numbers attributed to each page in the system, and those numbers that can be seen printed on the pages of the hard copy. This imposes a new sequence onto the pages and makes browsing difficult between numbers. The project was funded as part of Collect Britain by the British Government's New Opportunities Fund, with the purpose of making some of the cultural resources of the British Library accessible to life-long learners.[14] Even though the articles within

---

14 N. Smith, 'Digitising Documents for Public Access', in L. MacDonald (ed.), *Digital Heritage: Applying Digital Imaging to Cultural Heritage* (Oxford: Elsevier Butterworth-Heinemann, 2006).

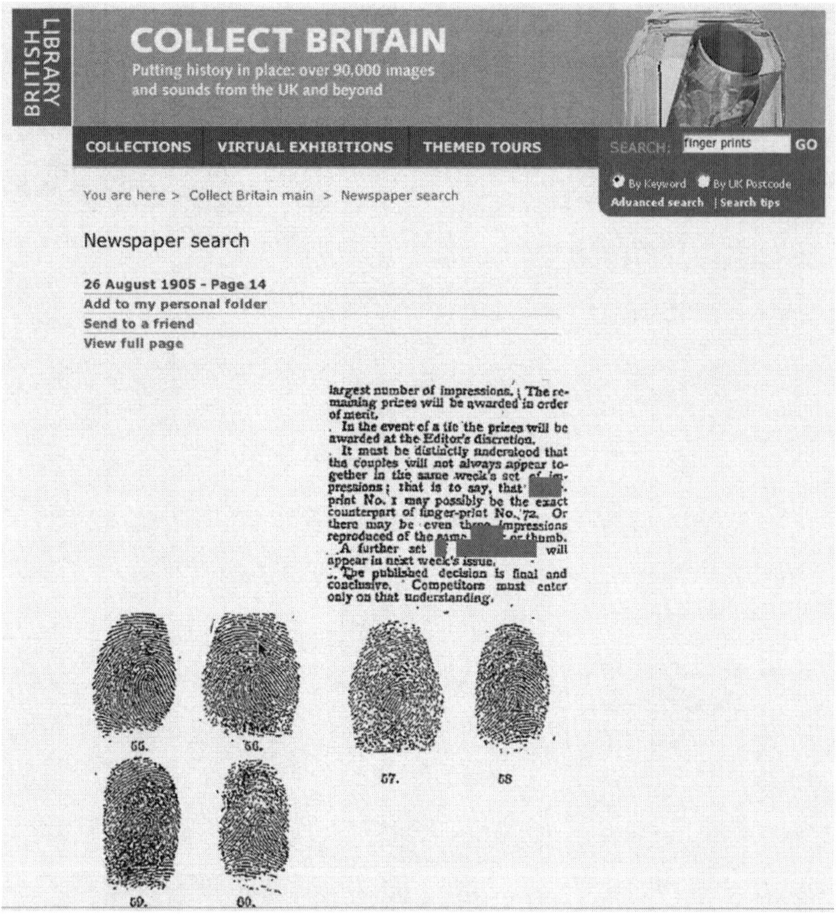

Figure 9.6   Article View, *Penny Illustrated Newspaper*

Source: <http://www.collectbritain.co.uk/system/paper/index.cfm?fuseaction=paper.articl e&refId=%2FPEN%2F1905%2F08%2F26%2F14%2FAr01403%2Exml&collection=PEN &searchtext=finger%20prints&place=>, accessed 30 May 2007. © British Library Board. All Rights Reserved.

the *Penny Illustrated Newspaper* can be searched separately, the user interface presents them as discrete objects so that they can be returned in global searches across the whole of Collect Britain. In light of its wider strategic aims, the British Library's *Penny Illustrated Newspaper* not only successfully provides users with easy access to the millions of articles within its 40,000 pages within two clicks of a mouse, but also presents these articles in a way that is interoperable with the other, diverse contents within Collect Britain. However, as we have argued, in the periodical the meaning of an article is lost when it is separated from its context,

Figure 9.7   Detail of 'Full page view', *Penny Illustrated Newspaper*

Source: <http://www.collectbritain.co.uk/system/paper/index.cfm?fuseaction=paper.
page&refId=PEN/1905/08/26/14/PG014.xml&collection=PEN>, accessed 30 May 2007.

whether on the page or within the number, volume or run of which it is a part. The attractive simplicity of the British Library's *Penny Illustrated Newspaper* comes at the cost of representing the structural integrity of the genre.

The British Library's *Penny Illustrated Newspaper* is based within a long tradition of indexing periodicals for content retrieval. Well-known nineteenth-century paper indexes such *Palmer's Index to the Times Newspaper*, *Poole's Index to Periodical Literature* and the various incarnations of W.T. Stead's *Index to the Periodical Literature of the World*, not to mention archives of scholarly journals such as JSTOR and Project Muse, all seek to organize the contents of periodicals according to the content of the articles within them.[15] However, there are alternative traditions of periodical indexing. Catalogues such as the *British Union Catalogue of Periodicals* list journals by title and the same is true of the nineteenth-century press directories such as *Mitchell's Newspaper Press Directory* or *Sell's Dictionary of the World's Press*, which often combine simple alphabetical lists of titles with divisions according to the genre of the periodical.[16] The most recent attempt to list every nineteenth-century periodical by title is the *Waterloo Directory*. This ongoing project currently contains over 50,000 entries, arranged alphabetically in its paper incarnation. In its online version, however, access can be by journal title, or through fields such as 'Issuing Body', 'County/Country', or 'People'.[17] The presence of these other traditions of indexing and archiving periodicals makes explicit the type of editorial decisions that are often elided when looking at finished archives and indexes. Whereas these decisions are embodied in the paper editions, the flexibility of the online version of the *Waterloo Directory* demonstrates that in the digital domain they can remain dynamic. Searchable databases, metadata schema (whether user-defined or contributed by editors) and well-structured Extensible Markup Language (XML) with appropriate style sheets, all offer the potential to reorder large corpora on the fly.[18]

---

15 *Palmer's Index to the Times Newspaper* (Samuel Palmer, 1790–1941); W.F. Poole et al., *Poole's Index to Periodical Literature*, 7 vols (Boston: Osgood, 1882–1908); W.T. Stead and E. Hetherington (eds), *Index to the Periodical Literature of the World*, 11 vols (Review of Reviews, 1891–1900).

16 J.D. Stewart et al., *British Union-Catalogue of Periodicals: A Record of the Periodicals of the World, from the Seventeenth Century to the Present Day, in British Libraries*, 5 vols plus supplements (London: Butterworth Scientific Publications, 1955).

17 North, *Waterloo Directory*. The digital version is at <http://www.victorianperiodicals.com>, accessed 10 March 2008.

18 J.J. McGann, 'The Rationale of Hypertext' at <http://www.iath.virginia.edu/public/jjm2f/rationale.html>, accessed 10 March 2008. See also J.J. McGann, 'The Rationale of Hypertext', in K. Sutherland (ed.) *Electronic Text: Investigations in Method and Theory* (Oxford: Clarendon Press, 1997), pp. 19–46.

Recent developments in social networking associated with web 2.0 applications have demonstrated that editors need not make such decisions at all. For a functional example of a

The recent attention to print forms that have been marginalized in the past – whether as part of scholarly projects such as those encouraged by the *Wellesley Index* or those aimed at a broader audience such as the British Library's Collect Britain – provides a timely reminder that the material culture of print is as worthy of editorial attention as the writing it contains. When considering the creation and publication of digital resources, which involve such extensive transformations of material form, such timely reminders become pressing. Form – whether conceived in terms of paper, typography, spatial layout, size or genre – not only provides the mechanism for a text to travel through time, but also records the interactions between a text and its historical contexts. Inseparable from content, form bears not only the marks of a text's production – whether this is the contributions of those responsible, the materials in which it is constituted or the way it imagines it will be used – but also the marks of its cultural life, from those designed by its producers, to those perhaps more accidental marks left by its readers.

Editing form, editing ncse

The very title of the *Nineteenth-Century Serials Edition* incorporates our awareness of the necessary editorial role in republishing periodicals: part of the project's remit is to investigate strategies and tools for scholarly editions of periodicals. As such, the formal diversity of the six titles in the edition is as important as their individual historical significance. Indeed, their historical importance necessitates that we preserve the formal components that make up their respective identities and not simply treat them as repositories of articles. Although there is a bias towards nineteenth-century reform journals, each is quite distinct: the *Monthly Repository* was an influential Unitarian monthly magazine that developed over its run into a pioneering literary and philosophical journal; the *Northern Star* was the weekly newspaper of the Chartist movement; the *Leader* was an intellectual weekly review of news, politics and the arts that was edited by members of the mid-century intellectual avant garde; the *English Woman's Journal* was a pioneering feminist monthly; *Tomahawk* was a more progressive satirical alternative to illustrated journals such as *Punch*; and the *Publishers' Circular* was a long-running trade publication for the print trade.

As you can see from Figure 9.8, this diversity is captured by the front pages of each title. Not only do they look different, they also all contain different ratios of text and image, genres of content, and they are all situated differently with regard to other print genres such as books and newspapers. However, these differences are located within certain identifiable generic categories. For instance, despite their variations, the mastheads are still identifiable as types of masthead. Although

---

user-defined archival model for nineteenth-century studies see NINES <http://www.nines. org>, accessed 10 March 2008.

Figure 9.8   Front pages of the six periodicals that make up ncse

Source: Images from the *Nineteenth-Century Serials Edition* <www.ncse.ac.uk>, accessed 7 August 2007.

it is the diversity of such features that distinguishes one title from another, the differences are structured relationally and so it is incumbent upon editors to facilitate the necessary comparisons. This task is complicated as most formal clues to genre are visual or structural: whereas facsimile pages can display some presentational features, and OCR-generated text can provide a useful index to bring out connections between types of content, most formal aspects of the press require more intensive editorial scrutiny and intervention. Visual components, whether pictures or fancy typography, are rarely legible in OCR transcripts, and structural relationships remain invisible. Rather than simply apply digital tools to text and image, editing this material requires the application of tools to the periodical as an object – including all its components in all their structural complexity – in order to bring out their constitutive relationships.

Olive software specializes in producing seamless digital editions of diverse content that can be accessed via web browsers. An important feature of this – effectively utilized in the *Penny Illustrated Newspaper* – is the division of page elements into segments, displayed in Hypertext Markup Language (HTML) but structured within XML repositories. By connecting text and image, and then structuring this relationship in larger hierarchies, it is possible to design projects using Olive applications that can implement abstract maps of periodical form. However, when we began to design ncse, we found that the form of the periodical did not neatly fit into Olive's existing applications. We initially used two applications, Active Paper Archive and File Cabinet: Active Paper Archive is used primarily to digitize newspapers, and Olive has extensive experience in digitizing historical newspapers including the British Library's *Penny Illustrated Newspaper*; File Cabinet is used to structure large libraries of material right down to the level of the page, and is well-suited to the publication of books.[19] Although periodicals are not strictly mixtures of books and newspapers, we found aspects of each of these existing applications essential to represent periodical form, and we worked with a new Olive product, Viewpoint, that combines aspects of both.

We also found periodical form difficult to conceptualize theoretically. Our initial attempts to map all the generic aspects of the periodical produced a set of relationships so unwieldy as to challenge visual representation.[20] We tested parts of our schema with Olive and, after much work, achieved some positive results. Figure 9.9 shows a screenshot from an early pilot that identifies, without human markup, four levels of hierarchy on the page. The first of these levels – which is itself located in specific number, volume and title – is the department 'Portfolio.' Next is the first component within the department, a serial novel entitled 'The Apprenticeship of Life'. The subsequent level is a heading that states which instalment of the novel we are reading, 'First Episode'. Last, comes the chapter itself, 'Chapter One. The Young Skeptic'. This hierarchy is represented schematically in the Table of Components on the left of the image, and 'First Episode' is highlighted on the page on the right.

Working to develop a system that could identify formal categories and locate them in a hierarchy encouraged us to ask questions of the periodicals. For instance, although the hierarchy described above seems intuitive and is apparent to the eye, the level that denotes the instalment 'First Episode' largely repeats information contained in the title of the chapter itself, 'Chapter One. The Young Skeptic'. Such redundancies, and the problems with connecting generic categories that appear differently across titles (and indeed, moments within runs of single titles), encouraged us to develop a more stripped down structural model:

ncse > title > volume > number > department > item

---

19 For an overview of Olive applications see <http://www.olivesoftware.com/products/>, accessed 10 March 2008.

20 See <http://www.ncse.ac.uk/redist/pdf/data_map.pdf>, accessed 10 March 2008.

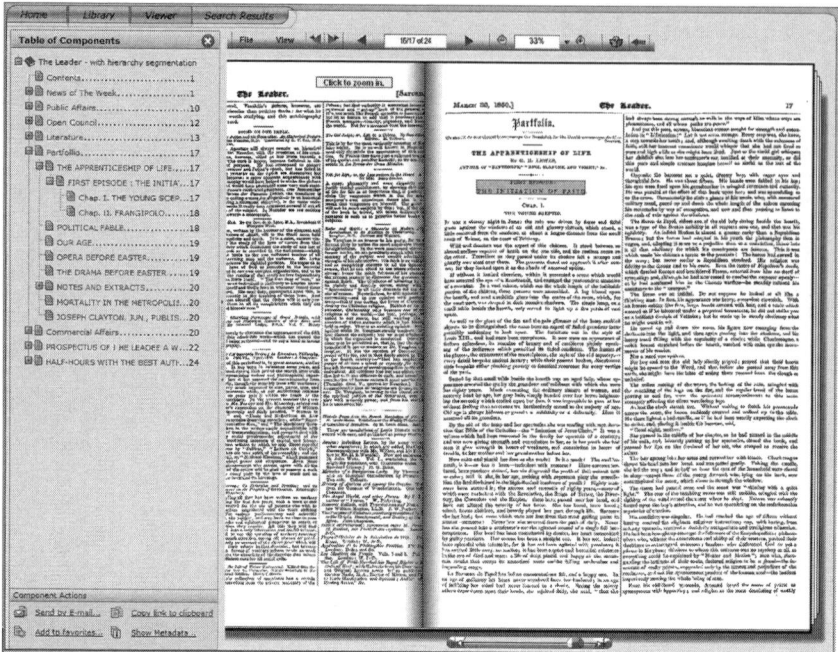

Figure 9.9   **An early pilot, displayed in File Cabinet, which shows four levels of hierarchy: Leader > Portfolio > The Apprenticeship of Life > First Episode > Chap. I. The Young Sceptic**

Source: Nineteenth-Century Serials Edition.

The first four levels are represented in a folder tree. The highest is the edition of six titles (plus nineteenth-century supplementary material and our own discursive essays); next are the titles themselves; then the bound volume; and finally the individual number that might be one of a number of editions. The final two levels are located on the page and the departments displayed in a Table of Components similar to the one on the left in Figure 9.9. The item remains the basic unit in ncse, but, as it also identifies components such as mastheads, handwriting, images and newspaper stamps, it is not synonymous with the article. Rather, the item describes any component on the page, and we use metadata to ensure that non-textual items can be returned in searches. As we generate thematic and formal metadata for each item, so users can compare types of item from across the edition.

Conclusion

In editing nineteenth-century periodicals today, we, like our nineteenth-century predecessors, are simultaneously editors, publishers and hawkers. When considering the periodical as genre, figures such as the author do not offer a suitable organizing principle; rather, the complex relationships that underpin periodical publication force editors to attend to the object as a whole. Whereas authors are conventionally responsible for their words, editors – both of nineteenth-century periodicals and twenty-first century digital editions – must make those words into an object. This involves identifying content, organizing it, developing presentational tools, identifying users, and then making it available to them. As always, this must be achieved under the constraints of time and money. Editing is always located at this intersection between an existing object and a new object: negotiating the relationship between them is not simply about reproduction, but also about transformation. What is important is to remember that such transformations entail losses as well as gains, and a fundamental part of the editorial process is identifying where these losses occur. In the digital domain, the transformation between media means we not only edit the source material, but also the means of making it into something new.

Chapter 10
Digitizing Inscribed Texts

Charlotte Roueché

For a scholar in the humanities, it can be intimidating to embark upon a project with a substantial technical component and then to formulate the experience in writing. My expertise is in Roman and late Roman epigraphy, the study of inscribed stones, and I am a relative newcomer to humanities computing. My contribution to the interrogation of the humanist's use for electronic resources is largely confined to my experience on one particular project and the issues that this has raised. This chapter therefore provides a narrative account of the project, setting out the practical issues, while trying to draw attention to the generic and methodological issues.

The material

Aphrodisias[1] in south-western Turkey, is a Graeco-Roman city which flourished from the late Hellenistic period (second century BC) to the end of antiquity (sixth-century AD). While the city does not often feature in literary accounts of the period, it is outstandingly rich in an excellent local marble. This had the consequence that it produced an unusually large quantity of sculpture, and of inscribed texts: even simple prohibitions or public notices are inscribed rather than painted.

Western visitors began to record inscribed texts at the site in the early eighteenth-century; and several hundred inscriptions had been published, by various authors, before the current excavations began, in 1960.[2] In the early 1960s New York University established a programme of systematic excavations, which still continue. In 1966 Joyce Reynolds, of Cambridge, began to record the inscriptions found by the current excavations; in the early 1970s I joined her, and we continued to record and publish inscriptions until 1995, when Angelos Chaniotis (of Heidelberg, now of All Souls' College, Oxford) took over.

This places upon us a basic responsibility. All scholars who gain access to remote and unique material acquire a duty to witness to what they have seen. Eighteenth and nineteenth-century travellers did what they could in the often

---

1 See <http://www.nyu.edu/projects/aphrodisias/>. All urls current at the time of writing, September 2007.

2 For a full account of the publications, see <http://insaph.kcl.ac.uk/bibliography/index.html>.

very difficult circumstances, transcribing as many texts as they were able. At Aphrodisias, Wood, a traveller in the eighteenth-century, copied texts on the pages of his interleaved Homer, presumably to save his supply of paper. Fellows, in 1840, mentions that there was plague in the village when he visited Aphrodisias; his transcriptions are not particularly accurate. J. Kennedy Bailie, an Irish divine, transcribed some inscriptions himself, but many more which he had lifted, without acknowledgement, from earlier publications.[3] In 1893 two Austrian scholars, Kubitschek and Reichel, spent ten days at Aphrodisias. Kubitschek transcribed over 80 texts; Reichel only transcribed 40, but produced far more careful and detailed renderings of the appearance of the texts and their monuments.[4] All these copyists had to choose what material to copy, and how fully to record it: they tended to focus, quite understandably, on longer or more complete texts. From the mid nineteenth-century some supplemented their copies with paper impressions, squeezes, which require time to produce. Squeezes are made by wetting sheets of absorbent paper, usually filter paper, and placing them over the face of an inscription which is then rubbed with a brush. The result is an excellent impression of the texture of the stone, of other markings, and of the letters of the inscription. The squeezes are also three-dimensional, unlike a photograph or drawing, and they scan particularly well.[5] Late in the century, photography started to be used at excavations; after the First World War, epigraphers started to transport cameras to more remote sites, but squeezes and drawings continued to be very important.

Compiling a full and accurate record, therefore, is an essential element of epigraphy; and the quality of data expected in such a record has steadily increased with the improvement in recording technologies. The total corpus of the inscriptions of Aphrodisias now includes about 2,000 texts – many very fragmentary. There are substantial practical problems in publishing such a corpus. The sheer volume of material is not very attractive to a publisher; and the situation is complicated by modern expectations. Modern editions provide far more information about each text than the early editions based on notebook copies; they are expected to include photographs, representing not only the texts themselves, but also their archaeological context. For an inscription has two identities: it is both a text – to be handled in the same way as any other text – but also an archaeological object, with a context.

Since most conventional publications are not easy to combine with illustrations, epigraphers have developed protocols for indicating information about the physical state of a text – square brackets to enclose missing material, underdots to indicate uncertain letters, etc. These evolved over more than a century; a standard set, for papyri and subsequently inscriptions, was eventually agreed during the 1930s (the

---

3 See L. Robert, *Hellenica* 13 (Limoges: A. Bontemps, 1965), pp. 152–4.

4 For a fuller account see C. Roueché, 'History and Bibliography of the Inscriptions', <http://insaph.kcl.ac.uk/bibliography/index.html>.

5 For an excellent collection of examples see 'Images from the Squeeze Collection of the Ohio State University' <http://omega.cohums.ohio-state.edu/epigraphy/inscriptions/>.

so-called Leiden conventions).[6] Discussions and refinements have continued ever since.[7] The resultant texts are not very easy reading for scholars who are unused to these conventions, and a consequence has been that inscribed texts are normally excluded from the canon of literary texts. One category of text which has received some attention is that of verse inscriptions, but even these have only received patchy consideration. At Aphrodisias, for example, we have a block carrying two verse inscriptions; one of them entered the literary tradition in antiquity, was recorded in the Greek Anthology and can be found in the Thesaurus Linguae Graecae (TLG), which is a collection of literary texts. The other adjacent text was only recorded on stone, and so is excluded, as 'only' an inscription. This kind of categorization reflects one of the aspects of paper publication, where the pressure must always be to reduce the scope of categories, in order to save space.[8]

Apparatus

There are no significant differences between the modern copies. In line 6, for ξυνὸν, AP has κοῖλον. The Byzantine copyist perhaps chose to 'improve' the text, and wrote κοινὸν which was subsequently corrupted to κοῖλον (as editors since Boeckh have conjectured); but see commentary, V.8.

Photographs

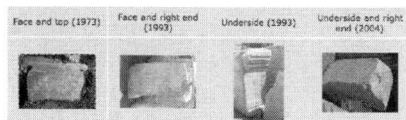

Commentary

For Asclepiodotus see also 54; see discussion at V.8 following.

Locations

› **Found:** Village: '*In muro apud Turcam domum in orientali pagi parte*' (Picenini); 'built into a village house, which has since been demolished' (NYU).
› **Original:** Unknown.
› **Last Recorded:** Museum.

Figure 10.1   Verse honours for Asclepiodotus

Source: http://insaph.kcl.ac.uk/iaph2007.

The project

It was for me, as I think it often is for others, the sheer question of volume which led me to start considering electronic publication. Working at King's, with colleagues in the Centre for Computing in the Humanities (CCH), undoubtedly made me

6 B.A. van Groningen, 'Projet d'unification des systèmes de signes critiques', *Chronique d'Égypte*, 7 (1932): 262–9.

7 So S. Dow, *Conventions in Editing: A Suggested Reformulation of the Leiden System* (Durham, NC: Duke University, 1969); H. Krummrey and S. Panciera, 'Criteri di edizione e segni diacritici', *Tituli*, 2 (1980): 205–15; S. Panciera, 'Struttura dei supplementi e segni diacritici dieci anni dopo', *Supplementa Italica* 8 (Rome: Quasar, 1991).

8 See <http://insaph.kcl.ac.uk/ala2004/inscription/eAla053.html> and <http://www.tlg.uci.edu>.

more aware of such possibilities. But my initial concept was a very simple one: I envisaged presenting a set of texts in HTML, accompanied by photographs and plans. When I first started thinking along these lines, in the early 1990s, the largest problem seemed to be the difficulty of finding a standard fount for Ancient Greek. To begin with I imagined presenting material on CD-ROM; it gradually became clear that the internet was likely to provide a better vehicle. By the early 2000s, a Unicode character set for ancient polytonic Greek had been agreed.[9]

In 1999 I was granted a two-year Research Readership by the British Academy to develop this project. I started by approaching an old pupil and colleague Charles Crowther, at the Oxford Centre for the Study of Ancient Documents.[10] This was an invaluable example of the importance of communication between projects; the Centre has acted for some time as a clearing-house for news of electronic projects in this field. Charles was able to put me in touch with Tom Elliott, of the Ancient World Mapping Centre, at the University of North Carolina at Chapel Hill,[11] who had just published a proposal for the publication of inscriptions in TEI-compliant XML – EpiDoc.[12] These were acronyms that I had heard at CCH, without any real understanding; and I doubt whether I would have engaged with the concepts involved if they had not been presented to me in terms of their direct application to my particular concerns. I see that as a recurrent problem: how do we bring together the specialist scholar and the person with the knowledge of how computing might contribute? Charles Crowther and Tom Elliott are among the few scholars in my field who combine both epigraphic and computing skills. It may be that the next generation of scholars will combine them as a matter of course; but it may equally be that the demands of both fields will continue to require partnerships of expertise, and that it will continue to be essential to establish channels of communication and dissemination.

In this instance there was an obvious case for partnership. Tom Elliott and I applied to the Leverhulme Trust for a one-year grant to test his EpiDoc by publishing some of my inscriptions; this was successful and the resultant Epidoc Aphrodisias Project (EPAPP)[13] began. We decided to start with a second edition of a volume that I had already published, *Aphrodisias in Late Antiquity* (London: Society for the Promotion of Roman Studies, 1989). The volume was out of print, and there was sufficient new material to make a second edition worthwhile; but the bulk of the academic work had been done, so that its conversion would be achievable in the time. Also, the resultant publication (which we referred to as *eALA*) would be something that could be directly compared with a book.

---

9 For a useful description see J. Kalvesmaki, 'Guide to Unicode Greek' <http://www.doaks.org/publications/unicodegreekguide.pdf>.

10 Oxford Centre for the Study of Ancient Documents <http://www.csad.ox.ac.uk/>.

11 Ancient World Mapping Centre, University of North Carolina at Chapel Hill <http://www.unc.edu/awmc/>.

12 See <http://www.epapp.kcl.ac.uk/desc.html> for a full description of the EpiDoc encoding standard.

13 Epidoc Aphrodisias Project (EPAPP) <http://www.epapp.kcl.ac.uk/>.

The Leverhulme grant allowed us to appoint Gabriel Bodard as a research assistant; Gabriel was completing a PhD on Greek tragedy, and had worked for a year at the TLG project (mentioned above). By the end of the year (in 2002) we had an online version assembled, although it was rather crude; and we had held two very useful workshops, in Chapel Hill and London, to talk to other epigraphers with similar interests.[14] In winter 2003 we were given a second three-year grant by the Arts and Humanities Research Council, to develop the project further and extend it to all the corpus of Aphrodisias inscriptions (*InsAph*); the grant also included provision for three workshops each year, to be held in the UK, mainland Europe and the USA.[15]

During the first year of the new project we developed and refined the *eALA* website, with particular focus on indexing and other functions which were essential for the next corpus. In early 2005 we published it as *ala2004*.[16] The site is stable, and will only be subject to non-content-bearing alterations. One of the principal aims of this second stage has been to develop, stabilize and disseminate internationally agreed protocols for such publication, and having *ala2004* online and available immediately made a great difference to this process: it was striking to me how difficult many people found it to imagine in advance what the site would be like, even though most of its functionality was paralleled elsewhere on the web. This suggests the importance, for this generation, of abundant and well-publicized pilot projects.

The funding for the project ended in April 2007. The first months of 2007, therefore, were taken up with completing the full corpus for publication – tasks which are really no different from those normally required to bring a publication to completeness. The electronic medium makes various kinds of checking and controlling easier, while at the same time introducing its own possibilities of error. But the essential work is what it always was – careful scholarly analysis for errors and lacunae, chasing references, deciding on spellings, etc. The whole point of the enterprise is to publish a scholarly work to the highest of standards. However, there will be some level of unfinishedness. We will not be able to provide full translations of every one of the 1,750 texts – simply because we have not had the time. But there we can exploit one of the great strengths of digital publication: we can make the essential information richly available before we have dotted the very last t, or reached the letter Z – we propose to produce at least one further edition of the corpus with this additional material. For large bodies of data of this type, this should prove to be an extraordinarily useful precedent – although it will be interesting to see how reviewers respond.

---

14 For details of these meetings, see <http://www.epapp.kcl.ac.uk/calendar.html>.

15 Inscriptions of Aphodisias Project <http://insaph.kcl.ac.uk>.

16 See <http://insaph.kcl.ac.uk/ala2004>.

Integration

Perhaps the single most recalcitrant task has been disseminating knowledge of the publication. We gave it an ISBN number, since it is the second edition of a book; but it remains a challenge to persuade librarians to catalogue it, particularly since it is free, and therefore does not trigger the usual accessioning process. Library practice in this area clearly varies widely; at King's the print version first edition and the online second edition are catalogued together (at my request!). In the British Library catalogue there are two copies of the first edition and no mention of the second. It is, I think, very important for this issue to be addressed. The silence of the catalogues reflects, and reinforces, a widespread sense among our peers that these are not 'real' publications: only a book is that.

Another crucial aspect of the project is its relationship to other digital undertakings in the field. Epigraphers have been exploring ways of using computers to organize their data for at least 20 years. Much of the pioneering work was done with Latin texts, since there were no fount problems. There are two large databases which put such material online, grouped as the Electronic Archive of Greek and Latin Epigraphy.[17] Of these, the database that has the simplest structure is the one in Rome, under the direction of Silvio Panciera.[18] At a meeting in Rome in October 2006, we undertook to make the EpiDoc schema compatible with the design of the Rome database. This will enable us to set up 'cross-walks' for material published in EpiDoc to be transferred directly into that database. Material in the database could also be exported, and transformed into other formats, via EpiDoc. This has taken some extra time, but it seems to us intrinsically valuable and an important part of making EpiDoc a fully accepted tool among epigraphers.

In Greek epigraphy the pattern has been somewhat different: the lead was taken by David Packard, who sponsored the development of a collection of epigraphic texts in electronic form. This was originally published on CD-ROM, but since 2005 it has been available online.[19] The site is a test site and contains a very rich collection of material, including all the texts from Aphrodisias published through 1993. In autumn 2006 we had a meeting with the administrators, and we are now working towards creating a link between their site and ours. The aim is that we should embed their identification numbers in our XML; that they should be able to obtain, automatically, from our site, new and updated texts; and that the users of their site should be offered a link directly to our publication.

Most important of all to us is that we illustrate what we are doing in our publication, and so encourage the take-up of EpiDoc by others for their own publications. Agreed standards are essential, but they do have to be agreed by the academic community concerned, not imposed by external 'experts'. We have worked hard to organize meetings where epigraphic colleagues would feel

---

17 See <http://www.eagle-eagle.it/>.

18 See <http://www.edr-edr.it/index_it.html>.

19 <http://epigraphy.packhum.org/inscriptions/>.

welcome, not threatened. Over the last three years we have held nine workshops, and given lectures, seminars and training sessions. The aim is to get epigraphers to perceive that EpiDoc encoding simply represents an extension of the approach which produced the Leiden conventions. As often in humanities computing, it is important to demonstrate that the intellectual activities and processes in what appear to be separate fields are in fact closely related.

Our essential aim in this process has been to establish a dialogue. Many epigraphers, and other humanities scholars, still expect to define a problem, hand it over to a group of 'technicians' and receive a shiny new machine in return. This is an approach that has made many software manufacturers and consultants very rich, but it is not financially viable for non-profit-making enterprises, and it is also not the way to develop resources that can grow and be sustained. The challenge is to persuade people to work together with humanities computing experts to devise solutions. Only rarely can there be a complete sharing of expertise, but there must be a shared area of interest and discussion. The barriers are often institutional: 'expertise' in computing is often seen as a separate skill, housed in a separate department.

Over the first two years of the project, therefore, we focused our workshops principally on reaching and involving 'stakeholders' – people working with inscriptions in excavations, in museums, in published corpora, in the search for onomastics, or for grammar. In the last year of the project we slightly shifted our focus to concentrate more on the production of a set of clear and usable tools. In March 2006 we organized a different kind of workshop: a week-long 'sprint', to work on a set of tools and guidelines for Epidoc. Twelve of us assembled: three epigraphers; six people who work on Greek or Latin and computing; one expert programmer; and two TEI experts. Directed by Tom Elliott, the sprint was hard work, but extremely fruitful.[20]

We held a second, smaller sprint in Chapel Hill in December 2006. Since then, I have been principally engaged in the activities which normally engage an author in the last stages of a publication – cross-checking, correcting, etc. In doing so, I have been able to use the tools created by my colleagues in the workshops, which meet my needs as an epigrapher.

The core element in the development of standards, therefore, is communication. It is not enough to assume that the internet will somehow magically disseminate good practice. It is necessary to discuss and debate in a real dialogue, without either kind of 'expert' assuming superiority. One element in this must be a matter of language. Both epigraphers and computing experts have their own acronyms – CIL, XML; it will be valuable, but difficult, to develop a shared language which is not rendered impenetrable by over-use of such conventions. This requires a certain amount of confidence on both sides, so that the experts do not feel that they need to assert their expertise through obscurity.

---

20 See <http://epidoc.sourceforge.net/development.shtml> for the results of this work.

A further essential element is that one should be able to demonstrate the true added value of the process, and this must reside in scholarly advantages for epigraphy. For me, starting with a vision of a few static HTML pages with lots of photographs simply to accommodate the volume of information, very little of the additional added value was initially apparent, but I have learned – and am still learning – a lot. One striking benefit of publishing in this way is being able to open out the possible avenues of approach for users. My web monograph is a linear progression, reflecting the design of my book, and is accompanied by a linear commentary. But the material can also be reached by date, by findspot, by type of monument, by type of text. This allows for far richer presentation and exploitation of the material. Now an honorific decree inscribed on a sarcophagus, which would in a conventional corpus have been located either under 'honorific' or under 'funerary' can be found under either heading. Experts with very different interests, looking for material relevant to the archaeological context, or to the literary resonances, can both be accommodated. Another important feature for material from an excavation which is still continuing is that in due course Professor Chaniotis, and our future successors, will be able to add material to the corpus, with no clumsy separate fascicules.

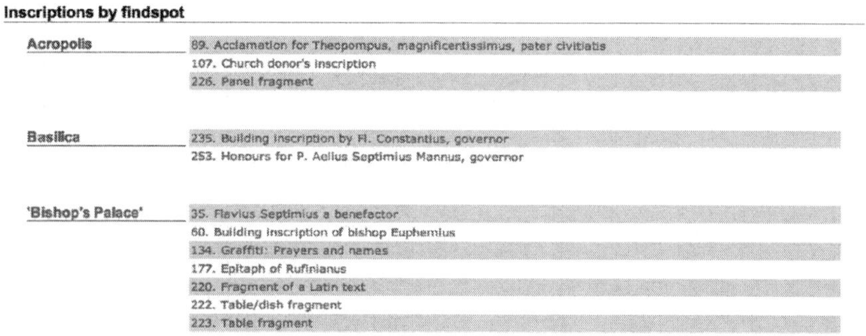

Inscriptions by findspot

Acropolis	89. Acclamation for Theopompus, magnificentissimus, pater civitatis
	107. Church donor's inscription
	226. Panel fragment
Basilica	235. Building inscription by Fl. Constantius, governor
	253. Honours for P. Aelius Septimius Mannus, governor
'Bishop's Palace'	35. Flavius Septimius a benefactor
	60. Building inscription of bishop Euphemius
	134. Graffiti: Prayers and names
	177. Epitaph of Rufinianus
	220. Fragment of a Latin text
	222. Table/dish fragment
	223. Table fragment

Figure 10.2   Inscriptions by findspot

Source: http://insaph.kcl.ac.uk/iaph2007.

A further aim for the new project was the possibility that several scholars – in our case in London, Cambridge, Oxford, Heidelberg, Paris and New York – could work within a single online workspace, contributing their particular expertise. This is something that we are still developing at present: the protocols are as important as the technology. Interestingly, the barrier has not been technological; what have to be overcome are issues of ownership of data, and the sense of authorship. What is the status of any one scholar's contribution to such a resource? These are issues that scientists have dealt with; but in the humanities such scholarly boundaries remain, even when the technology would make it possible to ignore them.

Inscriptions by date

Very uncertain	?128. Prayer of the builders
Second/third century	147. Epitaphs of anonymus, tabernarius, and of Euarestus
	148. Epitaph of Aurelia Dionysia
Third/fourth century	?8. Verse honours for a governor
	?147. Epitaphs of anonymus, tabernarius, and of Euarestus
	?148. Epitaph of Aurelia Dionysia
	?149. Epitaph of MMM. Aurrr. Peritianus, Eutyches and Heracleus
	?150. Epitaph of Vitus, also called Asterius, cursor of the phylae
	?193. Place inscription of Aelianus
	?196. Place inscription of men of Hierapolis
	?197. Place inscription of men of Hierapolis
	?220. Fragment of a Latin text

Figure 10.3   Inscriptions by date

Source: http://insaph.kcl.ac.uk/iaph2007.

More widely, an attraction for me is that these texts will be marked up in a schema compatible with other texts, whether they are written on stone or papyrus or transmitted by the manuscript tradition. We have been working closely with groups developing similar protocols for papyri; we have had very fruitful discussions with scholars involved in publishing Byzantine seal impressions, and others working on publications of coins. In the longer term, this should help to break down what have been essentially false distinctions between texts which all originate from the same cultural milieu, but are recorded on different media.

Dissemination

Integration, for me, describes the process of reaching colleagues and academics with such a resource. But the use of the new medium means that academic work is now in fact – not just in theory – accessible in quite a different way to the outside world. This raises the familiar question of accessibility, and the closely related one of authenticity. The publication of material in this way transforms the status of the scholar from guardian of treasured and expensive truths. To colleagues in London or Oxford our current project appears to be a luxurious extra addition to the normal tools of scholarship; but meetings with scholars and students from such countries as Turkey, Russia or Japan have brought home to me how transforming it can be to be offered direct access to primary sources, from which they have been effectively excluded by publishing costs and geographical constraints. Moreover, such material becomes accessible to a far wider circle than just scholars and students – one email I received came from the proprietor of an olive farm about 30 minutes from Aphrodisias.

This accessibility entails responsibilities. Firstly, once a resource of this kind is openly accessible to all, it needs to be far more lucidly and fully explained than a resource intended only for colleagues. An example of this is provided by the Prosopography of the Byzantine World (PBW).[21] This publication is the latest in a long series, and the first to be published online: it is instructive to look at the parent publication, Prosopographia Imperii Romani,[22] where the entries, written in Latin, are limited to brief references to publications described by acronyms. At the opposite end of the scale, the PBW includes an abundance of contextualizing text, with translations and a glossary. A question for the future must be: how much explanatory material must the original editor now provide? Is there a need for a new kind of interface publication to help intelligent interested people use the resource?

The other issue is that of authenticity – how do I know what I am reading? What is its status? What can I expect from it? As to authenticity, it is my belief that authentication mechanisms will develop. One of my hopes is that the various learned societies will consider whether they do not have a role here, similar to the kind of authentication which was once provided by a publisher's imprint. I see this as a question which requires rather more attention than it has received. There is much talk of peer review, but in this discussion, the principal concern seems to be that of academics as to whether they will receive due credit for work published in this way. The issue of accessibility means that scholars must also find ways to communicate the reliability of what they are reading to a wider public. It is easy to see this is as relatively unimportant in the area of humanities. But it is only necessary to consider what the situation would be if the inscriptions of Aphrodisias included a text which appeared to mention a visit by St Paul (unlikely but not impossible). This would interest a far wider audience than the normal readership for such material. How would they know how well to trust what they were reading? The Dan Brown[23] effect – and the range of resultant websites – can serve as a reminder that it may be as important to provide people with ways of finding reliable information about ancient history as about painkillers. At present we are a very long way from this.

And finally, I suppose, there is the issue of what this entity is. I do not know what to call my publication. Perhaps eMonograph? Web monograph? eCorpus? I assume that conventions will develop. And I imagine, too, that answers will develop to another intractable question: when a medium is so unlimited, how do I, the author, determine what I must do, and what I should leave to others? Very specifically, how deeply do I mark up the text? Do I just lemmatize words or start marking up past participles? Perhaps we come back to the word 'expert': my intervention should be limited to those matters on which I am uniquely expert, and other experts will take the material forward. I am certainly very grateful for the opportunity to explore these questions with real experts in humanities computing.

---

21 Prosopography of the Byzantine World <http://www.pbw.kcl.ac.uk>.

22 Prosopographia Imperii Romani <http://www.bbaw.de/bbaw/Forschung/Forschungsprojekte/pir/de/Startseite>.

23 Author of *The Da Vinci Code*, published in 2003, which has sparked widespread interest in biblical history, ancient history, grail legends and archaeology, but is steeped in consistent historical inaccuracy.

Chapter 11

Digital Genetic Editions: The Encoding of Time in Manuscript Transcription[1]

Elena Pierazzo

Writing, which includes correcting and rewriting, is a process that occurs in time as well as space. This simple and obvious statement involves many complex issues, both theoretical and practical, for the transcription and encoding of manuscript texts; it is ultimately, however, a matter of scholarly decision and tact, determined to a large extent by the kind of manuscript to be transcribed, whether to pursue these issues or not.

When a scholar examines a written text, especially a manuscript, the object of the investigation is usually to discover the final result of that writing and rewriting process. The examination can take various forms: it can be approached from a codicological/documentary point of view, 'photographing' the resulting product; from a textual point of view; or from a genetic point of view, by trying to describe the flow of authoring. The first approach is more typically taken in the transcription of scribal fair copies, the latter in dealing with autograph working or draft manuscripts, while the second can be applied to any kind of text product. All these points of view translate into different editorial practices and outcomes: for instance, diplomatic, critical and genetic editions. In recent years these editorial practices have been tested in the digital framework, and although many high-quality results have been achieved, not all issues have been positively considered and resolved. This is especially the case with timed genetic editions of modern working and draft manuscripts.

Digital editions of manuscripts (medieval or modern) have opened new possibilities to scholarship as they normally include fully searchable and browsable transcriptions (following one or more of the methodologies outlined above) and, in many cases, some kind of digital facsimile of the original source documents, variously connected to the edited text. Technical improvements in digital photography have for the first time allowed the international community to

1 The present essay contains an enlarged and revised version of a paper presented at *Digital Humanities 2007*, the 19th Joint International Conference of the Association for Computers and the Humanities, and the Association for Literary and Linguistic Computing held at the University of Illinois, Urbana-Champaign, 4–8 June 2007. I would like to thank all who have helped me in the preparation and revision of the present work: Arianna Ciula, Marilyn Deegan, Eleonora Litta Modignani Picozzi and Kathryn Sutherland.

enjoy easy access to high-quality reproductions of primary sources, deposited in libraries all over the world and otherwise inaccessible to the majority of scholars; printed photo-facsimile editions, though long available, have always been rare and extremely expensive. The wide availability and relatively low cost of the representation of sources in a digital environment is dramatically influencing editorial practice, not least in offering the possibility of reproducing and verifying the scholarly work done on the text, and effectively overruling the compactness of the critical apparatus. This is even truer for modern manuscript editions, where access to autographic source material has made genetic criticism more easily exploitable by a large community of scholars.

Furthermore, the new information technologies are leading to the creation of a different kind of edition, able to represent the different features of a text in a much more effective way. Textual editions based on digital encoding can, for instance, be easily presented on a website in different layout formats (readable version, diplomatic version, semi diplomatic version, and so on), some of them even offering to users the possibility of building their own visualization of the text. On the other hand, printed diplomatic, semi–diplomatic and genetic editions are rare and limited to the work of only a few important authors, as the high costs of their publication are not supported by the restricted specialist public towards whom they are targeted.

> The project of publishing the draft documents of texts in extenso (outline, scenarios, rough drafts, manuscripts, etc.) does not seem realistic, given the actual conditions of publishing and the existing norms in the marketplace of books, except in the case of short works (short stories, novellas, poems, etc.) that do not have a very developed genetic material.[2]

As an example, the critical edition of the juvenile notebooks, working and draft manuscripts of Jane Austen edited by R.W. Chapman[3] can be usefully mentioned here. The text Chapman had printed is a 'clean' final version, with all the authorial workflow that can be reconstructed through a deep investigation of the original source material relegated to notes at the end of the book. A digital research project on Jane Austen's autograph manuscripts began in 2006.[4] This will produce, as one

---

2 P.-M. de Biasi, 'Toward a Science of Literature: Manuscript Analysis', in J. Depmann, D. Ferrer and M. Groden (eds), *Genetic Criticism: Texts and Avant-textes* (Philadelpia: University of Pennsylvania Press, 2004), p. 62.

3 Single editions of Austen's working and draft manuscripts were published by Chapman from the 1920s; in 1954 they were collected in a volume – J. Austen, *Minor Works Now First Collected and Edited from the Manuscripts by R. W. Chapman, with Illustrations from Contemporary Sources* (1954) – from which the notes containing the deleted passages and other authorial phenomena are missing.

4 The Austen Project is a three-year AHRC-funded collaborative venture between Oxford University, the Bodleian Library, the British Library and King's College London, co-directed by Kathryn Sutherland and Marilyn Deegan.

of its outcomes, a website from which a multi-layout diplomatic–genetic edition will be available for browsing and searching. The transcribed texts will be placed side by side with high-quality facsimiles of the manuscripts. It is evident that this new edition (or multi-edition) will dramatically enhance the research possibilities for scholars of Jane Austen, as the editorial work will be offered in a transparent way, allowing other scholars to replicate, and therefore validate, or debate it in a more effective and detailed way than heretofore.

Many digital editions of (autographic) manuscripts already available on the web or on other kinds of digital support frames offer more or less the same possibilities, but most of them still avoid the crucial task of representing the different layers of authorial correction that occurred at different points in the authorial workflow.[5] A scholarly evaluation of timing is crucial in the case of modern autograph draft and working manuscripts (indeed, the 'restor*ation* of a temporal dimension to the study of literature' is considered as the main aim of genetic criticism itself by Jeb Deppman[6]). This is because the stratification of corrections, deletions and additions can give insights into an author's way of working, into the work itself, the evolution of the author's *Weltanschauung*, the meaning/interpretation of the text, and because (*mostly* because, according to genetic critical theorists) working and draft manuscripts, as well as final versions, are texts worth exploring in themselves. These are all issues highlighted in genetic criticism since the 1970s.[7] Genetic criticism (or *critique génétique*) has characterized the French school of philology over the last decades, concentrating around the activities promoted by ITEM (*L'Institut des Textes et Manuscrits Modèrnes*).[8] The theories and practices of genetic criticism have spread beyond France, and are now considered as fundamental scholarly approaches to any draft or working manuscript (*brouillons*). Yet while the scholarly methodologies of the French school have generally been positively appraised, their outcomes, in the shape of printed genetic editions, have been criticized as unreadable, unusable, time-consuming and, in general, deceptive. The obscure, intricate symbolism that necessarily characterizes such editions is perhaps the principal reason for their cold reception by the academic community; and indeed the need to represent the intricate stratifications of textual manipulations on a printed page may lead to an obscurity even greater than that recorded in the erasures and interlineations of the source manuscript. The new multi-layout edition model enabled by digital technologies may be the right answer to these

---

5 The Austen Project is indeed considering marking up timed sequences of corrections.

6 Depmann et al. (eds), *Genetic Criticism*, p. 2.

7 The argument is too complex to give more than basic references: A. Grésillon, *Eléments de critique génétique. Lire les manuscrits modernes* (Paris: Presses Universitaires de France, 1994) offers a good starting point; and Depmann et al. (eds), *Genetic criticism* offers a historical overview of the French school of genetic criticism.

8 More information about ITEM can be found at the Institute web site at <http://www.item.ens.fr/>, accessed 23 September 2007.

justifiable criticisms, but only with the understanding that the essential axis along which textual variation develops – time, that is – needs to be incorporated.

Medieval manuscripts, copied by one or more scribes, are also, of course, the result of a process occurring in time, but the different kind of authorship issues involved in such cases seems to imply a difference in the evaluation of the cultural weight of the possible recorded variants and corrections. Furthermore, as we will see below, modern draft and medieval fair-copy manuscripts are distinguished by different types of temporal axis as well as different usage functions, helping us to differentiate and characterize even more clearly the two different handwritten products.

Types of transcription (and edition)

Modern genetic critical theory differentiates between at least three kinds of transcription:

1. *Diplomatic transcription*: the text is transcribed with the intention of reproducing in the transcription all the features of the source document, including existing punctuation, marginal insertions reproduced in the exact position where they occur in the original, special characters and so on. The goal of such transcription is the reproduction of the actual appearance of the *document*.
2. *Linear transcription*: the text is transcribed in order to obtain a 'readable' version of the text, restoring, if necessary, the flow of writing and correction, inserting the eventual additions in the position where the author intended (or probably intended) them to be (with or without marks indicating their actual position), either marking in some way, or ignoring, deletions, either providing, or not providing, a critical apparatus. The goal of the transcription is the *text*.
3. *Timed transcription*: the transcription intends to witness all the different moments in which the author applied corrections, deletions and insertions to an original draft text. The goal of the transcription is the description of the *process*.

The first two types of transcriptions have been used and supported alternatively by genetic scholars: the diplomatic transcription being considered at the same time more faithful and not so worthy as it merely deciphers any writing obscurity without offering greater readability to the user; the linear transcription being more readable but open to the accusation of teleologism. Dirk Van Hulle, reporting the debate, suggests two possible strategies to solve the dispute: if a transcription is presented in combination with a facsimile, the linear transcription should be preferred 'precisely because it turns the image into a text'; and, even better, if 'the transcription is encoded in a markup language, the transcribed page can be presented in many ways',[9] meeting everyone's wishes. A third option has never been exploited in practice due to the impossibility for the printed page to effectively represent the time flow.

In a digital environment it is nowadays commonly assumed that text editions imply the application of some kind of markup, and in particular an XML markup conformant with the Text Encoding Initiative (TEI) Guidelines, the benefits of which are well understood in the humanities community: the ensuing transcription will share a common framework comprehensible to a large body of users and scholars; and the transcribed text can be presented in many ways, thanks to the application of different style sheets.[10]

Current encoding practice based on TEI Guidelines traditionally deals with the first two kinds of edition outlined above (diplomatic and linear); the first somewhat problematically, the second with much more ease. A recent development in the TEI encoding schema has now made possible the third kind of transcription. The difficulties presented by the diplomatic/documentary approach are to be detected in the default structural TEI framework which emphasizes the semantic structure of the text rather than its layout. A default TEI text structure allows the inclusion within the <body> element of a sequence of structural divisions (<div>s) that can be nested, either a sequence of paragraphs (<p>) and verses (<l>), or a sequence of anonymous blocks (<ab>).[11] A <p>-focused text,[12] where lines and page boundaries are marked by milestones, implies that of the two basic concurrent hierarchies (semantic and physical layout), the stressed one is <p>-based (that is, any segment of text is described by its meaning and function more than by its appearance), and an eventual page-based visualization is resolved through style sheets or any other kind of post-processing scripting language.

---

9 D. Van Hulle, *Textual Awareness: A Genetic Study of Late Manuscripts by Joyce, Proust and Mann* (Ann Arbor: University of Michigan Press, 2004), p. 36. Strangely enough, among the several possibilities offered by applying computing to genetic criticism, including computational text statistics and text mining, de Biasi did not include the transcription or the digital edition (de Biasi, 'Toward a Science of Literature: Manuscript Analysis', pp. 64–6).

10 See E. Vanhoutte, 'Editorial Theory in Crisis: The Concepts of Base Text, Edited Text, Textual Apparatus and Variant in Electronic Editions', paper presented at *DRH 2005*, Lancaster, 4–7 September 2005. Available online at <http://www.drh.org.uk/drh2005-abstracts.pdf>, accessed 23 September 2007; and E. Pierazzo, 'Just Different Layers? Stylesheets and Digital Edition Methodology', paper presented at *Digital Humanities 2006*, Paris, 5–9 July 2006. Available online at <http://www.allc-ach2006.colloques.paris-sorbonne.fr/DHs.pdf>, accessed 23 September 2007.

11 The TEI encoding model allows for many other layouts: for instance, for drama, the transcription of speeches, dictionaries and so on, but these possibilities are not relevant to our discussion.

12 The expression '<p>-focused text' is here used to exemplify any kind of semantically structured markup that is normally used in any TEI-encoded document, including encoding based on <ab>.

This approach works well only in the case of 'clean' texts, such as classical or medieval fair-copy manuscripts; but the results are limited in the case of chaotic modern draft manuscripts. Accordingly, many projects have adopted their own textual approach, by customizing the TEI environment and creating folio elements (or page or any other similar elements), as well as specific elements for lines (or using the <l> element) and liminal regions. This is the case, for instance, of the model presented by Aurèle Crasson and Jean–Daniel Fekete:[13]

```
<folio id="folio-18v"
rend="image(jabs/images/manuscrits/m18versog.jpg) width(1008)
height(1134)">
    <fragment id="folio-18v-2-33" rend="rect(179 473 916 664)">
    <l id="folio-18v-2-9">on le verra
    <del id="folio-18v-2-10">dans</del>
    <add id="folio-18v-2-11" place="supralinear">visiter</add>
    le Musée <del id="folio-18v-2-12">puis</del> et
    </l>
    <l id="folio-18v-2-13">en sortir, peu <del>aprés</del> de temps
aprés ;          <del>et</del> y
    </l>
    <l id="folio-18v-2-14">penétrer, à nouveau, mais,
    <del id="folio-18v-2-15">cette fois</del>,
      par la
    </l>
    <l id="folio-18v-2-16">Grand pyramide.</l>
    </fragment>
</folio>
```

This situation may change, even considerably, when the first release of the new TEI P5 becomes generally available for use in future digital editions.

The new version, in fact, includes a new element <facsimile> able to contain detailed information about the digital facsimile of the source manuscript that often (if not always) is provided beside the transcribed text in digital editions.[14] Such an element provides a way of defining areas (<zone>) of the image to be referenced from the transcribed text by identifiers (the ID/IDREF mechanism) delimiting the start and the end of a zone. This will allow the connection of text and images at any desired level of granularity; but it will still not support the transcription of manuscripts that hardly fit into the semantic <p>-based TEI model, even if it constitutes a good basis for further developments.

---

13 A. Crasson and J.-D. Fekete, *Structuration des manuscrits: Du corpus à la région* (2004). Available online at <http://www.lri.fr/~fekete/ps/CrassonFeketeCifed04-final.pdf>, p. 4, accessed 23 September 2007.

14 Available at <http://www.tei-c.org/release/doc/tei-p5-doc/en/html/PH.html#PH FAX>, accessed 23 September 2007.

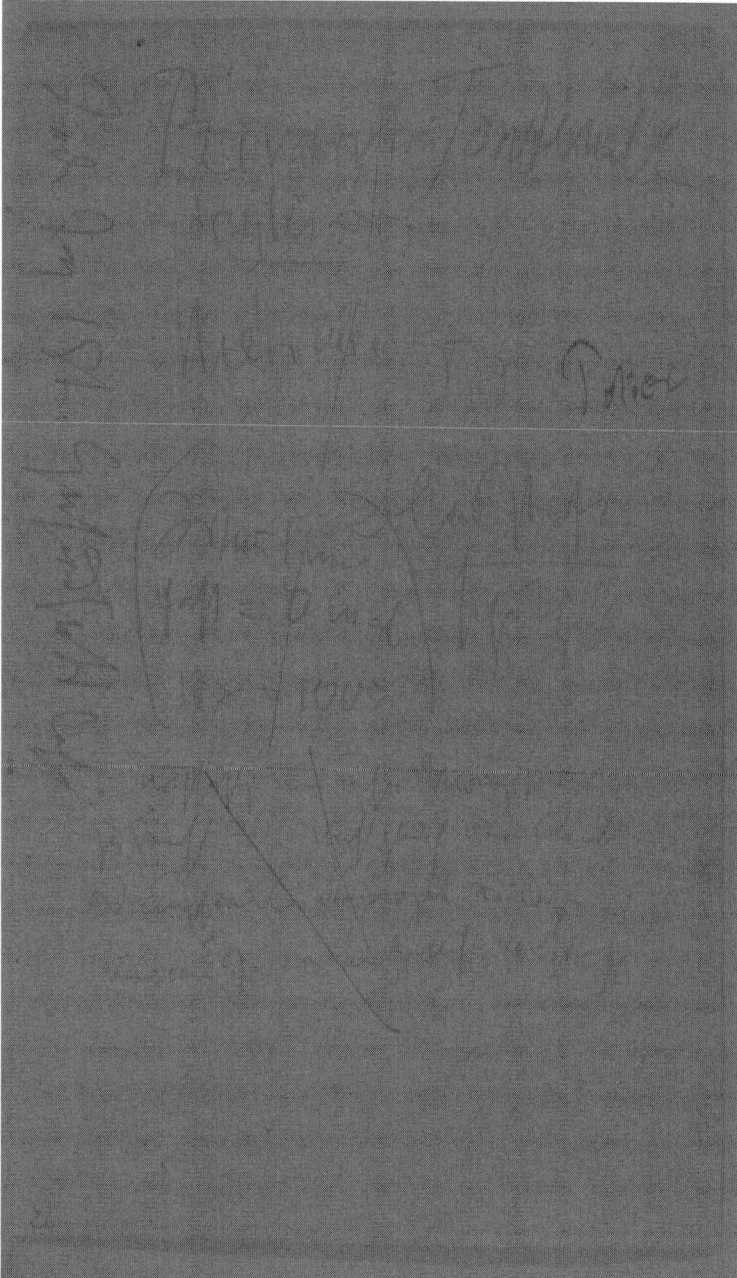

Figure 11.1   Notebook N IV 1, p. 50

Source: © Stiftung Weimarer Klassik und Kunstsammlungen, Goethe- und Schiller-Archiv, Weimar 2003.

In the case of some working manuscripts it is, in fact, extremely difficult to determine the semantic nature of a block of text (a paragraph? an item? a floating fragment?) and its relations with other blocks (see, for instance many examples from the Nietzsche notebooks published and transcribed by the HyperNietsche Project).[15] In these situations a descriptive layout approach (instead of a semantic approach), with anonymous blocks geographically referenced might be more suitable. So, for instance, a structural markup based on <page> (or <leaf> or <div type="page">), <region> (or <ab type="region">) and <line> (or <seg type="line">) can probably describe the document without forcing the interpretation of the content.

Table 11.1   Customized geographical markup versus TEI standard markup

Customized (semantic sugar)	Standard TEI markup
<page>	<div type="page">
<region place="margin-left"	<ab type="region-margin-left"
direction="top-to-bottom">	subtype="top-to-bottom">
<line></line>	<seg type="line"></seg>
<line></line>	<seg type="line"></seg>
</region>	</ab>
<region place="main"	<ab type="region-main"
direction="left-to-right">	subtype="left-to-right">
<line></line>	<seg type="line"></seg>
<line></line>	<seg type="line"></seg>
</region>	</ab>
</page>	</div>

Linear transcriptions (the second editorial option) are normally very well supported by the TEI encoding model. The Guidelines recommend the transcription of insertions and deletions exactly where they were placed by the author, the @place attribute of the <add> and <addSpan> elements providing the location of the insertions and @hand for <add>-like and <del>-like elements providing the means of describing the hand/responsibility of the correction. Other attributes such as @rend and @type (and some others) complete the range of possibilities for describing peculiar features in the text.

For timed transcriptions (the third editorial option), on the contrary, nothing (or very little) really existed until November 2007, either by way of markup practice or general guidelines. This kind of transcription has always constituted the secret

---

15 Available at <http://www.hypernietzsche.org/type_list.php?type=notebook>. The image has been downloaded from <http://www.hypernietzsche.org/egrepalysviola-101>, accessed 21 September 2007.

dream of genetic scholars, but it has virtually never been realized in print as time-based editions are extremely difficult to represent in that medium, because of the bi-dimensionality of paper sheets.

On voudrait représenter dans la bidimensionalité des pages un processus génétique dont on s'est pourtant appliqué à montrer que sa propriété est d'ajouter à l'écrit, qui est bidimensionel, une troisième dimension, qui est celle du temps![16]

In a digital framework, however, bi-dimensionality can be overruled by a hypertextual/multimedia approach that allows the creation of a more flexible context for the presentation of a genetic edition.

The problem of time-based encoding has been intensively discussed in recent years (for example, by the TEI Manuscripts SIG Meeting Report 01,[17] and by Edward Vanhoutte,[18] who suggests that the markup solution employed in the transcription of speech might be adapted for timed written records). A first detailed proposal was advanced by Pierazzo in 2007,[19] and only with TEI P5 1.0 (released on November 2007) has a comprehensive encoding model been offered to the community of scholars.

Temporal axes

Genetic scholars have outlined the existence of two different types of temporal axes involved in the writing process:

1. *Syntagmatic axis*: represents the teleological text flow, not only from a content (tale's time flow) point of view, but principally from a writing (writing the text from the first to the last word) point of view. It represents the 'normal' time of writing.

---

16 'You would like to represent in the bi-dimensionality of pages a genetic process to which you have strained to demonstrate that its feature is to add to writing, which is bi-dimensional, a third dimension, that is time': Grésillion, *Eléments de critique génétique*, p. 121.

17 The TEI 'Special Interest Group' on manuscripts met for the first time in Nancy (8 November 2003). Minutes and documents produced there are available from the TEI website at <http://www.tei-c.org.uk/Activities/SIG/Manuscript/mssigr01.xml.ID=body.1_div.3>, accessed 23 September 2007.

18 E. Vanhoutte, 'Putting Time Back in Manuscripts. Text Ontology, Critique Génétique and Modern Manuscripts', in *ALLC/ACH 2002*, Tübingen, Germany, 24–28 July 2002.

19 E. Pierazzo, 'The Encoding of Time in Manuscript Transcription: Towards Genetic Digital Editions', in *Digital Humanities 2007*, Urbana Champaign, USA, 4–8 June 2007. Available online at <http://www.digitalhumanities.org/dh2007/abstracts/xhtml.xq?id=172>, accessed 23 September 2007.

2. *Paradigmatic axis*: represents the choice between different versions of the text. In temporal terms, it represents the rewriting of the same segment.

It is very difficult to find cases in which we have values in just one of the two axes; nevertheless, their relevance may vary with different kinds of manuscript. A 'clean' or fair copy will have a high rate on the syntagmatic axis, but a very low one on the paradigmatic axis. In contrast, a draft autograph modern manuscript will have a variable value on the syntagmatic axis (very low in the case of miscellaneous notebooks) but a very high rate on the paradigmatic one. Correspondence is a peculiar kind of manuscript source, and, according to temporal analysis proposed so far, letters normally have a high value on the syntagmatic axis, though they may have high values on the paradigmatic axis as well, according to the degree of formality of a particular letter (the higher the formality, the lower the values in the paradigmatic axis). (See Figure 11.2.) The different relevance of the two temporal axes is perhaps more reliable than other criteria by which to distinguish modern draft from medieval (or classic) manuscripts. The distinction is of great importance since these two kinds of artefact require different methods and approaches.

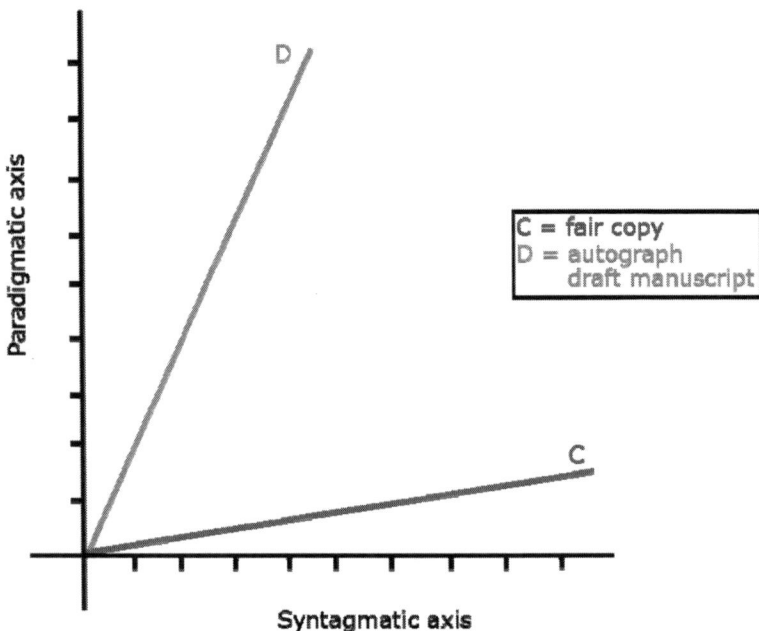

Figure 11.2   Temporal axis

The introduction of print eventually saw the relegation of the manuscript state mainly to the role of the draft, though of course there were exceptions. Consequently, when we speak of 'modern manuscripts', we normally imply autograph or holograph draft manuscripts, along with the assumption that, once the authoring process is completed, the text takes on a printed or some other kind of 'stable' form. The manuscript is accordingly considered mainly as a support for authoring or proofreading and the printed format is reserved for reading. Furthermore

> the most fundamental difference between these two kinds of documents [i.e. modern and medieval manuscripts] is the private nature of modern manuscripts. While scribal copies were means of communication, written manuscripts gradually lost this public status, especially after the invention of print technology.[20]

There are, of course, modern texts that continue to circulate in manuscript form or to have an initial manuscript circulation and a subsequent print circulation, but they are a minority of cases.[21]

Temporal analysis of authorial corrections

The segmentation of the text into paradigmatic syntagms (i.e. chunks of text in which some paradigmatic alteration has occurred) and the detection of the temporal sequence of such alterations are major editorial tasks and sometimes simply hopeless in practice. It is not, however, the objective of this chapter to deal with the difficulties of de-coding the authorial workflow, but how to handle it once that the segmentation has been satisfactorily carried out.

Let us consider a couple of examples taken from page 3595 of Giacomo Leopardi's *Zibaldone*.[22]

Example 1

Figure 11.3   Leopardi, *Zibaldone*, p. 3595, line 6

Transcription: 'che e' si rechi a' dotti denti l'un d'essi cibi' ('that you bring to learned people teeth one of those provisions').

---

20 Van Hulle, *Textual Awareness*, p. 8.

21 Let us think, for instance, of works condemned and prohibited by the Inquisition (or by any other institution) that broadly circulated in manuscripts up to the nineteenth-century, such as the manuscripts of Pietro Giannone.

22 G. Leopardi, *Zibaldone di pensieri. Edizione fotografica dell'autografo con gli indici e lo schedario*, ed. E. Peruzzi, 10 vols (Pisa, 1989), vol. 8, p. 3595.

In the above line we can detect two corrections: (1) deletion of the line under 'si' and (2) deletion of 'dotti' corrected into 'denti'. However, the authorial flow is more complex than this. We can try to draw the timing of the creation of the segment as follows:

- Time 1: writing 'che e' si rechi a' dotti'
- Time 2: deletion of 'dotti'; consequent writing of 'denti'
- Time 3: underlining of 'si'
- Time 4: deletion of the line under 'si'
- Time 5: underlining of 'rechi' and 'denti'
- Time 6: writing of 'l'un d'essi cibi'

Other timetable combinations could also be possible, but let us assume this is the more probable. Such a transcription tries to model the real flow of writing, but such a model may not be workable. In fact, it will fragment the flow of the plain writing (syntagmatic axis) into potentially infinite pieces. To simplify (and modelling is indeed a simplification process), we can assume as Time 0 (default) the time of the normal plain writing flow, timing only subsequent corrective interventions (paradigmatic axis). The schedule will then be modified as follows:

- Time 0: writing 'che e' si rechi a' dotti'
- Time 1: deletion of: 'dotti'
- Time 0: writing of 'denti'
- Time 2: underlining of 'si'
- Time 3: deletion of the underline under 'si'
- Time 4: underlining of 'rechi' and 'denti'
- Time 0: writing of 'l'un d'essi cibi'

A further simplification is also possible: assuming that – in genetic critical terms – so-called 'writing variants' (deletion of a single word substituted by another that immediately follows on the same line) occur while the normal writing flow takes place, the following model can be drawn:

- Time 0: writing 'che si rechi a' dotti'; deletion of: 'dotti'; writing of 'denti'; writing of 'l'un d'essi cibi'
- Time 1: underlining of 'si'
- Time 2: deletion of the underline under 'si'
- Time 3: underlining of 'rechi' and 'denti'

This last assumption should not imply that any in-line correction is to be considered to have been done at Time 0, but just the one followed by its correction. In fact, in the case of the deletion of an adjective or of any other word not essential from a syntactical point of view, the correction can occur at any time. Writing variants are connoted by the paradigmatic axis, but can also be considered as a sort of perturbation on the syntagmatic axis.

Example 2[23]

Figure 11.4   Leopardi, *Zibaldone*, p. 3595, line 11

Transcription: 'che di due ° più Eroi a̶ ° più quanto si voglia pari di' ('that of two [or more] heroes t̶o̶ o̶r̶e̶ m̶o̶r̶e̶ as good as').

This passage can be timed as follows:

- Time 1: writing 'che di due Eroi a';
- Time 2: deletion of 'a';
- Time 3: writing of 'quanto si voglia pari di'
- Time 4: interlinear addition of 'o più' after 'Eroi'
- Time 5: deletion of the addition
- Time 6: interlinear addition of 'o più' after 'due'

Or, in the simplified version, as follows:

- Time 0: writing of 'che di due Eroi a'; deletion of 'a'; writing of 'quanto si voglia pari di'
- Time 1: interlinear addition of 'o più' after 'Eroi'
- Time 2: deletion of the addition
- Time 3: interlinear addition of 'o più' after 'due'

Example 3

Example 3 (Figure 11.5) is taken from the initial page of the surviving fragment of Jane Austen's working manuscript of *Persuasion*.

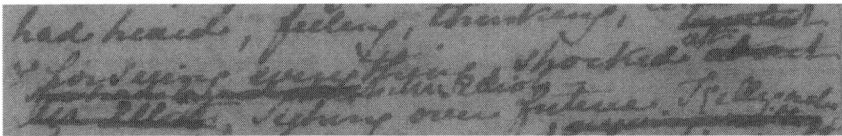

Figure 11.5   Austen, *Persuasion*, British Library Ms. Egerton 3038, p. 1

Transcription: '& forseeing everything, shocked at b̶y̶ w̶h̶a̶t̶ a̶b̶o̶u̶t̶ /
M̶r̶ E̶l̶l̶i̶o̶t̶ l̶e̶a̶r̶n̶e̶d̶ a̶b̶o̶u̶t̶ M̶r̶ E̶l̶l̶i̶o̶t̶ Mr Elliot, sighing over future Kellynch'

---

23 Ibid.

- Time 0: writing of '& forseeing everything, shocked about Mr Elliot, sighing over future Kellynch'
- Time 1: deletion of 'about Mr Elliot' and addition of 'by what learned about Mr Elliot'
- Time 2: deletion of 'by what learned about Mr Elliot'; addition of 'at' and 'Mr Elliot'

What we can infer from this model is that the syntagmatic axis (including perturbations as writing variants) should be considered as the default time flow and, from a genetic point of view, neutral and not relevant. Indeed, the aim of time-based encoding ought to be the evaluation of the corrections on the paradigmatic axis.

The encoding

A timed digital genetic edition of the above-mentioned texts needs to enable users to browse among different versions of the text that – in a given time – existed on the author's page. Once the text has been encoded in XML (TEI), through the application of different style sheets (and/or other scripts, such as JavaScript, for instance) to the encoded texts, it will be possible to show all the different stages and to give the user the possibility of browsing among them.

Example 1

- Time 0: che e' si rechi a' ~~dotti~~ denti l'un d'essi cibi
- Time 1: che e' <u>si</u> rechi a' ~~dotti~~ denti l'un d'essi cibi
- Time 2: che e' <u>si</u> rechi a' ~~dotti~~ denti l'un d'essi cibi
- Time 3: che e' <u>si</u> <u>rechi</u> a' ~~dotti~~ <u>denti</u> l'un d'essi cibi

Example 2

- Time 0: che di due Eroi a quanto si voglia pari di
- Time 1: che di due Eroi a ° più quanto si voglia pari di
- Time 2: che di due Eroi a ° più quanto si voglia pari di
- Time 3: che di due ° più Eroi a ° più quanto si voglia pari di

Example 3

- Time 0: & forseeing everything, shocked about / Mr Elliot, sighing over future Kellynch
- Time 1: & forseeing everything, ~~shocked~~ by what ~~about / Mr Elliot~~ learned about Mr Elliot, sighing over future Kellynch
- Time 2: & forseeing everything, ~~shocked~~ at by what ~~about / Mr Elliot~~ learned about ~~Mr Elliot~~ Mr Elliot, sighing over future Kellynch

To mark up these textual segments many customized models could be chosen,[24] but only the TEI proposal will be discussed here in detail as it provides an exemplification of the way such matter could be handled and as it is destined – due to the key role held by the TEI in the humanities – to influence deeply any subsequent research project, regardless of whether the model has been embraced or consciously refused. The new release of TEI P5 (version 1.0, November 2007[25]) offers scholars the facility to encode time sequences in a shareable way. It has been introduced in response to the requests of many users who, in recent years, have strongly pushed for a means to encode genetic dossiers in a convenient and unified way. The model is certainly a good attempt to address such needs, but there is still room for improvement: as users test it in practice and challenge its boundaries, new requirements will arise and new solutions will have to be found.

The TEI model is based on the introduction of the element <subst> to wrap a couplet of deletion and addition, but this binary model is hardly enough to describe the complexities of the writing and the rewriting process. I suggest that a new element <revision> should be implemented to wrap a textual segment (or, in other words, a paradigmatic syntagm) in which corrections have occurred. This element has to be used in combination with a @seq attribute carried by <add> and <del> elements to mark the temporal sequence of authorial interventions. According to this model, the first example presented above may be encoded as follows:

```
<snippet>
     che e' <revision [in bf]>
     <del type="underline deletion" seq="2">
     <hi rend="underline" seq="1">si</hi>
     </del>
     <hi rend="underline" seq="3">rechi a'</hi>
     <del type="overstrike">dotti</del>
     <hi rend="underline" seq="3">denti</hi>
</revision [in bf]> l'un d'essi cibi
</snippet>
```

The above markup nevertheless assumes an extension in the usage of the @seq attribute to the <hi> ('highlight') element, as the underlining is being considered as a part of the correction process.[26] These small extensions clearly show the kind of adjustment the proposed model will require to fit real-life projects. It is inevitable, though, that

---

24 See for instance, the ones proposed by Vanhoutte, 'Putting Time Back in Manuscripts'; and by Pierazzo, 'The Encoding of Time in Manuscript Transcription'.

25 And therefore not yet public at the time of writing (September 2007). I would like to thank Arianna Ciula, member of the TEI Council, who kindly allowed me to access the working draft.

26 In this case, the underlining clearly occurred *after* the normal flow of writing (syntagmatic axis), otherwise 'dotti' (writing variant) would also have been underlined as well.

any abstract and generalized model, such as the TEI necessarily needs to be, will require continuous tweaks and implementation to suit the needs of real texts.[27]

The second example may be encoded as follows:

```
<snippet>
    <revision [in bf]>
    che di due <add place="intralinear" seq="3">o più</add> Eroi <del
type="overstrike">a</del>
    <del type="overstrike" seq="2">
    <add place="interlinear" seq="1">o più</add>
    </del> quanto si voglia pari di
    </revision [in bf]>
</snippet>
```

And the third:

```
<snippet>
    <abbr>&amp;</abbr> forseeing everything, shocked
    <revision [in bf]>
    <del rend="overstrike" seq="1">about</del>
    <add place="superlinear" seq="2">at </add>
    <del rend="overstrike" seq="2">
    <add place="superlinear" seq="1">by what</add>
    </del>
    <lb/>
    <del rend="overstrike" seq="1">
    <abbr>M<am rend="sup">r</am></abbr> Elliot
    </del>
    <del rend="overstrike" seq="2">
    <add place="superlinear" seq="1">learned about <abbr>M<am
rend="sup">r</am></abbr>
    Elliot –
    </add>
    </del>
    <add place="superlinear" seq="2">
    <abbr>M<am rend="sup">r</am></abbr> Elliot
    </add>
    </revision [in bf]>, sighing over future Kellynch
    <lb/>
</snippet>
```

---

27 And, indeed, the TEI provides a simple mechanism to customize and extend the core schema, also providing clear Guidelines on how to do this in a compliant 'clean' way. See L. Burnard and S. Bauman (eds), *TEI P5: Guidelines for Electronic Text Encoding and Interchange* (2007), in particular 'Using the TEI', available at <http://www.tei-c.org/release/doc/tei-p5-doc/en/html/USE.html>, accessed 23 September 2007.

The TEI Guidelines also provide another encoding for timed corrections, based on the critical apparatus model where a @varSeq attribute is provided for the <app> element with almost the same meaning as @seq. The text of the Guidelines suggests here that the usage of the two models is equivalent.[28] In this case one might argue that normally a critical apparatus is built in order to register variants from other witnesses of the same text[29] and not for transcribing the variants provided by the same source document. And indeed a critical edition and a genetic dossier have different goals and methods, and therefore the two models should not be contaminated.[30] The idea of 'variant' itself (recorded in a critical apparatus, implying one text with alternative formulations) is to be refused in a genetic critical framework, to be replaced by paradigmatic substitutions.

Relative or absolute?

The first two examples examined above from Leopardi's *Zibaldone* occur on the same page: should we then consider Time 1 of the first example the same as Time 1 of the second example? The answer should be: no – very little can be said about the timing of editorial/authorial interventions in two different segments. The possibility of establishing an absolute timing for corrections is applicable only where we have strong palaeographic evidence or authorial declarations dating or describing a revision. For instance, we can imagine that authors might be in the habit of typewriting their texts and then correcting them by hand: in this case the assumption of an absolute time is possible. But since different layers of hand corrections can also occur, there will be, even in this case, the necessity of considering relative timed interventions.

The model proposed by TEI fits a relative-time framework only, as from the Guidelines, the @seq values are reset within any <revision> group of corrections, and no mention of an absolute framework is made. Certainly a way can be found

---

28 A previous version of P5 (version 0.8, generated 25 July 2007), that did not include the <subst> element or the @seq attribute, recommended the <app> method to deal with complex situations: 'As a rule, it is recommended that the <app> method be used for encoding substitutions of any complexity. It is also desirable that the one method be used throughout any one transcription. Accordingly, the <app> method is recommended for text-critical transcription of primary textual materials requiring encoding of instances of other than straightforward substitution' <http://www.tei-c.org/release/doc/tei-p5-doc/en/html/PH.html, accessed on 21 September 2007; no longer available from the TEI website but still downloadable as source file from <http://sourceforge.net/project/showfiles.php?group_id=106328&package_id=141127>.

29 And, indeed, so state the Guidelines: 'Scholarly editions of texts, especially texts of great antiquity or importance, often record some or all of the known variations among different *witnesses* to the text' <http://www.tei-c.org/release/doc/tei-p5-doc/en/html/TC.html#TCTR>, accessed 23 September 2007.

30 See Van Hulle, *Textual Awareness*, part 1 for a thorough exposition and comparison between different editorial schools.

to encode an absolute-time sequence, either by extending the usage of the @seq attribute, or by creating some new elements or attributes. But this option needs to be carefully considered before being endorsed.

As already suggested, an electronic edition is able to display the third editorial dimension, but this possibility needs to be managed with care as an incorrect consideration of time as absolute or relative can bring to display texts that never existed. Let us imagine for a moment that we build a tool able to display at one time all variants of a given text that are marked as either Time 1, Time 2 or Time 3 and so on: the results could consists in the display of textual stages that never existed in practice, including variants that might have existed at different points in time. In the absence of explicit authorial declarations or of graphic evidence, the only possible display and encoding would be to show the timing of variants segment by segment: that is, to give evidence only of relative timed corrections.

Genetic criticism can discover great advantages in new information technologies, not only because the multiple layout of the transcribed text and the possibility of connecting it to facsimile representations of the source manuscript can cater for diversified user needs, but because the temporal dimension can be better represented in digital than in print format. Digital solutions must therefore be accompanied by an accurate appraisal of the kind of temporality that the encoding needs to consider. An incorrect assessment of the temporal phenomena involved may lead to an unfruitful and misleading complication of the encoding or to versions of a text that never existed.

Bibliography

ABM-Utvikling, *Digitalisering og tilgjengeliggjøring for kultur og læring*, Prosjektrapport (Oslo: ABM-Utvikling, 2006).

Andersen, J., 'The Materiality of Works: the Bibliographic Record as Text', *Cataloguing and Classification Quarterly*, 33 (2002): 39–65.

Anon., 'Address', *Unitarian Chronicle and Companion to the Monthly Repository* (1832): 1–2.

Atkinson, R., 'An Application of Semiotics to the Definition of Bibliography', *Studies in Bibliography*, 33 (1980): 54–73.

Austen, J., *Minor Works Now First Collected and Edited from the Manuscripts by R. W. Chapman, with Illustrations from Contemporary Sources* (London: Oxford University Press, 1954).

Austin, J.L., *How to Do Things with Words*, ed. J.O. Urmson (Oxford: Clarendon Press, 1962).

Avalle, D.S., *Principi di critica testuale* (Padova: Antenore, 1972).

Barchas, J., *Graphic Design, Print Culture and the Eighteenth-Century Novel* (Cambridge: Cambridge University Press, 2003).

Bédier, J., 'La tradition manuscrite de Lai de l'ombre', *Romania*, 54 (1928).

Beetham, M., *A Magazine of Her Own? Domesticity and Desire in the Woman's Magazine, 1800–1914* (London: Routledge, 1996).

Berrie, P., Eggert, P., Barwell, G. and Tiffin, C., 'Authenticating Electronic Editions', in L. Burnard, K. O'Brien O'Keefe and J. Unsworth (eds), *Electronic Textual Editing* (New York: Modern Language Association, 2006), pp. 436–48.

Bevan, E.R., *The House of Ptolemy* (London: Methuen, 1927). Available online at <http://penelope.uchicago.edu/Thayer/E/Gazetteer/Places/Africa/Egypt/_Texts/BEVHOP/4F*.html>.

de Biasi, P.-M., 'Toward a Science of Literature: Manuscript Analysis', in J. Depmann, D. Ferrer and M. Groden (eds), *Genetic Criticism: Texts and Avant-textes* (Philadelpia: University of Pennsylvania Press, 2004), pp. 36–68.

Bjelland, K., 'The Editor as Theologian, Historian and Archaeologist: Shifting Paradigms within Editorial Theory and their Sociocultural Ramifications', *Analytical and Enumerative Bibliography*, 1 (2000): 1–43.

Bowers, F., *Textual and Literary Criticism: The Sandars Lectures in Bibliography 1957–1958* (Cambridge: Cambridge University Press, 1966).

Bowers, F., 'Principle and Practice in the Editing of Early Dramatic Texts', in F. Bowers, *Textual and Literary Criticism: The Sandars Lectures in Bibliography 1957–1958* (Cambridge: Cambridge University Press, 1966), pp. 117–50.

Brake, L., *Subjugated Knowledges: Journalism, Gender and Literature 1837–1907* (New York: Macmillan, 1994).

Brake, L., *Print in Transition, 1850–1910: Studies in Media and Book History* (Basingstoke: Palgrave, 2001).

Brake, L. and Demoor, M. (eds), *Dictionary of Nineteenth-century Journalism* (London and Ghent, British Library and Academia Press, forthcoming).

Brake, L., Jones, A. and Madden, L. (eds), *Investigating Victorian Journalism* (Basingstoke: Macmillan, 1990).

Burnard, L., 'An Introduction to the Text Encoding Initiative', in D. Greenstein (ed.), *Modelling Historical Data* (St. Katharinen: Max-Plank-Institut für Geschichte i.K.b. Scripta Mercaturae Verlag, 1991), pp. 81–91.

Burnard, L., 'On the Hermeneutic Implications of Text Encoding', in D. Fiormonte and J. Usher (eds), *New Media and the Humanities: Research and Applications* (Oxford: HCU, 2001), pp. 31–8.

Burnard, L. and Bauman, S., *TEI P5: Guidelines for Electronic Text Encoding and Interchange* (2007). Available online at <http://www.tei-c.org/release/doc/tei-p5-doc/en/html/index.html>.

Burnard, L., O'Brien O'Keeffe, K. and Unsworth J. (eds), *Electronic Textual Editing* (New York: Modern Language Association of America, 2006).

Burnard, L. and Sperberg-McQueen, C.M., *Living with the Guidelines: An Introduction to TEI Tagging*, Text Encoding Initiative, Document Number: TEI EDW18, 13 March 1991.

Bush, V., 'As We Might Think', *Atlantic Monthly*, August (1945).

Buzzetti, D., 'Digital Editions: Variant Readings and Interpretations', in *ALLC-ACH'96: Conference Abstracts* (Bergen: University of Bergen, 1996), pp. 254–6. Available online at <http://gandalf.aksis.uib.no/allc/thaller.pdf>.

Buzzetti, D., 'Text Representation and Textual Models', in *ACH-ALLC'99 Conference Proceedings* (Charlottesville, VA: University of Virginia, 1999), pp. 219–22.

Buzzetti, D., 'Digital Representation and the Text Model', *New Literary History*, 33/1 (2002): 61–87.

Buzzetti, D., 'Diacritical Ambiguity and Markup,' in D. Buzzetti, G. Pancaldi and H. Short (eds), *Augmenting Comprehension: Digital Tools and the History of Ideas* (London: Office for Humanities Communication, King's College, 2004), pp. 175–88.

Buzzetti, D. and McGann, J.J., 'Electronic Textual Editing: Critical Editing in a Digital Horizon', in L. Burnard, K.O. O'Keefe and J. Unsworth (eds), *Electronic Textual Editing* (New York: Modern Language Association of America, 2006), pp. 51–71.

Buzzetti, D. and Rehbein, M., 'Textual Fluidity and Digital Editions,' in M. Dobreva (ed.), *Text Variety in the Witnesses of Medieval Texts*, Proceedings of the International Workshop (Sofia, 21–23 September 1997) (Sofia: Institute of Mathematics and Informatics of the Bulgarian Academy of Sciences, 1998), pp. 14–39.

Caton, P., 'Form, Content and the Philosopher's Stone', paper presented at the Sixteenth Joint International Conference of the Association for Literary and Linguistic Computing and the Association for Computers and the Humanities. Abstract in *ALLC/ACH 2004: Computing and Multilingual, Multicultural Heritage, The 16th Joint International Conference, Göteborg University, 11– 16 June 2004, Conference Abstracts* (Göteborg: Göteborg University, 2004), pp. 40–42.

Cerquiglini, B., *In Praise of the Variant: A Critical History of Philology*, trans. B. Wing (Baltimore: The Johns Hopkins University Press, 1999).

Conscience, H., *De Leeuw van Vlaenderen of de Slag der Gulden Sporen. Tekstkritische editie door Edward Vanhoutte, met een uitleiding door Karel Wauters* (Tielt: Lannoo, 2002).

Coombs, J.H., Renear, A.H. and DeRose, S.J., 'Markup Systems and the Future of Scholarly Text Processing', *Communications of the ACM*, 30 (1987): 933–47.

Council of Biology Editors, *Scientific Style and Format: The CBE Manual for Authors, Editors and Publishers* (Cambridge: Cambridge University Press, 1994).

Cover, R., 'XML and Semantic Transparency' (1998). Available online at <http:// www.oasis-open.org/cover/xmlAndSemantics.html>.

Cover, R., Duncan, N. and Barnard, D.T., 'The Progress of SGML (Standard Generalized Markup Language): Extracts from a Comprehensive Bibliography', *Literary and Linguistic Computing*, 6 (1981): 197–209.

Cox, J.N., *Poetry and Politics in the Cockney School: Keats, Shelley, Hunt and their Circle* (Cambridge: Cambridge University Press, 1998).

Crane, G., 'Classics and the Computer: An End of the History', in S. Schreibman, R. Siemens and J. Unsworth (eds), *A Companion to Digital Humanities* (Oxford: Blackwell, 2004), pp. 46–55.

Crane, G., Bamman, D. and Babeu, A., 'ePhilology: When the Books Talk to their Readers', in R. Siemens and S. Schreibman (eds), *Blackwell Companion to Digital Literary Studies* (Oxford: Blackwell, 2007).

Crasson, A. and Fekete, J.-D., 'Structuration des manuscrits: Du corpus à la région' (2004). Available online at <http://www.lri.fr/~fekete/ps/ CrassonFeketeCifed04-final.pdf>.

Dahlström, M., 'Drowning by Versions', *Human IT*, 4 (2000): 7–38.

Dahlström, M., 'How Reproductive is a Scholarly Edition?', *Literary and Linguistic Computing*, 19/1 (2004): 17–33.

Davidson, D., *Essays on Actions and Events* (Oxford: Oxford University Press, 1980).

Day, A.C., *Text Processing* (Cambridge: Cambridge University Press, 1984).

De Mauro, T., *Minisemantica dei linguaggi non verbali e delle lingue* (Bari: Laterza, 1982).

De Mauro, T., *Prima lezione sul linguaggio* (Bari: Laterza, 2002).

Depmann, J., Ferres, D. and Groden, M. (eds), *Genetic Criticism: Texts and Avant-textes* (Philadelphia: University of Pennsylvania Press, 2004).

DeRose, S.J., Durand, D.D., Mylonas, E. and Renear, A.H., 'What is Text, Really?', *Journal of Computing in Higher Education*, 1/2 (1990): 3–26.

Dow, S., *Conventions in Editing: A Suggested Reformulation of the Leiden System* (Durham, NC: Duke University, 1969).

Dubin, D., 'Object Mapping for Markup Semantics', in B.T. Usdin (ed.), *Proceedings of the Extreme Markup Languages 2003 Conference* (Montreal, Quebec, 2003). Available online at <http://www.mulberrytech.com/Extreme/Proceedings/xslfo-pdf/2003/Dubin01/EML2003Dubin01.pdf>.

Dubin, D. and Birnbaum, D., 'Interpretation Beyond Markup', in B.T. Usdin (ed.), *Proceedings of the Extreme Markup Languages 2004 Conference* (Montreal, Quebec, 2004). Available online at <http://www.mulberrytech.com/Extreme/Proceedings/xslfo-pdf/2004/Dubin01/EML2004Dubin01.pdf>.

Eaves, M., Essick, R. and Viscomi, J. (eds), 'William Blake Archive'. Available online at <http://www.blakearchive.org>.

Eggert, P., 'The Work Unravelled', *TEXT*, 11 (1998): 41–60.

Eggert, P., 'Text-encoding, Theories of the Text and the "Work-site"', *Literary and Linguistic Computing*, 20 (2005): 425–35.

Eggert, P., 'What E-Textuality Has To Tell Us about Texts', unpublished paper given to the Society for Textual Scholarship conference, March 2005, New York.

Flynn, P., 'Beginning *Blackwood's*: The Right Mix of Dulce and Utilité', *Victorian Periodicals Review*, 39 (2006): 136–57.

Gleßgen, M.-D. and Lebsanft, F., 'Von alter und neuer Philologie: Neuer Streit über Prinzipien und Praxis der Textkritik', in M.-D. Gleßgen and F. Lebesanft (eds), *Alte und neue Philologie*, Beihefete zu editio 8 (Tübingen: Max Niemeyer Verlag, 1997), pp. 1–14.

Goldfarb, C.F., *The SGML Handbook* (Oxford: Oxford University Press, 1990).

Grafton, A., *The Footnote: A Curious History* (Cambridge, MA: Harvard University Press, 1997).

Graham, G., *The Internet: A Philosophical Inquiry* (London: Routledge, 1999).

Greetham, D.C., *Textual Scholarship: An Introduction* (New York and London: Garland Publishing, 1994).

Greetham, D.C., *Theories of the Text* (Oxford: Oxford University Press, 1999).

Greg, W.W., *Collected Papers* (ed.) J.C. Maxwell (Oxford: Clarendon Press, 1966).

Grésillon, A., *Eléments de critique génétique. Lire les manuscrits modernes* (Paris: Presses Universitaires de France, 1994).

Grey, V., *Charles Knight: Educator, Publisher, Writer* (Aldershot: Ashgate, 2006).

Grigely, J., *Textualterity: Art, Theory and Textual Criticism* (Ann Arbor: University of Michigan Press, 1995).

van Groningen, B.A., 'Projet d'unification des systèmes de signes critiques', *Chronique d'Égypte*, 7 (1932): 262–9.

Harney, G.J., 'To the Readers and Friends of the "Star of Freedom"', *The Star of Freedom*, 1, 7 August (1852).

Haugeland, J., 'Semantic Engines: An Introduction to Mind Design', in J. Haugeland (ed.), *Mind Design: Philosophy, Psychology, Artificial Intelligence* (Montgomery, VT: Bradford Books, 1981), pp. 1–34.

Hayles, N.K., 'Translating Media: Why We Should Rethink Textuality', *Yale Journal of Criticism*, 16/2 (2003): 263–90.

Hayles, N.K., 'What Cybertext Theory Can't Do', *Electronic Book Review*, posted 15 February 2001, modified 8 March 2003 <http://www.electronicbookreview.com>.

Hayles, N.K., *My Mother Was a Computer: Digital Subjects and Literary Texts* (Chicago: University of Chicago Press, 2005).

Henrikson, P., 'Kampen om litteraturhistorien: romantikerna som filologer', in L. Burman and B. Ståhle Sjönell (eds), *Text och tradition. Om textedering och kanonbildning* [Text and Tradition. On Text Editing and the Creation of a Literary Canon]. Nordiskt Nätverk för Editionsfilologer. Skrifter. 4 (Stockholm: Svenska Vitterhetssamfundet, 2002).

Hjelmslev, L., *Prolegomena to a Theory of Language*, trans. F.J. Whitfield (Madison: University of Wisconsin Press, 1961), pp. 47–70.

Hjelmslev, L., *Language: An Introduction* (Madison: University of Wisconsin Press, 1970).

Houghton, W.E. (ed.), *Wellesley Index to Victorian Periodicals, 1824–1900*, 5 vols (Toronto: University of Toronto Press, 1966–1979).

Huitfeldt, C., 'Multi-dimensional Texts in One-dimensional Medium', *Computers and the Humanities*, 28 (1995): 235–41.

Huitfeldt, C., 'Scholarly Text Processing and Future Markup Systems', *Jahrbuch für Computerphilologie*, 5 (2003): 219–36. Available online at <http://www.computerphilologie.uni-muenchen.de/jg03/huitfeldt.html>.

Hume, R.D., 'The Aims and Uses of "Textual Studies"', *Papers of the Bibliographical Society of America*, 99 (2005): 197–230.

Hunt, A.S., 'A Note on the Transliteration of Papyri', *Chronique d'Égypte*, 7 (1932): 272–4.

Hunter, I., 'The Regimen of Reason: Kant's Defence of the Philosophy Faculty', *Oxford Literary Review*, 17 (1995): 51–85.

IFLA, *Functional Requirements for Bibliographic Records: Final Report*, UBCIM publications, vol. 19 ns (München: Saur, 1998). Available online at <http://www.ifla.org/VII/s13/frbr/frbr.pdf>.

Jackson, K., *George Newnes and the New Journalism in Britain, 1880–1910* (Aldershot: Ashgate, 2001).

Janko, R. review of T. Kouremenos, G.M. Parássoglou and K. Tsantsanoglou (eds with intro. and comm.), *The Derveni Papyrus*, Studi e testi per il 'Corpus dei papiri filosofici greci e latini', vol. 13, Florence: Casa Editrice Leo S. Olschki, 2006, *Bryn Mawr Classical Review*, 29 October (2006). Available online at <http://ccat.sas.upenn.edu/bmcr/2006/2006-10-29.html#n9>.

Jones, H.L. (trans.), *The Geography of Strabo* (Loeb Edition, Cambridge, MA: Harvard University Press, 1924).

Jónsson, M., 'Utgiverisk impotens', paper presented at the conference *Nordiske middelaldertekster – Utgivere & brukere*, Oslo, Centre for Advanced Studies at the Norwegian Academy of Sciences and Letters, 27–29 April 2001; rev. Icelandic edn, 'Getuleysi útgefenda?', *Skírnir*, 175 (2001): 510–29.

Kalvesmaki, J., 'Guide to Unicode Greek' <http://www.doaks.org/publications/unicodegreekguide.pdf>.

Kant, I., *Kritik der reinen Vernunft* ([1781]; Hamburg: Meiner Verlag, 1998).

Kanzog, K., *Prolegomena zu einer historisch-kritischen Ausgabe der Werke Heinrich von Kleists: Theorie und Praxis einer modernen Klassiker-Edition* (München: Hanser, 1970).

Kelly, E., 'The Jerilderie Letter' (1879), facsimile images at <http://www.slv.vic.gov.au/collections/treasures/jerilderieletter>.

Kichuk, D., 'Metamorphosis: Remediation in *Early English Books Online (EEBO)*', *Literary and Linguistic Computing*, 22/3 (2007), 291–303.

King, A. and Plunkett, J. (eds), *Victorian Print Media: A Reader* (Oxford: Oxford University Press, 2005).

Kirschenbaum, M.G., 'Editing the Interface: Textual Studies and First Generation Electronic Objects', *TEXT*, 14 (2002): 15–51.

Kirschenbaum, M.G., 'Materiality and Matter and Stuff: What Electronic Texts Are Made Of', *Electronic Book Review*, posted 1 October 2001, modified 30 November 2003 <http:// www. electronicbookreview.com>.

Kirschenbaum, M.G., *Mechanisms: New Media and the Forensic Imagination* (Cambridge, MA: MIT Press, 2008).

Krummrey, H. and Panciera, S., 'Criteri di edizione e segni diacritici', *Tituli*, 2 (1980): 205–15.

Latour, B., 'Visualization and Cognition: Thinking with Eyes and Hands', in *Knowledge and Society: Studies in the Sociology of Culture Past and Present*, 6 (1986), pp. 1–40.

Leopardi, G., *Zibaldone di pensieri. Edizione fotografica dell'autografo con gli indici e lo schedario* (ed.) E. Peruzzi, 10 vols (Pisa: Scuola Normale Superiore, 1989).

Ludäscher, B., Marciano, R. and Moore, R., 'Preservation of Digital Data with Self-validating, Self-instantiating Knowledge-based Archives', *ACM SIGMOD Record*, 30/3 (2001): 54–63. Available online at <http://users.sdsc.edu/~ludaesch/Paper/kba.pdf>.

Maas, P., *Textual Criticism*, trans. B. Flower (Oxford: Clarendon Press, 1958).

McCarty, W., 'Data Modelling for the History of the Book?', *Humanist Discussion Group* 16 (26 February 2003), 509 (King's College, Centre for Computing in the Humanities, 2003). Available online at <http://www.kcl.ac.uk/humanities/cch/humanist>.

McGann, J.J., *The Textual Condition* (Princeton, NJ: Princeton University Press, 1991).

McGann, J.J., 'What Is Critical Editing?', in *The Textual Condition* (Princeton, NJ: Princeton University Press, 1991).

McGann, J.J., 'The Rationale of Hypertext', in K. Sutherland (ed.), *Electronic Text: Investigations in Method and Theory* (Oxford: Clarendon Press, 1997), pp. 19–46.

McGann, J.J., *Radiant Textuality: Literature after the World Wide Web* (New York: Palgrave, 2001).

McGann, J.J., 'Rethinking Textuality', <http://www.iath.virginia.edu/~jjm2f/old/jj2000aweb.html> (undated).

McKenzie, D.F., *Bibliography and the Sociology of Texts* (Cambridge: Cambridge University Press, 1999).

McLaverty, J., 'Warburton's False Comma: Reason and Virtue in Pope's *Essay on Man*', *Modern Philology*, 99 (2002): 379–92.

Mason, N. et al. (eds), *Blackwood's Magazine 1817–1825: Selections from Maga's Infancy*, 6 vols (London: Pickering and Chatto, 2006).

Miller, C.R., 'Genre as Social Action', *Quarterly Journal of Speech*, 70 (1984): 151–67.

Nelson, T.H., *Literary Machines* (privately published, 1986).

Newth, E., 'All litteratur til folket nå! Om Nasjonalbibliotekets digitalisering, Google Book Search og brukerne', *Prosa*, 3 (2007), 6–12.

North, J.S. (ed.), *Waterloo Directory of English Newspapers and Periodicals: 1800–1900*, 2nd series (20 vols) (Waterloo, ON: North Waterloo Academic Press, 2003).

Nowviskie, B., (2000). 'Interfacing the Edition', talk given at the Conference 'Literary Truth and Scientific Method', Charlottesville, VA: University of Virginia. Available online at <http://jefferson.village.virginia.edu/~bpn2f/1866/interface.html>.

Nunberg, G., 'The Places of Books in the Age of Electronic Reproduction', *Representations*, 42 (1993): 13–37.

Ore, E.S, (1999) 'Elektronisk publisering: forskjellige utgaveformer og forholdet til grunntekst(er) og endelig(e) tekst(er)', in: L. Burman and B. Ståhle Sjönell (eds), *Vid texternas vägskäl: textkritiska uppsatser* (Nordiskt Nätverk för Editionsfilologer. Skrifter: 1) (Stockholm: Svenska Vitterhetssamfundet, 1999), pp. 138–44.

Ore, E.S., 'Monkey Business–or What is an Edition?', *Literary and Linguistic Computing*, 19/1 (2004): 35–44.

Ore, E.S. and Cripps, P., 'The Electronic Publication of Wittgenstein's *Nachlass*' in L. Burnard, M. Deegan and H. Short (eds), *The Digital Demotic* (London: Office for Humanities Communication, King's College, 1997), pp. 111–18.

Palmer, S., *Palmer's Index to the Times Newspaper* (1790–1941).

Panciera, S., 'Struttura dei supplementi e segni diacritici dieci anni dopo', *Supplementa Italica* 8 (Rome: Quasar, 1991), pp. 9–21.

Peckham, M., 'Reflections on the Foundations of Modern Textual Editing', *Proof*, 1 (1971): 122–55.

Pichler, A., 'Advantages of a Machine-readable Version of Wittgenstein's *Nachlass*', in K. Johannessen and T. Nordenstram (eds), *Culture and Value: Philosophy and the Cultural Sciences* (n.p.: The Austrian Ludwig Wittgenstein Society, 1995).

Pierazzo, E., 'Just Different Layers? Stylesheets and Digital Edition Methodology', paper presented at *Digital Humanities 2006*, Paris, 5–9 July 2006. Available online at <http://www.allc-ach2006.colloques.paris-sorbonne.fr/DHs.pdf>, pp. 158–60.

Pierazzo, E., 'The Encoding of Time in Manuscript Transcription: Towards Genetic Digital Editions', in *Digital Humanities 2007*, Urbana Champaign, USA, 4–8 June 2007. Available online at <http://www.digitalhumanities.org/dh2007/abstracts/xhtml.xq?id=172>, pp 150–52.

Poole, W.F. et al., *Poole's Index to Periodical Literature*, 7 vols (Boston: Osgood, 1882–1908).

Postman, N., *Technopoly: The Surrender of Culture to Technology* (New York: Vintage Books, 1993).

Raymond, D.R., Tompa, F.W. and Wood, D., 'Markup Reconsidered', paper presented at the First International Workshop on Principles of Document Processing, Washington DC, 22–23 October 1992, Abstract available online at <http://softbase.uwaterloo.ca/~drraymon/papers/markup.ps>.

Raymond, D.R., Tompa, F.W. and Wood, D., 'From Data Representation to Data Model: Meta-semantic Issues in the Evolution of SGML', *Computer Standards and Interfaces*, 10 (1995): 25–36. Available online at <http://softbase.uwaterloo.ca/~drraymon/papers/sgml.ps>.

Recki, B., 'Kritik', *Religion in Geschichte und Gegenwart*, 4 (2001): 1781–2.

Renear, A., 'Out of Praxis: Three (Meta)Theories of Textuality', in K. Sutherland (ed.), *Electronic Text: Investigations in Method and Theory* (Oxford: Clarendon Press, 1997), pp. 107–26.

Renear, A., 'The Descriptive/Procedural Distinction is Flawed', *Markup Languages*, 2/4 (2001): 411–20.

Renear, A., 'Theory Restored', paper presented at the Sixteenth Joint International Conference of the Association for Literary and Linguistic Computing and the Association for Computers and the Humanities, abstract in *ALLC/ACH 2004: Computing and Multilingual, Multicultural Heritage, The 16th Joint International Conference, Göteborg University, 11–16 June 2004, Conference Abstracts* (Göteborg: Göteborg University, 2004), pp. 110–12.

Renear, A., Dubin, D., Sperberg-McQueen, C.M. and Huitfeldt, C., 'Towards a Semantics for XML Markup', in R. Furuta, J.I. Maletic and E. Munson (eds), *Proceedings of the 2002 ACM Symposium on Document Engineering*, McLean, VA, November 2002 (New York: ACM Press, 2002), pp. 119–26.

Robert, L., *Hellenica* 13 (Limoges: A. Bontemps, 1965).

Robinson, P., 'Is There a Text in These Variants?', in R. Finneran (ed.), *The Literary Text in the Digital Age* (Ann Arbor: University of Michigan Press, 1996), pp. 99–115.

Robinson, P., 'What Is a Critical Digital Edition?', *Variants: The Journal of the European Society for Textual Scholarship*, 1 (2002): 43–62.

Robinson, P., 'Where We Are with Scholarly Editions, and Where We Want To Be', *Jahrbuch für Computerphilologie*, 5 (2003): 126–46. Available online at <http://computerphilologie.uni-muenchen.de/jg03/robinson.html>.

Robinson, P., 'Current Issues in Making Digital Editions of Medieval Texts – or, do Electronic Scholarly Editions have a Future?', *Digital Medievalist*, 1/1 (2005). Available online at <http://www.digitalmedievalist.org/article. cfm?RecID=6>.

Robinson, P., 'A New Paradigm for Electronic Scholarly Editions' (2006) <http://www.methodsnetwork.ac.uk/activities/es03abstracts.html>.

Rockwell, G., 'What Is Text Analysis, Really?', *Literary and Linguistic Computing*, 18/2 (2003): 209–219.

Ryan, M.-L., 'Cyberspace, Virtuality and the Text', in M.-L. Ryan (ed.), *Cyberspace Textuality: Computer Technology and Literary Theory* (Bloomington: Indiana University Press, 1999).

Ryle, G., *The Concept of Mind*, 2nd edn ([1949], Harmondsworth: Penguin Books, 1963).

Scheibe, S., 'Zu einigen Grundprinzipien einer historisch-kritischen Ausgabe', in G. Martens and H. Zeller (eds), *Texte und Varianten: Probleme ihrer Edition und Interpretation* (München: Beck, 1971), pp. 1–44.

Scheibe, S., 'Diskussion zu Theorie und Praxis der Edition. Aufgaben der germanistischen Textologie in DDR', *Zeitschrift für Germanistik*, 4 (1981): 453–63.

Scheibe, S., 'Quelles éditions pour quels lecteurs?' in L. Hay (ed.), *La Naissance du Texte* (n.p.: José Corti, 1989), pp. 77–86.

Searle, J.R., *Speech Acts: An Essay in the Philosophy of Language* (Cambridge: Cambridge University Press, 1969).

Searle, J.R., 'A Taxonomy of Illocutionary Acts', in K. Gunderson (ed.), *Language, Mind and Knowledge*, Minnesota Studies in the Philosophy of Science, 7 (Minneapolis: University of Minnesota Press, 1975), pp. 344–69, repr. in J.R. Searle, *Experience and Meaning: Studies in the Theory of Speech Acts* (Cambridge: Cambridge University Press, 1975), pp. 1–29.

Segre, C., *Avviamento all'analisi del testo letterario* (Torino: Einaudi, 1985); Engl. edn, *Introduction to the Analysis of the Literary Text*, trans. J. Meddemmen (Bloomington: Indiana University Press, 1988).

Shattock, J. and Wolff, M. (eds), *The Victorian Periodical Press: Samplings and Soundings* (Leicester: Leicester University Press, 1982).

Shillingsburg, P., *Scholarly Editing in the Computer Age: Theory and Practice*, 3rd edn (Ann Arbor: University of Michigan Press, 1996).

Shillingsburg, P., *From Gutenburg to Google* (Cambridge: Cambridge University Press, 2006).

Smiraglia, R.P., *The Nature of a 'Work': Implications for the Organization of Knowledge* (Lanham, MD: Scarecrow Press, 2001).

Smith, M.N., 'Electronic Scholarly Editing', in S. Schreilbman, R. Siemens and J. Unsworth (eds), *A Companion to Digital Humanities* (Oxford: Blackwell, 2004). Available online at <http://www.digitalhumanities.org/companion/>.

Smith, N., 'Digitising Documents for Public Access', in L. MacDonald (ed.), *Digital Heritage: Applying Digital Imaging to Cultural Heritage* (Oxford: Elsevier Butterworth-Heinemann, 2006), pp. 3–31.

Sperberg-McQueen, C.M., 'Text in the Electronic Age: Textual Study and Text Encoding, with Examples from Medieval Texts', *Literary and Linguistic Computing*, 6 (1991): 34–46.

Sperberg-McQueen, C.M. and Burnard, L. (eds), *Guidelines for Electronic Encoding and Interchange* (Chicago: Text Encoding Initiative, 1994).

Sperberg-McQueen, C.M. and Burnard, L., *TEI P4 Guidelines for Electronic Text Encoding and Interchange: XML-compatible Edition (P4)* (Oxford, Providence, Charlottesville, and Bergen: The TEI Consortium, 2002). Available online at <http://www.tei-c.org/P4X/>.

Sperberg-McQueen, C.M., Dubin, D., Huitfeldt, C. and Renear, A., 'Drawing Inferences on the Basis of Markup', in B.T. Usdin and S.R. Newcomb (eds), *Proceedings of the Extreme Markup Languages 2002 Conference* (Montreal, Quebec, 2002). Available online at <http://www.mulberrytech.com/Extreme/ Proceedings/xslfo-pdf/2002/CMSMcQ01/EML2002CMSMcQ01.pdf>.

Sperberg-McQueen, C.M., Huitfeldt, C. and Renear, A., 'Meaning and Interpretation of Markup', *Markup Languages*, 2/3 (2000): 215–34.

Stead, W.T. and Hetherington, E. (eds), *Index to the Periodical Literature of the World*, 11 vols (Review of Reviews, 1891–1900).

Steding, S.A., *Computer-based Scholarly Editions: Context – Concept – Creation – Clientele* (Berlin: Logos Verlag, 2002).

Stewart, J.D. et al., *British Union-Catalogue of Periodicals: A Record of the Periodicals of the World, from the Seventeenth Century to the Present Day, in British Libraries*, 5 vols plus supplements (London: Butterworth Scientific Publications, 1955).

Strout, A.L., 'James Hogg's "Chaldee Manuscript"', *PMLA*, 65 (1950): 695–718.

Stuart, L. (ed.), *His Natural Life*, by Marcus Clarke, the Academy Editions of Australian Literature (St Lucia: University of Queensland Press, 2001).

Sutherland, K., *Jane Austen's Textual Lives: From Aeschylus to Bollywood* (Oxford: Oxford University Press, 2005).

Svedjedal, J., *The Literary Web: Literature and Publishing in the Age of Digital Production. A Study in the Sociology of Literature* (Stockholm: The Royal Library, 2000).

Swift, J., *Gulliver's Travels*, (ed.) C. Rawson and I. Higgins (Oxford: Oxford University Press, 2005).

Tanselle, G.T., *The Life and Work of Fredson Bowers* (Charlottesville: Bibliographical Society of the University of Virginia, 1993); repr. from *Studies in Bibliography*, 46 (1993): 1–186.

Tanselle, G.T., 'Critical Editions, Hypertexts and Genetic Criticism', *The Romanic Review*, 86/3 (1995): 581–93.

Tanselle, G.T., 'The Varieties of Scholarly Editing', in D.C. Greetham (ed.), *Scholarly Editing: A Guide to Research* (New York: MLA, 1995), pp. 9–32.

Thaller, M., 'Text as a Data Type', in *ALLC-ACH'96: Conference Abstracts* (University of Bergen, 1996), pp. 252–4. Available online at <http://gandalf. aksis.uib.no/allc/thaller.pdf >.

Thaller, M., 'Strings, Texts and Meaning', in *Digital Humanities 2006*, 1st AHDO International Conference Abstracts (Paris: Université Paris-Sorbonne – Centre de Recherche Cultures Anglophones et Technologies de l'Information, 2006), pp. 212–214.

Timpanaro, S., *The Genesis of Lachmann's Method* (ed. and trans.) G.W. Most (Chicago: University of Chicago Press, 2005).

Treadwell, M., 'Benjamin Motte, Andrew Tooke and *Gulliver's Travels*', in H. Real and H.J. Vienken (eds), *Proceedings of the First Münster Symposium on Jonathan Swift* (München: Fink, 1985), pp. 287–304.

Turner, E., *Greek Papyri: An Introduction* (Oxford: Oxford University Press, 1980).

Turner, M., *Trollope and the Magazines: Gendered Issues in Mid-Victorian Britain* (Basingstoke: Macmillan, 2000).

Unsworth, J., 'What is Humanities Computing and What is Not?', in G. Braungart, K. Eibl and F. Jannidis (eds), *Jahrbuch für Computerphilologie*, 4 (2002). Available online at <http://computerphilologie.uni-muenchen.de/jg02/ unsworth.html>.

Van den Branden, R., Vanhoutte, E. and Roelens, X., *Johan Daisne. De trein der traagheid op CD-ROM. Elektronische editie* (Gent: KANTL, 2007).

Vanhoutte, E., 'Where is the Editor?: Resistance in the Creation of an Electronic Critical Edition', *Human IT*, 3/1 (1999): 197–214. Available online at <http:// www.hb.se/bhs/ith/1-99/ev.htm>.

Vanhoutte, E., 'Putting Time Back in Manuscripts. Text Ontology, Critique Génétique and Modern Manuscripts', paper presented at *ALLC/ACH 2002*, Tübingen, Germany, 24–28 July 2002.

Vanhoutte, E., 'Display or Argument: Markup and Visualization for Electronic Scholarly Editions', in T. Burch, J. Fournier, K. Gärtner and A. Rapp (eds), *Standards und Methoden der Volltextdigitalisierung. Beiträge des Internationalen Kolloquiums an der Universität Trier, 8./9. oktober 2001* (Stuttgart: Franz Steiner, 2003), pp. 71–96.

Vanhoutte, E., 'Editorial Theory in Crisis: The Concepts of Base Text, Edited Text, Textual Apparatus and Variant in Electronic Editions', paper presented at *DRH 2005*, Lancaster, 4–7 September 2005. Available online at <http://www.drh. org.uk/drh2005-abstracts.pdf>.

Van Hulle, D., *Textual Awareness: A Genetic Approach to the Late Works of James Joyce, Marcel Proust and Thomas Mann*, PhD thesis (Antwerp: University of Antwerp, 1999).

Van Hulle, D., *Textual Awareness: A Genetic Study of Late Works by Joyce, Proust and Mann* (Ann Arbor: University of Michigan Press, 2004).

West, M.L., 'The Textual Criticism and Editing of Homer', in G.W. Most (ed.), *Editing Texts: Texte edieren*, Aporemata 2 (Göttingen: Vandenhoeck and Ruprecht, 1998), 94–110.

Williams, W.P. and Abbot, C.S., *An Introduction to Bibliographical and Textual Studies*, 2nd edn (New York: Modern Language Association of America, 1989).

Witkowski, G., *Textkritik und Editionstechnik neuerer Schriftwerke. Ein methodologischer Versuch* (Leipzig: H. Haessel Verlag, 1924).

Woolley, D., 'The Textual History of *A Tale of a Tub*', *Swift Studies*, 21 (2006): 7–26.

Youtie, H., 'The Papyrologist: Artificer of Fact', *Greek, Roman and Byzantine Studies*, 4 (1963): 19–32.

Index